XHOSA

a cultural grammar for beginners

Patricia Schonstein Pinnock

African Sun Press

"Without understanding there can be no friendship. If one wishes to understand a people one must identify oneself with them. One must study their language, customs and culture. To do this with the amaXhosa of today one must know something of them as they were in the past and as one may yet meet them in their own territories." *Joan Broster*

For Don and our children. And for my parents, Giannina and Emerich Schonstein, from whom I learnt a love of languages.

Xhosa: A cultural grammar for beginners
by Patricia Schonstein Pinnock
Layout and design: Donald Pinnock
Cover and decorations: Gillian Mathew

ISBN Number 1-874915-03-2
Published by African Sun Press, P.O.Box 16415, Vlaeberg 8018, Cape Town, South Africa.

Reproduction by Unifoto, Cape Town.
Printed in Hong Kong by South China Printing Company (1988) Limited.

Contents

Part one: Culture and history

Part two: Language

Acknowledgements

I am indebted to the children who attended Rivendell Children's Centre in Grahamstown between 1985 and 1990 for introducing me to their exquisite language. Special mention must be made of Piwe Mdoko, Phathuxolo Ngeleza and Chuma Koliti.

My warm and special thanks go to Dr Jeff Peires for the encouragement and help he gave me and for allowing me to quote extensively from his books. I also thank Joan Broster for her inspiring friendship and for the insight into Xhosa culture which she gave me. Her works and those of Dr Peires inspired and moved me deeply, filling me with a sense of pathos at the passing of a once timeless culture and way of life.

My thanks to Sandy Rowoldt and Zweliyanyikima Vena of the Cory Library at Rhodes University in Grahamstown as well as to Marijke Cosser and Fleur Way-Jones of the 1820 Settler Museum, Grahamstown, for their help with historical and cultural material and for tracing out-of-print grammar books. I am grateful for being allowed to look through the museum's archives and for the help given by Marijke in selecting suitable pictures.

I am indebted to the many people who contributed time, advice and expertise in their various fields - Professor Peter Mtuze, Professor Buyiswa Mini, Dr Cecil Manona, Dr Russell Kaschula, Dr John Claughton, Nomakomani Zinnia Baai, Kholeka Nkwinti, Fazana Qwakanisa, Shealagh Ryan, Shelley Roodt, Issy Pinchuck, Vuyiswa Totobela, Nozizwe Mngqibisa, Ray Black, Anthony Greyling, Cathryn Pinnock, Lou Moore, Gillian Mathew, Michael Heuermann, Julius Mfete, Helmut Thomsen, Ben Maclennan, Julian Cobbing, Lalou Meltzer, Kerrie Shepherd and most especially Shaun Benton for his extensive help with the final manuscript.

I also thank my dear friend Ntombi Mzuzo, whose Xhosa was as pure and as old as the patterns in the grass mats she wove. Her dignity, eloquence and sparkling wit rang out, like the songs of many birds, enticing me so that I could never rest until I had unravelled the splendour of her language and will never feel accomplished until I can speak it as eloquently and enchantingly as she.

My special thanks and love go to my husband, Don, for teaching me research and computer skills, for designing this book and for the encouragement and support which he gave me.

I thank the Stella and Paul Lowenstein Educational Trust, the Standard Bank Foundation, the Mackenzie Foundation, the Nedcor Chairman's Fund and the Equal Opportunity Foundation for contributing towards the research costs of this book. Finally I wish to thank the VW Community Trust who contributed towards printing costs of the first edition.

Patricia Schonstein Pinnock

Cape Town 1994

Part 1

Culture and history

1 Historical overview

Reports by Portuguese survivors of shipwrecks along the south-east coast during the 16th and 17th centuries describe the Xhosa people as cattle herders who hunted game and cultivated sorghum. They lived in beehive-shaped huts in scattered homesteads which were ruled by chiefs. According to oral tradition, the ancestors of the Xhosa lived in the foothills of the Drakensburg mountains before moving slowly to the coast.[1] They are thought to have moved westward over a period of 300 years from about 1550 to 1850. The boundaries of the territory they occupied fluctuated considerably over time, but in the years between 1700 and 1850 they did not often extend west of the Sunday's River or east of the Mbashe River along the coastal strip which separates South Africa's inland plateau from the Indian Ocean.[2] By the beginning of the 16th century they had probably already settled as far south as the Umzimvubu River, near present-day Port St Johns.

The Xhosa were pastoralists and their slow movement was more in the nature of an expansion than a migration. One of the main reasons for this movement was simply the hiving off of the sons of reigning chiefs to found new chiefdoms of their own, relieving political pressure at the centre of the kingdom.[3] Over the centuries various chiefdoms formed through inner turmoils and divisions, through unions with Khoisan groups whose territories the Xhosa overran and conquered and through the arrival in their midst of refugees from wars in Natal.

The people known today as Xhosa actually consist of various centuries-old societies called Mpondo, Bomvana, Bhaca, Thembu, Mpondomise, Xesibe, Mfengu, Hlubi, the Xhosa proper and others, which were bound century after century by ties of marriage as well as by diplomatic, military and political alliances. Their customs and ways of life were, and still are today among traditionalists, built around their heads of cattle and the oral tradition of their origin at the Dedesi River. This river is no longer identifiable, but is described as having been a headwater tributary of the Umzimvubu River. Common to all these societies is their language.[4]

1 Interview with J.B. Peires, Umtata, 1992.
2 J.B. Peires, 1981, page 1.
3 Ibid., page 20.
4 Noel Mostert, 1992, pages 81 and 184.

Sandile's kraal in the Amatole, by Thomas Baines, c.1849

Because of these linguistic and cultural similarities it has been the practice to apply the name 'Xhosa' not only to the Xhosa themselves but to all Africans indigenous to the Eastern Cape and resident in the old Cape Province, including Ciskei and Transkei. The designation Xhosa is now widely used by all the groups, particularly when they live in multi-ethnic cities such as Johannesburg, Cape Town and Durban. Among themselves, however, the people still tend to refer to themselves as Gcaleka, Hlubi, Thembu, Mpondo, etc. Many prominent contemporary Xhosa politicians are still identified by these affiliations. For instance, Nelson Mandela was born a prince of the Thembu royal house, Winnie Mandela is Mpondo and the martyred Steve Biko was Xhosa.[5]

In its narrower definition, however, the name Xhosa is correctly applicable only to the societies ruled over by chiefs of the Tshawe family who claim descent from a great 16th century hero named Xhosa. The first modern historian of the Xhosa people, J.H. Soga, speculated in the early 1930s that Xhosa's heroic stature derived from the fact that he was a 'Moses' figure who brought his people from some remote inland point to the coastlands, which were to become their home.[6] However, it is unlikely that such a person ever existed as there are no legends or stories of any kind about him.[7] It is more probable that the word 'Xhosa' is derived from the Khoi '//kosa', meaning 'angry men'.[8]

Oral tradition holds that the first king of the Xhosa was Cirha and

5 Ibid., page 186.
6 Ibid., page 81.
7 Interview with J.B. Peires, Umtata, 1994.
8 J.B. Peires, 1981, page 13.

View of a Xhosa settlement

that, because of his stinginess, he was dethroned by his younger brother, Tshawe. This incident occurred some time before 1600. Tshawe became a distinguished chief who established the amaTshawe as the royal clan of the Xhosa nation. They remain so today.

The Xhosa kingdom was not very centralised and each Tshawe chief was relatively autonomous within his own chiefdom. As the generations passed the chiefs dispersed over a wide area, expanding the Xhosa kingdom by subjecting the Khoisan and other independent clans to Tshawe authority. They formed the vanguard of the descent of the cattle-owning Xhosa speakers along the south-eastern coast. Their westward drift accelerated rapidly during the 18th century until, in the last quarter of that century, particular groups of Xhosa found themselves in the path of the eastward-moving white colonists.[9] The Xhosa found themselves selected by history and upon them fell the brunt of the experience of contact, violent or otherwise, with the outside world.[10] It changed them forever and set them quite apart in experience from the Thembu, for instance, who were less drawn into contact with the colonists, and the Mpondo, who were hardly drawn in at all.[11] The Mpondo were especially remote from contact with whites. Pondoland, on the border between the Cape Province and Natal, is a ruggedly wild area. Its rough coast provided no sea links and the rough landscape discouraged road and rail connection. These physical circumstances effectively took the Mpondo out of mainstream 19th century events. In

9 Noel Mostert, 1992, page 185.
10 Ibid.
11 Ibid.

ancient times the Mpondo were said to be great, fierce and feared warriors, but they kept out of the colonial wars. They were the last Africans to come under Cape colonial administration, and this only happened in 1894.[12]

One of Tshawe's successors was Phalo, who ruled during the 18th century. He had two sons, Rharhabe and Gcaleka, who both laid claim to their father's position during his lifetime. The succession dispute resulted in war and a split between the two brothers. The Tshawe dynasty divided into two main branches - the Great House of Gcaleka, living east of the Great Kei River, and the Right-Hand House of Rharhabe, living west of the Great Kei.[13] Many Xhosa chiefdoms in the Transkei descended from Gcaleka, and those in the Ciskei from Rharhabe.

The amaRharhabe bore the brunt of the Frontier Wars and in the process were divided yet again between the followers of Ngqika, who collaborated with the colonial forces, and the followers of Ndlambe, who resisted them.

The settlement pattern of the Eastern Cape was much disrupted by the wars of the 19th century, both among the Xhosa themselves and against the whites. By 1880 a clear division had emerged between the Ciskei and the Transkei. In the Ciskei the Xhosa speaking people had lost most of their land and become increasingly integrated into the colonial culture and economy. The Transkei was swallowed whole by the colonial power, with the result that the original culture and settlement pattern remained intact to a much greater extent.[14]

During nine Frontier Wars between 1779 and 1878 the Xhosa received very little help from their neighbours. They were shattered by the Great Cattle Killing of 1856-1857 when, acting on the prophecies of a young girl called Nongqawuse, they slaughtered their cattle and stopped planting crops. According to the girl's prophecies these deeds would lead to the resurrection of their ancestors, the retreat of white colonisers and an era of idyllic prosperity. Instead, tens of thousands of people starved to death. The Xhosa nation was torn apart and the people were dispersed among the white farmers of the Karoo and the Eastern Cape.[15] They were the first African people to become widely known to Europeans. This is probably why the name 'Xhosa' became the name for all Africans in the Eastern Cape.[16]

12 Ibid.

13 During the 1850s the area west of the Great Kei River was known as British Kaffraria, and the area east of the Great Kei as Kaffraria.

14 Interview with J. B. Peires, Umtata, 1992.

15 J.B. Peires, 1989, summary on back cover.

16 Interview with J.B. Peires, Umtata, 1992.

2 The roots of the Xhosa language

Xhosa belongs to a large family of languages spoken from the southern point of Africa to as far north as Cameroon.[1] This family of languages was named 'Bantu' by Dr Wilhelm Bleek (1827-1875) in his book *'A Comparative Grammar of South African Languages'*, published in 1862. He took this name from the most common form of the word for 'people' in these languages, (abandu, batho, wuntu, anthu etc.) and it became a convenient academic description of Africa's principal linguistic family.

The name 'Bantu' fell into disfavour during the repressive apartheid years because it was used by the South African government to discriminate between black Africans and 'others'. Many scholars prefer to use the term 'Sintu' in naming these languages. This follows Dr Bleek's use of **ntu** for a person, prefixed with **isi-** to identify it as a

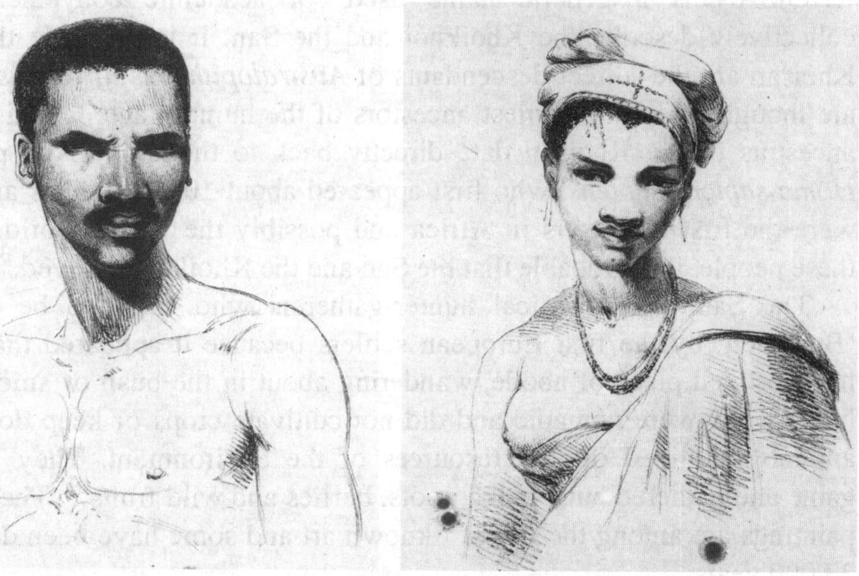

Xhosa man and woman, c.1804

1 "We have recently made large collections of vocabularies of words of the different dialects on this part of the coast, especially of those spoken between the Bight of Biafra and Benguela; and we find that they are all not only related to each other, but by comparing them with such vocabularies as we have of the languages of the Cape of Good Hope, Mozambique, and other parts of the Eastern coast, we learn, that though differing from each other materially as dialects, yet that they all undoubtedly belong to one general family." Rev. Wilson: *Annual Report of the American Board of Missions* for 1847, as quoted by Rev. J. Appleyard, 1850, pages 378-379.

language (language-person).[2] The great majority of the peoples of eastern, central and southern Africa today speak one of the more than 400 different Bantu languages. They comprise many nations and peoples and involve many cultures. The Bantu languages are not only numerous and widespread, they are also closely related to one another, sharing a similar vocabulary and grammatical structure. Xhosa speakers today form the largest single Bantu language group in southern Africa and their closest linguistic relatives are the Zulu, Swazi and Ndebele peoples. The Zulu and the Xhosa share four-fifths of their vocabulary. The following Bantu languages occur in southern Africa.

Eastern Cape	Xhosa
Natal and Zululand	Zulu
Matabeleland (southern Zimbabwe)	Ndebele
Malawi	Ngoni
Swaziland	Swazi
Lesotho	Sotho
Botswana	Tswana
Mashonaland (northern Zimbabwe)	Shona
Namibia	Herero
Angola	ki-Mbundu

Contact between the Xhosa and the Khoisan

KHOISAN is a generic name used for academic convenience to collectively describe the Khoikhoi and the San. It is probable that the Khoisan are the direct descendants of *Australopithecus africanus*, who are thought to be the earliest ancestors of the human race. Certainly the ancestors of the Khoisan date directly back to the Stone Age people, *Homo sapiens sapiens*, who first appeared about 100 000 years ago and were the first tool users in Africa and possibly the whole world. From these people it is probable that the San and the Khoikhoi evolved.[3]

The San were classical hunter-gatherers who came to be named 'Bushmen' by the first European settlers because it appeared that they had no fixed place of abode, wandering about in the bush or among the hills. They were nomadic and did not cultivate crops or keep domestic animals but lived off the resources of the environment. They hunted game and gathered nuts, bulbs, roots, berries and wild fruits.[4] Their rock paintings are among the oldest known art and some have been dated at 23 000 years.

Scholars believe that, about 2 000 years ago, San living in the area of northern Botswana may have come into contact with people from central Africa who possessed sheep, and from whom they may have later obtained cattle.[5] These domestic animals contributed to the physical,

2 Interview with John Claughton, Grahamstown, 1993.
3 Reader's Digest Illustrated History of South Africa, 1988, page 11.
4 Noel Mostert, 1992, page 25.
5 Reader's Digest, op. cit.

linguistic and social transformation of a group or groups of San into people who were to name themselves **'Khoikxoin'** and are now known as Khoikhoi. Different groups of Khoikhoi had different names, such as Damaqua, Gonaqua, Hessequa, Inqua, Gouriqua and others.[6] Khoikxoin meant 'the real people' or 'men-of-men' and they used this name to distinguish themselves from the San.[7] The milk diet derived from cattle caused the emergent Khoikhoi to grow taller and more robust, although they remained on the whole a light, wiry people. Their flocks and herds gave them different values of wealth, power and territory and their need for seasonal pastures brought them into conflict with the San, upon whose territory they encroached.[8] However, although the Khoikhoi prided themselves in their herds, they also hunted and gathered like the San, especially in times of drought. Both often lived closely together, with the San willing to act as herdsmen in return for milk.

The Khoikhoi tended to be coastal people and various groups lived around Table Bay. The Dutch called those who lived along the shore 'strandlopers' (beach-walkers). Some lived far inland and in 1752 an officer of the Dutch East India Company went as far east as the Kei River, where he met several Khoikhoi groups.[9]

According to Theophillus Hahn, a theologian who was one of the few people to study the Khoikhoi, they were named **Hottentots** by the early Dutch settlers of the Cape. 'Hottentot' was a word the Dutch used meaning 'gibberish' and referred to the language of the Khoikhoi, which the Dutch did not understand.[10] It was a language full of sounds which early European visitors to the Cape found difficult to pronounce.

Khoikhoi woman, c.1812

Khoikhoi settlement

6 Ibid., page 21.
7 Martin Roberts, 1990, page 3.
8 Noel Mostert, 1992, page 33.
9 Candy Malherbe, 1984, page 52.
10 Conrad Spamer, 1991, page 6.

However, there has been controversy about the name 'Hottentot' and some scholars believe it was in fact derived from the Khoikhoi use of the word **hautitou**, which they used when they danced.

Augustin de Beaulieu, whose fleet sailed from Honfleur in France to the Cape in 1619, wrote in 1620: "They speak from the throat, and seem to sob and sigh when speaking. Their usual greeting on meeting us is to dance a song of which the beginning, the middle and the end is 'hautitou'."[11] In 1623 Jon Olafsson, a visitor from Holland to the Cape, wrote: "Their dance was after this fashion - on uttering the word 'Hottentot!' they snapped two of their fingers and clicked with tongue and feet, all in time." [12] The name Hottentot became such a pejorative term that modern historians have discarded it.

Khoikhoi man c. 1804

The Xhosa name for the San, **Abathwa**, is still used today. The Xhosa called the Khoikhoi **Amaqheya** and **Amalawu**. **Amalawu** was probably a nickname signifying those who preferred eating their cattle to keeping them.[13] Both these names are still used today to name people of mixed race.

There is some controversy surrounding the term San as it was not a collective name used by the 'Bushmen' to describe themselves and was a pejorative term used by the Khoikhoi. Theophillus Hahn wrote in 1881: "The word (San) has acquired a low meaning and is not complimentary. The Khoikhoi speak of !UriSan, white Bushmen, and mean the low white vagabonds and runaway sailors who visit their country as traders." Modern historians have not found common ground in choosing an alternative name to 'Bushmen' although it never carried the same negative qualities as 'Hottentot'. Some scholars initially preferred a simple division of Khoikhoi, and called them Khoi, while others preferred to refer to them simply as 'hunter-gatherers'. The term Khoisan is accepted as a collective term for naming all southern African hunter-gatherers.[14]

The Khoisan spoke a variety of languages which were all related and which were extreme dialects of each other. All these dialects included various click sounds. Their speech richly influenced the language of the Xhosa, which absorbed almost the entire and extensive word stock of the Khoisan together with their 'clicks'.[15] The clicks were unknown to the

11 Raven-Hart (Ed.), 1967, page 101.
12 Emilia Potenza, 1992, page 47.
13 Rev. John Appleyard, 1850, page 9.
14 Noel Mostert, 1992, page 34.
15 The Xhosa word **igusha** (sheep) is an interesting borrowing from the Khoi. The Xhosa originally used the term **imvu.** Today **imvu** is generally only used in biblical and

Xhosa before they came into contact with the Khoisan and it is thought that most of the linguistic changes to Xhosa took place after the Xhosa people had settled in the coastal region.[16] Only the vocabulary and sound structure and not the grammar of the Xhosa language were affected by this contact. This large-scale borrowing of speech sounds was quite unique.

Although the Khoisan did not submit voluntarily to the Xhosa - and indeed there was active resistance - the wealth of Khoisan sounds and words which the Xhosa absorbed tell us of intermarriage and a sharing of cultures. However the Xhosa were at times brutal towards these little hunters and, as noted in chapter one, there is every reason to believe that the name 'Xhosa' is derived from the Khoikhoi word '//kosa' meaning 'angry men'.[17] The San were renowned rain makers and useful trading partners. Although those who entered Xhosa society were considered to be economically inferior, once they bettered themselves they became equals within Xhosa society.[18] The Gonaqua, Damaqua and Hoengiqua Khoi were not displaced from their ancient homes by the Xhosa but simply became Xhosa with full rights. The limits of Xhosadom were not ethnic or geographic but political. All people or groups who accepted the rule of the Xhosa thereby became Xhosa.[19]

A smallpox epidemic, unleashed among the Khoikhoi in 1713 by contaminated linen from an infected Dutch fleet, decimated the Khoikhoi population of the south-western Cape. Those who survived lost their old clan names and became known collectively as 'Hottentots'.[20]

---

ecclesiastical language. It is also used by the Zulu.

16 Rev. John. W. Appleyard (1850) questioned whether any Xhosa click-words themselves had actually come from 'Hottentot' dialects. He postulated that only a few nouns and perhaps a few particles were absorbed in their entirety. He suggested that perhaps the Xhosa absorbed only the clicks and that they incorporated them into words already existing in their own language, thus merely changing the form and sound of those words.

17 J.B. Peires, 1981, pages 13 and 24.

18 Ibid., page 23.

19 Ibid., page 19.

20 Reader's Digest Illustrated History of South Africa, 1988, page 45.

The influence of Dutch and English

THE DUTCH landed in what is now known as Cape Town in 1652, followed in 1806 by the English. Victorian scholars recognised the Xhosa language as being evolved, beautiful-sounding and lending itself to inspired use. George McCall Theal had this to say about it:

"The language has a very copious verb, and abstract nouns can be formed readily where they are not already in common use, so that any idea whatever can be expressed in it. As nearly every word ends in a vowel, and the enunciation of the people is clear and distinct, with the voice nicely modulated, the language is musical to the ear. Many individuals, especially among the chiefs and counsellors, display great ability in public speaking." [21]

The languages of both the Dutch and the English brought many changes to Xhosa, influencing it for three centuries and contributing a large number of words from their own cultures and civilizations. The names for artifacts, crops and animals which the Xhosa did not previously know of were taken into their language and in this way Xhosa absorbed Dutch, English and later Afrikaans words.

Engraved view of Table Bay and Mountain with a sketch of the Fort by O. Dapper, 1668

21 Noel Mostert, 1992, page 41. Unsourced.

Modern Xhosa

SO IT can be seen that Xhosa has taken in many words from other languages and has modified existing words to carry a modern meaning. It has had to enlarge its vocabulary to accommodate new objects, ideas and processes and has done so in a number of ways.[22] Objects were associated through the similarity of their shapes. For example, the name for a submarine, **inkwili**, comes from its shape which resembles the bird, the sombre bulbul, and electricity took its name from lightning, **umbane**. Sometimes a word imitated the sound associated with the object, as in **isithuthuthu**, a motorbike. The meaning of an existing word was sometimes extended to cover new ideas, many of them abstract and introduced by the early missionaries. A convert to Christianity was thought to have been pierced and to have collapsed like a burst bladder. He was called **igqoboka**, the dominant idea of the word being 'one who has been pierced' although the name has now lost its stigma. **Ngcwele**, which denoted limpid water or oil, was extended to mean purity of life or holiness. **Isono**, a wrong inflicted upon another, was extended to cover the abstract idea of sin.

A foreign word could also be transliterated with such changes of sound as required to bring it into harmony with Xhosa speech. So we have **ibokisi** (box), **isipeliti** (pin), **ipleyiti** (plate), **imoto** (car), **utitshala** (teacher) and **uloliwe** (train). Foreign words were also assimilated to a Xhosa expression of similar sound. For paper was used **iphepha**, the name of the thin bulb-leaf of **inyibibana**; rinderpest became **ulandipasi** and influenza became **umfulawenja** which literally means 'valley of the dog'. Bubonic plague became **ububani** , using the already existing Xhosa word **ukubhubha**, 'to die'. One can trace the association of tennis with **intenetya**, the rock hare. Sunglasses were called **idimas** (dimmers). Sweets became **iilekese** from the Afrikaans, 'lekker' meaning 'nice'. The Xhosas who embraced European ways of life and renounced their Xhosa heritage were called **amaTshipa**, 'the cheap ones'. All these adapted words satisfied a sense for euphony, or pleasing sound.

Living languages constantly undergo changes which reflect many of the changes within society itself. This can be seen in words formed during the last century. **Usiba**, 'feather' became the word for a pen and is still used today, although we no longer write with quills; **iponti** was formed from the British pound sterling and remained in use as the name for a two rand note, and more recently a two rand coin; **amajoni** was the

22 "Spoken language is not fixed, like a manufactured article, but is a living thing that has grown during the ages of development of the race, and continues to grow, as a plant does, in one direction or another. Outside influences may be brought to bear upon it; or, as in dress and manners, certain fashions may arise and prevail for a time, leaving behind them changes or tendencies that are suitable and necessary to meet new conditions, and therefore desirable; or that do violence to characteristic qualities that make it the proper expression of the spirit of the race.(We need) to discriminate, in these days of change, between changes that are desirable or... necessary...and those that arise from slovenliness of speech or thoughtless caprice of fashion, tending to lower the dignity of the language or spoil its beauty." W.G. Bennie, 1953 , page 1.

name given to British soldiers and is now used for all soldiers. It alludes to the name, Johnny, by which British soldiers familiarly addressed the Xhosa.

Words were also absorbed in different areas and were influenced by various languages. In the Eastern Cape the name for a pension became **umhlalaphantsi**, 'the sit down', whereas in the Transvaal a pension was called **idanki**, from the Afrikaans 'dankie', meaning 'thank you'.

In modern times the brand names of items often became general names, usually when that particular brand was the first of such items which the Xhosa encountered. Thus we have **icolgate** for toothpaste; **itsheka** (Checkers) for the plastic bags given out at supermarkets; **imamu** (Mum) for roll-on deodorant; **irama** for margarine; **i-omo** for washing powder and **i-jik** for bleach. The vans which began operating as taxis during the 1980s were named **iiZolabud** after the young athlete because, like her, they were small and fast!

Many new words developed or were modified during the political unrest of the 1980s: **iphimpi**, 'spitting cobra', became the name for a police informer; **ihagu**, 'a pig', the name for the large military vehicles which toured the townships; **abantu abadaka**, 'mud people', for the soldiers wearing military camouflage and **abehlangala** (after the large grey mongoose)[23] for the infamous council policemen, known in English as 'green flies'.[24]

Many Xhosa speakers who live in cities are trilingual (speaking also Afrikaans and English) and often incorporate the 'easier' words of the second or third language into their own. Inevitably the Xhosa spoken in towns and cities has modified and continues to change far more rapidly than Xhosa spoken in rural areas. Indeed, there is now a distinction between 'town' Xhosa and the 'pure' or 'regal' Xhosa spoken in rural areas. The substitution of Xhosa by English can be seen in words like **ukudanisa** and **ukujiva** (to dance in western style) instead of **ukuxhentsa,** which is used for traditional dancing only. **Ukushina** is used for 'to sparkle' instead of **ukukhanya**. There is also much interplay between urban Zulu and Xhosa. So, for example, we find the Zulu urban slang word, **spam**, used for a gun instead of the Xhosa, **umpu**.

23 The large grey mongoose, **umhlangala**, has a very decorative and highly coloured anus. It has the habit (authenticated by a number of zoologists) of lying on its back and exposing its anus which, surrounded by black hair, resembles a cluster of seeds or pips. It uses this to lure birds such as guinea fowls and even domestic fowls. As the fowl tries to pick at the 'pips' the mongoose leaps up and kills it. (Interview with Ray Black, Albany Museum, Grahamstown, June 1993.)

24 Interview with Vuyiswa Totobela, Grahamstown, 1992.

Xhosa and the media

CROSS-FERTILIZATION of languages is an exciting, creative and living process. By its very nature, language will take 'short cuts'. A person with the fluent use of two or three languages need not confine them to their own courses but might allow words and expressions to mingle and flow together. Because of this we might think that all new words form organically 'in the street'. But in fact many are 'composed' by the media to cope with new ideas and items.

Radio and television, particularly, have had a significant impact on the modification of words or the formation of new ones. The SABC, through its Xhosa broadcasting service, 'made' new words which did not occur in Xhosa. Often this was done by simply adding a Xhosa prefix to an English or Afrikaans word to transform it. Possibly the worst offenders are found in advertisements with words like **iradio**, **itaxi**, **ibus**, **isystem**, **idishwasher** and **ilife-insurance**. Words like these 'jar' the melodic sound of Xhosa and actually grate against the poetic flow within a sentence.

The media have a greater responsibility in the transformation of Xhosa than they imagine and perhaps they should exercise more care in this regard. Roots should be traced into already existing Xhosa words or concepts and these roots used to make new words. In this way Xhosa will not be 'Anglicised' or 'Afrikaanerised' but its own poetry and beauty will be acknowledged.

3 How people are named

Traditionally, Xhosa children are named by their fathers. They are usually given wonderful names which express joy and fruitfulness such as **Chwayita** (Rejoice), **Nwabisa** (Happiness), **Babalwa** (Favour), **Sipho** (Gift), **Chuma** (Flourish/Fruitful), **Xabiso** (Value) and **Mangaliso** (Marvel).

Xhosa names often express noble characteristics such as **Phathuxolo** (Bearer of peace), **Nonyaniso** (Truth), **Mandla** (Strength), **Mpumelelo** (Success) and **Zimasa** (Make strong/ Support). Names also express praise and thanksgiving to God, such as **Siyabonga** (We give praise), **Siyabulela** (We give thanks), **Sinethemba** (We have hope) or **Nomthandazo** (Prayer). In the past children might have been named after a natural occurrence, such as the sighting of a comet, a drought or a time of plenty. Nowadays a child will usually be given an English or Afrikaans name in addition to a Xhosa name.

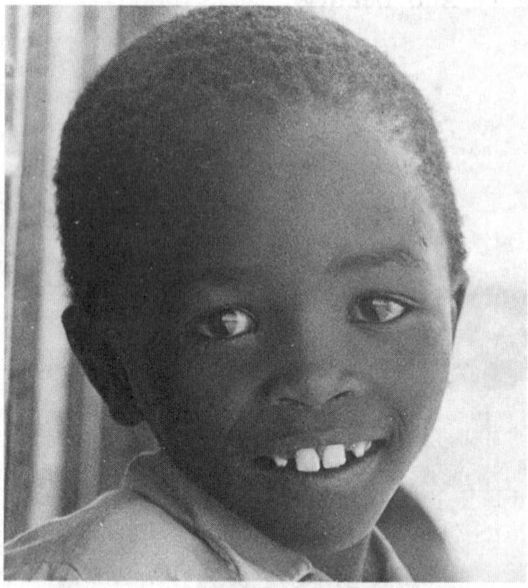

Early converts to Christianity had to give up their Xhosa names, surnames and clan names and these were generally replaced by biblical names. The first Xhosa people to be baptised at the Chumie Mission station during the last century were named after Europeans whom the missionaries wanted to honour. The first four to be baptised were renamed Robert Balfour (after the first secretary of the Glasgow Missionary Society), John Love (the secretary at the time), Elizabeth Love (his wife), Charles Henry (the Christian names of Lord Somerset) and Mary Ann, who was named after an unidentified person.[1]

In the early years of colonisation children were often named after great explorers or historical figures and one can still meet elderly people named **Livingstone**, **Columbus**, **Nelson**, **Kaiser**, **Wellington** and **Govan**.[2]

Often the Xhosa tradition of naming a child after a personal or physical characteristic is transposed into English or Afrikaans. So we meet people named **Goodman, Wiseman**, **Strongman**, **Whitey** or

1 R.H.W. Shepherd, 1940, page 61, quoting Glasgow Missionary Society Report, 1824, page 12.

2 William Govan was the first principal of Lovedale Mission, from 1841 to 1870.

Mooiplaas (Beautiful land), as well as **Beauty**, **Princess**, **Prudence**, **Patience** and **Queenette**.

A child's name might also reflect the situation within a family at the time of its birth. The last child of a large family might be called **Nondanele**, which means 'Enough', or **Daniswa**, 'Disappointment'. A third or fourth baby girl might be called **Ntombizandile** which means 'Lots of girls'. A long awaited baby might be called **Lindiwe,** meaning 'The one we have waited for'.

Girls' names often end in **-kazi** or **-iswa**. So we meet **Vuyokazi**, 'Joy', **Siphokazi**, 'Gift', **Kholiswa**, 'Satisfaction', **Phindiswa**,'Give in return', **Andiswa**, 'Expand/ Multiply', and **Faniswa**, 'Resemblance'. If a name does not have a special form for a girl, a boy's name, or a quality as described above, can be prefixed with **No-** to make it feminine. A girl takes her surname from her father. She will also have a clan name.

The clan, **isiduko**, is a conceptual kinship group. Normally all Xhosas have a clan name and it is considered to be more important than a surname. Family members are said to be the descendants of a common male ancestor whose name becomes the clan name. Although people cannot actually trace their genealogy as far back as the assumed clan founder, members of a clan share the same clan name and assume that they are related to each other. The clan name is the strongest way of identifying someone, even stronger than a father's or grandfather's surname because it identifies a person's whole family group and forebears. Traditional law does not allow people of the same clan to marry each other. **Isiduko** are relationships which cannot be demonstrated. The lineage through which ancestors can actually be traced is called **umnombo.**

When a woman marries she takes on her husband's surname. However, she keeps her clan name which becomes prefixed with **Ma-** after marriage. You can call a person by his clan name, it is a friendly and warm term and is often used. Some examples are **Radebe**, **Dlamini**, **Bhelke**, **Civa**, **Tshawe**, **Dlomo** and **Madiba,** which is Nelson Mandela's clan name.

A newly married woman may be given a new first name by her mother-in-law. They are usually names formed from nouns to do with homes, hearth and care.

Nokhaya	Name formed from the noun 'home'.
Nomzi	From the noun 'village' or 'homestead'. cf p64
Nobantu	From the noun 'people'.
Nobuntu	From the noun 'humanity'. It generally means all the good characteristics of human beings.
Nomthunzi	One who gives shade.
Nolungile	One who gives brightness.

Some Xhosa names

Boy	**Girl**	**Meaning**
Themba	Thembeka	Faith/ Trust/ Hope
Nkululeko	Nonkululeko	Freedom
Sizwe	Nosizwe	Nation
Zolile	Nokuzola	Tranquility
Lunga	Nokulunga	Everything is right

Names in action

HERE ARE the names of a real family, the Kitshanas, whose children were born between 1928 and 1958 in the Eastern Cape. Their firstborn died at birth so when the second baby was born healthy and strong there was great joy and she was named **Buyelwa** (from the word **ukubuya**, 'to return' or 'come back'). The third child, a boy, was called **Vuyisile**. His name meant 'joy' and expressed the parents' happiness at the birth of their first son. The fourth child was also a boy and was called **Phindile**. This meant 'again' ('We have done it again!'). The fifth child was a girl named **Vuyiswa** which also means 'joy' and is the feminine form of Vuyisile. The sixth child was called **Mzimkulu**, which meant the family was now large enough! It is formed from the words **umzi**, 'home' and **khulu**, 'big'.

Mr Kitshana himself was called **Mlungwana**, which means 'little white man' because he was very pale when he was born. When he married, his mother wanted to name his bride **Noluthango**, which is a rich and beautiful name, implying the care of one who embraces the homesteads and protects them as would a fence. Instead she named her daughter-in-law **Nofence** by translating the Xhosa **uthango** into the English 'fence' and turning it into a name by prefixing it with **No-**. Although the translation was accurate, the richness of meaning was lost.[3]

Some expressions

Ngubani igama lakho?	What is your name?
Igama lam nguSipho.	My name is Sipho.
NdinguPiwe igama lam.	My name is Piwe.
Ngubani ifani yakho?	What is your surname?
Ifani yam nguMdoko.	My surname is Mdoko.
Ngubani isiduko sakho?	What is your clan name?
Isiduko sam nguTshawe.	My clan name is Tshawe.
Ngubani?	Who is it?
Ungubani?	Who are you?
NdinguDonald.	I am Donald.

3 Interview with Vuyiswa Totobela, describing the names of her own family, Grahamstown, 1989.

4 Making first contact

In Xhosa, greeting is a much more formal and structured affair than in English. Indeed, the Xhosa set great store in conversation and it is considered ill-mannered to pass a friend or stranger on a road without greeting and exchanging news. If you meet a group of people and you can't greet each one in turn, or if you don't know the people at all, you should address the older member of the group. Traditionally, you cannot address someone older than yourself by his or her first name, but always by their term of respect. Someone as old as your parents would be addressed as **Bawo**, 'Father', a formal and dignified address for a man, or **Mama**, 'Mother'. **Tata** is a more colloquial form of 'Father'. An older woman would be addressed as **Dabawo**, 'Auntie' or even **Anti.** You would address someone as old as your grandparents as **Tat'omkhulu**, 'Grandfather', or **Makhulu**, 'Grandmother'.

Greet someone your own age as **Sisi**, 'Sister', or **Bhuti**, 'Brother'. It is disrespectful to use these two terms when addressing someone older than yourself, although in extended families children refer to their parents as **Sisi** and **Bhuti** and their grandparents as **Bawo** and **Mama**. A father might also be called **Tateyi**, which is similar to 'Daddy'. If you don't know a professional person's surname you would address them by their professional title such as **Titshalakazi**, 'Teacher', **Mfundisi**, 'Reverend', or **Novenkile**, 'Shopkeeper'. **Wethu**, 'you', is often used by women to greet children they don't know.

The first greeting is made by the person arriving or leaving. People will wait for you to greet them first when you enter a room. You must 'take your leave' when you go. You will notice that when a person is asked 'how are you' they usually answer **hayi,** 'no', before saying they are well and not **ewe,** 'yes'. It also seems quite common to have a complaint about something like the weather or work even if the person feels well. A person might also say **noko** after 'no, I'm fine': **Hayi, ndisaphila noko**. **Noko** has no direct English equivalent, although it could mean 'actually', 'really' or 'sort of'. It is used for texture. It implies there is a problem which can't be shared and ensures the listener's sympathy.

How to greet

TO GREET one person, say **molo!** To greet more than one person, say **molweni!**

Molo and **molweni** are used in the morning, afternoon and also at night. They can mean 'hello', 'good day', 'good morning', 'good afternoon', 'good evening' and 'hi'.

Molo and **molweni** are used when you meet someone, not when you say goodbye. Although you could say **molo ke,** which means 'greetings, then' or 'so, good day' as a form of goodbye.

Molo is probably borrowed from the Afrikaans **gooie more,** 'good morning', and the English **morrow** in 'good morrow'. Although they are no longer used now, it is likely that **bhota** and **bhotani** were the original ways of greeting before the absorption into Xhosa of **molo** and **molweni.** Nowadays only old people use this greeting although it is apparently sometimes used by the Mfengu as a more casual way of greeting. The Reverend Albert Kropf listed it in his dictionary of 1899 as a greeting used between lovers and also between women, but never by men to greet each other. A.C. Jordan tried unsuccessfully to re-introduce the popular use of this greeting through his book *'A practical course in Xhosa'*. **Bhota** and **bhotani** have all the same meanings as **molo** and **molweni.**

You can also greet by saying **yitsho!** which means 'say so!'. The plural form is **yitshoni!** This form of greeting is commonly used between people who are equal in age or status, especially between males.[1]

When you say goodbye, you actually say 'go well' or 'stay well'.

If you say 'go well' to one person, say **hamba kakuhle** or **uhambe kakuhle.**

If you say 'go well' to more than one person, say **hambani kakuhle** or **nihambe kakuhle.**

If you say 'stay well' to one person, say **sala kakuhle** or **usale kakuhle.**

If you say 'stay well' to more than one person, say **salani kakuhle** or **nisale kakuhle.**

Ukusala means 'to stay behind', so you'd be saying, 'stay behind well', but you could also say 'live well' and then you'd use **hlala kakuhle** or **uhlale kakuhle.** Another form of goodbye is **hlala kamnandi** or simply **kamnandi,** which means 'live pleasantly'. You could also say **sakubonana** or **sobonana,** which mean 'we'll see each other again'.

1 G. Owen Lloyd, in his paper *'A study of some Xhosa Words of Afrikaans Origin'* (1955) refers to two other forms of greeting used at his time of writing: **royindara** from the Afrikaans **goeie dag,** 'good day', and **ronani** from the Afrikaans **goeie naand,** 'good evening'.

Xhosa women, by F. T. I'Ons

Greeting by name

ALL XHOSA nouns have prefixes as described in the grammar section of this book. When you call, greet, instruct or respond to someone by name, the first vowel of the prefix of their name falls away. If you greet them by their title as 'children', 'parents', 'teacher', 'people', 'father' etc., the first vowel will also fall away.

Molo Fazana!	Hello Fazana!
Molweni bantwana!	Hello children!
Molweni bafazi!	Hello parents!
Molweni madoda!	Hello men!

If you want to be more emphatic when calling or addressing someone you simply add **-ndini** to the end of their name. **-ndini** can also mean (my) dear.

Mfazindini!	You, woman!/ (my) dear woman!
Mfondini!	You, fellow!/ (my) dear fellow!
Kwedin'! [2]	You, boy!/ (my) dear boy!

2 **Kwedin'**! can be a slightly offensive and derogatory form of address, if the person is not a 'little boy'. Strollers and street children are often addressed in this way.

Greeting the family

PEOPLE often use the plural form when greeting each other. This is to acknowledge other family members who are not present and to enquire how they are in their absence.

Molweni ekhaya!	Hello all at home!
Molweni Themba!	Hello Themba and all!
Molweni mama!	Hello mother and family!

How to answer when someone greets you

WHEN people are greeted they usually answer: **Ewe, molo!** which means 'Yes, hello!'.

Molo Mary!	Ewe, molo John!
Molweni bantwana!	Ewe, molo Vuyo!

After saying 'Hello', you should ask your friend how she is.

Kunjani?	How are you?
Ninjani?	How are you? (plural to include the family)
Usaphila?	Are you still well? (Do you still live?)
Nisaphila?	Are you still well? (plural to include the family)

Some expressions

Akukho nto imbi (ekhaya).	There's nothing wrong (at home).
Akuncedi ukukhalaza.	It doesn't help to complain.
Nawe.	'And you' when someone says 'hamba kakuhle' to you.
Uxolo.	Excuse me.
Ndiyavuya ukukubona.	I'm glad to see you.
Ndinovuyo ukukubona.	I have happiness to see you/ I am with joy to see you.
Ndiyavuya ukukwazi.	I am pleased to know you.
Mfan'am.	My little man/sonny - an affectionate term.
Nantso ke!	There, you have it!
Ndilapha.	I am here.
Uyandiqonda?	Do you understand me?
Ngena endlwini.	Come into the house.
Kulungile ke.	Alright then.
Kunjani kuwe?	How's it with you?
Uthini na?	What do you say?
Kunjani?	How are you? (singular)/ How's it?
Ninjani?	How are you? (plural)/ How's it?
Kunjani na?/ Ninjani na?	How's it? How're things going?
Uphila njani?	How are you?/ Do you live? (singular)
Niphila njani?	How are you? / Do you live? (plural)
Usaphila?	How are you?/ Do you still live? (singular)

Kunjani ngempilo?	How is your health? (singular)
Ninjani ngempilo?	How is your health? (plural)
Niyavuka?	How are you?/Are you awake? (plural)
Nivuka njani?	How are you? This is the way to ask someone how *everything* is and the respondent usually goes into a long explanation of the weather, work, illness, etc. before asking the same of his friend.
Yiz' apha, xhego.	Come here, old man. (Xhego can be used in a loving, teasing way to address a young boy.)
Ndisaphila noko nam.	I am well after all/ Notwithstanding things, I am also well.
Uphuma phi? /Niphuma phi?	Where are you from? (Where do you go out from?) Plural form implies family origin.
Usuka phi?	Where do you hail from?
Uvela phi?	Where do you come from?

Vocabulary

ukuthetha	to speak
ukuncokola	to chat
incoko	a conversation/dialogue
ukubulisa	to greet/salute
ukubulisela	to give greetings on behalf of another
umbuliso	a greeting
ukubuza	to ask
ukudibana	to meet/to mingle
ukuhleka	to laugh
ukubulela	to thank
ukubuya	to come back
umhlobo, imihlobo	a friend
ubuhlobo	friendship
ukuphendula	to answer/reply
impendulo	an answer/a reply
ukuphulaphula	to listen
uthando	love/affection
ukuthanda	to love
ukuthetha	to speak
ukuvuya	to be glad/to rejoice
ukusabela	to reply/to send back an echo
ukubuza impilo	to ask of health. (This asks after the health, well-being, doings, etc. of a person's family and himself/herself. It is the first long exchange after a greeting.)
ukufika	to arrive/to be at a new place (**Siyafika apha.** - 'We are new here.')
kakuhle	well
kanene	really/indeed/truly
ukuvela	to come from

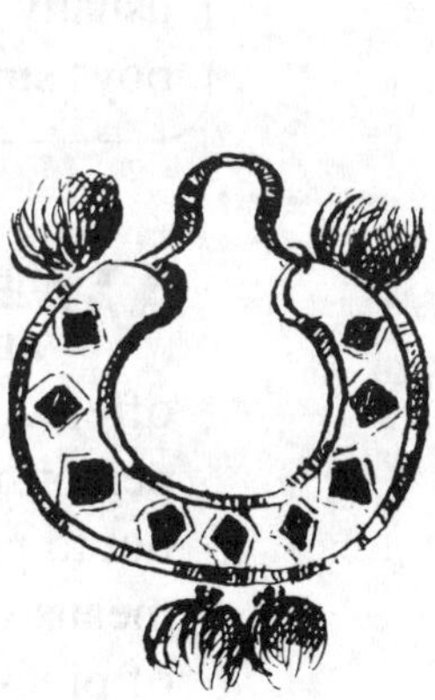

5 The sharing of tobacco

"They are passionately devoted to tobacco smoking. Men and women, although the former more so than the latter, smoke tobacco they have cultivated themselves, or they use the leaves of a certain other plant to which the Hottentots have given the name Dacha. The bowl of the pipe, which is cut from wood, has the same shape as that of an ordinary clay pipe, save that it is a great deal bigger; the barrel is straight and five to six inches long."

"Another type of tobacco pipe is seen less frequently. In that case the bowl and the mouthpiece, which in the latter case is longer than in the former, is not directly joined together, but is divided by a horn, usually that of an eland, which is filled with water, in which the smoke loses its sharpness. In company the pipe is passed round from one to the other, each one has a few strong draws and passes on the esteemed pleasure dispenser to his neighbour. The skin of a bluebuck, the smallest of the antelope family, which does not grow more than thirteen inches high, usually serves the purpose of a tobacco pouch. I never saw small girls and boys smoking."[1]

When people are gathered in a group it is customary to pass a pipe around for everyone to smoke. Tobacco is shared and if it is not offered someone will invariably ask whether anyone has a supply. Each person uses their own mouthpiece, not so much for reasons of hygiene but to prevent witchcraft. It is believed that a person can be bewitched by means of their body substances, such as spittle or hair. The significance of pipes in Xhosa society may be illustrated by the metaphor used when someone dies, **wayibeka inqawa**, 'he has laid down his pipe'.[2]

1 L. Alberti, 1807, pages 25-26.
2 T.S. Soga, 1931, page 344.

6 The traditional dress of the Xhosa

"The clothing consists of animal skins, which they are extremely handy at making. In general they use the skins of oxen or cows for their clothing. The principal apparel, in the case of both sexes, consists of a mantle. On long journeys and hunting expeditions the men protect the feet with soles made of ox-hide, which are secured by straps passed around the foot between the big toe, or otherwise by a top piece of leather which covers the whole foot, leaving the toes exposed. The women, unlike the men, do not go about bare-headed but wear caps made from the skin of some kind of antelope.

Apart from these pieces of apparel, one sees a quantity of ornaments of different kinds. Frequently the head is adorned with a shock of hair from the tail of an antelope. Some men wear a row of small copper or iron rings. Both men and women adorn themselves with necklaces of a variety of shells or with a number of strings of glass beads. Bracelets trimmed with shells, as well as rings of copper and iron, are worn by men and women chiefly over the wrists and both men and women adorn the amply pierced ears with strings of glass beads of the smallest variety, from which a number of larger ones are suspended." [1]

Woman wearing a kaross

The Xhosa originally wore skin garments. Men's cloaks were usually made of a single ox-hide and, reaching to the calves or to the ground, were just wide enough to close in front. Most cloaks were worn with the animal hair on the inside while the outside was curried, well greased and treated with ochre or dye. They were often worn over one shoulder and under the other arm. In warm weather they were slung back over the shoulders or not worn at all. Under their cloaks men wore only leather penis-sheaths attached to a loincloth.[2] Women wore more elaborate cloaks, joined together from three or four wedged pieces which almost formed a circle. They were narrow at the shoulders and covered a woman's body generously, allowing sufficient material to cover a child supported in a goat-skin sling or in the lap of a lightweight cloak bound at the waist with a thong.[3] Attached to the back of the cloak at the neck was a loose strip of skin, **isibhaca**, worn with the hair on the outside and

1 L. Alberti, 1807, page 29.
2 Lucy Alexander, 1990, page 32.

FAR LEFT: Mfengu girls by G. F. Angas, c. 1849.
LEFT: Xhosa woman in skirt by F.T. I'Ons, c.1846

ornamented with brass buttons in longitudinal rows. The central row was made up of rounded buttons while the others were flat. The amount of ornamentation of the **isibhaca** reflected the wealth of the wearer. In the 19th century the Xhosa and Mfengu attached fine steel chains as ornaments to their cloaks. A secondary wrap was sometimes worn under the cloak and this would be secured under the arms, around the waist or under the chin. Women wore a small apron around their loins but from 1820 onwards, as a result of European contact, they wore a skin skirt fastened at the waist and hanging just below the knees.[4]

Europeans introduced the Xhosa to cloth in the 19th century. Imported woven fabrics such as woollen blankets, cotton blanketing, melton cloth, cashmere and towelling started to take the place of skins, although skin garments survived for ceremonial dress.[5] The cloak was probably the first item to be altered by contact with Europeans and the nearer people lived to the Colony the sooner this occurred. By 1835 men of lower ranks began to use woollen blankets as cloaks.

The thick, loosely woven cotton cloth known as 'sheeting' became very fashionable and was made into garments and bags. The Mfengu

3 Ibid., page 34.
4 Ibid.
5 Ibid., page 32.

were the first to adopt cotton-sheeting as skirt material, probably around 1860, and by the end of the century all groups were using it, often coloured with ochre. By then mission converts wore skirts of European style with a blouse and headcloth.

The cotton-sheeting was originally imported from Lancashire but manufactured in East London from the 1930s. Its use continued well into the 20th century, but, with the increasing trend towards Western style fashion, the use of this fabric declined considerably and it is now no longer manufactured.[6] A blue, highly patterned cotton print, known as German Print, was in common use by the late 19th century and is still used today. It was originally dyed with indigo.

Married women covered their heads, usually with a cap made of antelope skin which was highly decorated with beads. Its last recorded use was in 1880 and it was rapidly replaced by highly coloured handkerchiefs, first recorded in 1827, or squares of spotted material, mentioned as early as 1844.[7] Women often carried a small leather pouch around their necks which contained an awl used for sewing or hairdressing. They sometimes wore circlets of cowrie shells around their heads or threaded beads and seeds into their hair. Metal bangles were popular ornaments for both men and women.[8]

The traditional form of clothing which developed through the use of cloth, beads and buttons is still seen today in remote areas. This traditional form of dress reflects, through ornamentation, the various social and life stages of the wearer.

Traditional babies usually go naked except for a simple string of beads and a pubic covering called **inkciyo**, worn from the age of one year.[9] Baby girls wear a little back apron as well. Children wear a pubic covering with a kaross for warmth made of either sheep-skin or a blanket. Young, uninitiated girls wear short skirts decorated with strips of black

6 Interview with Gail Boy, owner of Osher Bros. Trading Store, Grahamstown, 1992.
7 Lucy Alexander, 1990, page 35.
8 Ibid., page 35.
9 Joan Broster, 1976, page 6.

cotton fabric which are sometimes decorated with beads. Their breasts are left bare and a cotton-sheeting shawl is worn around the shoulders. They may also wear an **inkciyo**, often handed down from mother to daughter, and a head scarf.

Youths wear a loincloth and a blanket decorated with strips of fabric. If they have returned from working on the mines or other employment in the cities they wear black shorts and a blanket to show they have attained senior status. Young Bhaca men who have returned from the mines wear elegant, wide-legged trousers, bell-bottomed and tied at the ankles.[10] Youths and men alike carry sticks which have been decorated with beadwork or plastic tubing.

Xhosa chief and his wives, by F.T .I'Ons

Married women and women of marriageable age originally wore skin skirts called **izikhaka**. Now they wear a long wrap-around braided skirt called **umbhaco** made from cotton-sheeting or a blanket with a black strip woven into it. The number of rows of black braid sewn around the bottom of a skirt indicates the status of a woman in her household. Married women wear a narrow bib-like apron with their skirts. This is called **incebetha** and is made of cotton-sheeting. It is tied above the breasts and hangs down to the braiding on the skirt. A lightly braided cotton-sheeting shawl called **ibhayi** is worn over the shoulders. It takes its name from Algoa Bay (Port Elizabeth) the port through which the cotton-sheeting was originally imported. The Eastern Mpondo decorate these shawls with beadwork as well as braid. Skirts are held up by a beaded belt from which hangs a leather purse. Men wear a short braided skirt on ceremonial occasions, carrying a blanket over one shoulder.

Headgear, tobacco bags and pipes

TRADITIONAL youths and young girls wear coloured handkerchiefs or patterned scarves or sometimes simply a beaded headband. Newly initiated young men wear a simple black headscarf as they should not boast. A young wife wears a black headscarf tied closely to her head and well down over her eyes to indicate low status and the respectful attitude which is due to her husband's family. This is part of the **ukuhlonipha** tradition of respect for young brides. Men and older married women wear spectacular turbans.

Tobacco bags are part of ceremonial dress. Women's bags are usually made of cotton-sheeting decorated with beads and braid. Men often use tobacco bags made from goat-skin. In early days they would have used the skins of wild animals such as the dassie. Decorated tobacco bags and beaded pipes are considered essential for festive dress. Pipes are made by hand from wood and their shape and size differ for each age group. Old men usually smoke a short-stemmed, large, squat-bowled pipe. Youths and young women use slim pipes of medium length. Old women use

10 Joan Broster, 1976, page 18. Photograph page 93.

long pipes, which may reach to 50 centimetres, to show their age and prestige.[11]

Ochre and scarification

COLOUR has a deep religious significance amongst traditional Xhosa people. The people who worship ancestors are called **amaQaba**, 'the red people' because they paint themselves with red ochre or clay.[12] Red oxide called **imbola**, the colour of which is considered to be the blood of the earth, is used to colour the body, clothing and blankets. It is the emblem of happiness and faith because it is believed to be the colour beloved by the ancestral spirits. When it is used as a dye, the ochre is mixed in a basin of water and the clothing or blanket is kneaded in the mixture. The article is then laid out in the sun to dry. To keep the colour glowing, the process needs to be repeated often.[13]

The colour of the ochre varies from the orange-red used by the Bomvana to the brown-red favoured by the Mfengu and the deep brick-red of the Thembu. The Xesibe beat local earth into their garments to obtain a grey colour. The Eastern and some Western Mpondo prefer 'washing blue', small blocks of commercial bleach sold by traders. A strong solution produces a blue colour.[14]

Tradition has it that, at the turn of the last century, when the great chief Marhelane of Eastern Pondoland died, his people gave up the use of red ochre and wore white which is the traditional colour of mourning. One day, in an attempt to whiten her husband's blanket, a woman used a packet of washing blue. But she used too much and the blanket came out a very pretty blue. The colour was an immediate success and ever since then the Mpondo have blued their blankets and tribal dress. They use pale turquoise beads contrasted with white, black and orange.[15]

When ochre is not used by the 'red people' it means something abnormal or supernatural has happened. Then the red ochre is replaced by white ochre.[16] Sometimes a person is temporarily excluded from tribal life and this is shown by the use of white clay in place of ochre to cover the face, body and clothing. White clay is used by a breast-feeding mother to show that she is excluded from sexual relationships until her baby is weaned. It is used by the girl undergoing initiation into womanhood and the young man during circumcision rites as an effective signal to others of their condition.[17] The use of white clay shows that the wearer must be approached with decorum. White also has a special significance for the **amagqirha,** the traditional healers. They are called **abantu abamhlope**, 'the white people', which can be translated as

11 Joan Broster, 1967, page 76.
12 **Ukuqaba** means 'to paint with red ochre or red clay'.
13 Joan Broster, 1976, page 3.
14 Ibid.
15 Joan Broster, 1973, 1979, page 11.
16 Ibid.
17 Joan Broster, 1976, page 4.

'people of light'. They dress in white, use white clay, wear white beads and strips of white-haired goat-skin. They also carry the white brush or switch of the beast sacrificed on the day of graduation.

Use is also made of tattoo marks and scarification to enhance beauty. This practice is probably a relic from the days of tribal warfare, when women and girls were carried off and later, when rescued, could be identified by their marks. Girls of the Thembu tribe are scarified from the naval in three lines between the breasts and then in three diagonal lines above and below the breasts. Youths of the same age have the same horizontal lines.[18] Bhaca girls are scarified on their faces, Gcaleka girls on their shoulders and arms.[19]

18 Ibid., page 21.
19 Joan Broster, 1973, page 19 and unnumbered.

7 The language of beads

"How often on a cold winter's day in the shop I have heard a Qaba mother say, 'Oh my child has simply nothing to wear. I must buy him some beads.' "[1]

The wearing of beads goes back hundreds of years. Before the introduction of glass beads the Xhosa made them from natural materials such as teeth, horn, bone, ivory, wood, seeds, shells, ostrich egg shell and metal. They strung beads onto aloe fibre or twisted strands of animal sinew to make necklaces, belts, bracelets and anklets. Beads were scarce and highly valued because each was painstakingly made. They were used as currency, valued gifts and adornment.

The first glass beads were introduced to north Africa by Arab traders before 1500. These men also traded along the east coast of Africa, travelling in their dhows and introducing glass beads made in Venice by master craftsmen who had learnt their art from wandering Jewish and Byzantine glassworkers. Through existing indigenous trade routes, glass beads made their way down through Africa until some of them reached the Xhosa in southern Africa. These beads were scarce, difficult to obtain and very valuable. They were worn simply, in single strands.

From about 1500 until 1700 the Portuguese dominated the maritime trade of the Indian ocean and they used beads to pay for gold and ivory. In their voyages around the Cape both Bartholomew Dias and Vasco Da Gama exchanged glass and carnelian beads for fresh supplies of meat and water.[2] Agate and carnelian were mined in India where the town of Cambay in the west was the main centre for bead manufacture and distribution.[3] Carnelian and agate beads were highly prized for many centuries, not only for adornment but also because they were believed to have religious and magical properties. These 16th and 17th century trade values will give an idea of how prized carnelian and agate were.

Six to eight beads = one fat ox.
A girdle of agate or carnelian beads = one slave.
A copper bar or 40 - 50 beads = 4 clothes (sic).[4]

1 Joan Broster, 1967, page 22.
2 Ibid., page 20.
3 Carnelian is the geological name for the mineral, but the beads are often referred to as cornelian.
4 East London museum, 1993 exhibition on shipwrecks along Eastern Cape coast.

Carnelian and agate are varieties of chalcedony. Carnelian is clear red or reddish-brown and agate varies in colour. Selected stones were exposed to the sun and then baked to deepen their colour. They were then chipped and polished by hand into a variety of shapes and holes were drilled from each end with a bow drill.

Many Portuguese ships returning home from India were wrecked along the Indian Ocean coast.[5] On these shores, particularly along the Pondoland coast, one can still find the ancient carnelian stone beads from India and the early glass beads from Arabia, washed ashore from wrecks which have lain on the ocean floor for centuries.[6]

Large numbers of beads have been found at the site of the Sao Bento wreck (1554) at Msikaba near Port Edward and the Santo Esprito site (1608) at Haga Haga near East London, indicating that the vessels had substantial bead cargoes. From information gathered from local farmers and traders it has been ascertained that at least 5 000 carnelian beads were collected from the site of the Santo Esprito wreck alone.[7] During the 1920s and 1930s large numbers of beads were collected along the stretch of beach immediately north-east of the Umzimvubu River from the Belem wreck and the beach was appropriately called Agate Terrace.[8] No beads have been found at sites dated later than 1643 because by then the Portuguese trade in beads was already in decline. By the last part of the 17th century the trade in carnelian beads had virtually ceased.

After the Dutch and English settled at the Cape glass beads became more freely available but remained expensive. Initially the Xhosa obtained glass and metal beads through the Khoi who got them from the Dutch at the Cape. By the 1800s the supply of beads to the Xhosa had increased as a result of direct contact with Dutch colonists and the establishment of trade fairs by the British. Beads became more common and much cheaper as white traders set up trading stations in areas occupied by the Xhosa. Once the price of beads dropped they became more accessible to more people and an extensive beadcraft developed. Beads became an integral part of Xhosa culture and yielded an art which had a beauty rich in imagination and aesthetic appeal. More complex designs and stringing methods evolved and the use of beads as currency declined. Being illiterate, the people used beads as a form of communication to record messages and they developed a form of symbolism contained in colour combination and motif. Each tribe had its own colour preference and used none other.[9] Their different colours and designs portrayed tribal traditions and defined the social status, religious

---

5 Shipwreck sites which yielded beads: Sao Joao (1552), Port Edward; Sao Bento (1554), Msikaba; Santo Alberto (1593), Sunrise on sea - only one bead known from this wreck; Nossa Senhora de Belem (1635), Port St Johns; Santo Esprito (1608), Haga Haga; Santa Maria Madre de Deus (1643), Bonza Bay; Sao Goncalo (1630), Plettenberg Bay.

6 Fine specimens of these can be seen in the East London museum.

7 Axelson, 1988, pages 60- 61.

8 Ibid., page 73.

9 Joan Broster, 1967, page 21.

status, rank and wealth of the wearer. They identified initiated, courting or married people and told who had children. From birth to old age the beads told a story and blended subtly into the social structure.[10] They were worn by men, women and children but made exclusively by women, especially young girls and unmarried women.

In more recent times beads were threaded on 'Coates Number 10 strong stranded cotton'. Originally a method called **usinga**, 'sinew', was used. The long sinew taken from either side of the backbone of a beast was dried before being carefully teased into threads. These were rounded and rolled and were thick enough to thread beads without a needle.[11] Although glass beads were essentially foreign to the Xhosa, they became such an integral part of their culture that their use is accepted as being traditional.[12]

Bead wearing began with the simple strings of beads worn by children and young teenagers. As adolescence advanced so bead wearing

10 Ibid., page 171.
11 Ibid., page 20.
12 Dawn Costello, 1990, page 3.

progressed until it reached its high period during courtship when it had a deeply emotional significance.

Beads were woven together into flat shapes to cover mirrors, leather purses, belts, bottles, pipes, whistles, sticks, tin cans, blanket pins and anything else that could be worn or used. The flat bead articles were further combined with multiple ropes of beads to make body harnesses and gay trappings for the head, neck and limbs. Finally, all tribal dress - aprons, shawls, skirts, blankets, bags, even umbrellas, were decorated and edged with beads.[13]

The different Xhosa societies used blue, pink, red and white beads in different combinations with the addition of various specific other colours, according to custom. The Thembu used deep turquoise with red, white and navy. Mature persons used navy with white and pink. The Mfengu preferred pink, blue and white with a deeper blue and pink combination for wide collars. They also used red, black, and dark blue beads worked on a white background for large beaded tabs decorated with animal and human shapes. The Mpondomise worked mainly with blue, pink, red and white. The Xesibe liked green and orange. The Gcaleka preferred bright turquoise with red, navy and white, with older persons using pink instead of red. Mpondo beadwork was predominantly blue with contrasts of white, orange and black. The Xhosa proper used white, pink, blue and red with black and navy for outlining.

Early missionaries saw beadwork as an outward sign of paganism. In order to break pagan practices they forbade their Christian converts to wear beads, use ochre or wear tribal dress. They were also forbidden to take part in tribal dances or sacrifices.[14]

In modern times, with increasing Christianisation and modernisation, traditional beadwork has all but vanished. With the introduction of sanctions against South Africa during the apartheid years the importation of glass beads became expensive and difficult. Trade embargoes imposed from the 1960s ended the supply of Venetian beads which had reached the Xhosa since the 16th century and Czechoslovakian beads which had been imported since the 1940s. Glass beads could only be bought through agents acting as 'middlemen' who clandestinely broke trade restrictions. This meant that beads could only be bought expensively by the ton and small traders could no longer afford to stock them. Trade restrictions also limited the choice of colour.

In 1975 the cultural historian, Joan Broster, saw a Thembu woman buying orange beads at Ally Sheppard's trading store near Clarkebury: "This is not a colour traditionally worn by the Thembu. I asked her why she was using this colour. She shrugged in resignation, saying, 'what can we do when this is all there is to buy?' "[15]

13 Joan Broster, 1967, page 32.
14 Ibid., page 171.
15 Interview with Joan Broster, Gonubie, 1991.

8 Trade

From the earliest times Xhosa people used cattle, copper, iron and beads as forms of currencies which were both interchangeable and could be exchanged for other goods and services. Xhosa trade with the north-west Tswana tribes, the Kwena and Tlhaping (known to the Xhosa as the 'Briqua' or 'goat people') goes back to the 17th century. The Xhosa were at the southern end of a trade network in which iron, copper, cattle, tobacco and dagga were the main commodities.[1]

In their trade with the east they received iron which probably originated from the Zizi and Hlubi in Natal. Beads introduced into East Africa by the Portuguese circulated in Xhosaland and from the Mpondo came blue antelope skins, rare shells and shark skin.[2]

There are records of Xhosa trading honey with the Khoi in exchange for small stock and Xhosa tobacco which was specially cultivated for Khoi trade.[3] One report states that parties of Khoi travelled to the Xhosa every year to trade copper and beads for dagga at a designated time and place.[4]

Colonisation brought a new kind of economy into southern Africa - one based on gold and coinage. This new system of exchange ran alongside the pre-colonial Xhosa economy for quite some time without crushing it. But this new system presented special problems for the Xhosa. It did not recognise the exchange value of any of its own commodities once they had been traded out to the Xhosa, so a man could trade ivory for beads but he could not buy a blanket or pot with those beads.

Exchange between the Boers and the Xhosa began in the early 18th century. By 1752 there was already a considerable trade in ivory and by 1770 there was a well-beaten wagon road into Xhosaland.[5] Copper, iron and beads from the Colony were bartered for cattle and ivory.

The Xhosa chiefs were primarily interested in the cattle trade and competed with each other for potential trading partners from the Colony. Certain Boers kept trade goods and were visited by Xhosa wishing to exchange these for cattle.

The Dutch East India Company government at the Cape tried at

1 J. B. Peires, 1981, page 97.
2 Ibid.
3 J. B. Peires, 1981, page 97, quoting W. Paterson, 1789, page 93.
4 Ibid., quoting S.J.K. van Maaslandsluys q. G. Harinck, 1969, page 165.
5 Ibid., page 98, quoting D.Moodie, 1840.

Wagons on Market Square, Grahamstown by Thomas Baines, 1850

certain times to prohibit trade because it feared that quarrels over value might result in war. Yet at other times it must have encouraged trade because the Xhosa were regarded as one of the two chief suppliers of meat during times of shortfall in Cape Town.[6]

After the British took over the Cape in 1806 there were concerted attempts, particularly by Governor Sir John Cradock, to end trade with the Xhosa and Khoi, but these were generally unsuccessful.[7] With the arrival of the British settlers in 1820 the illegal cattle and ivory trade was soon in full swing and the colonial government, unable to stop the trade, decided to institute official trade fairs.[8]

The Xhosa insisted on beads and buttons being available for barter at these fairs. This was because, among themselves, these items were convertible into the only form of wealth that interested the Xhosa - cattle. With beads received for a single hide they could get a living beast further inland. For the Xhosa this was not barter but a money exchange. They were selling their cattle dear and replacing them with cattle bought cheaply elsewhere.[9] Another reason for the demand for beads and buttons was that they enabled profit to be shared among several people, for

6 J.B. Peires, 1981, page 99, quoting minutes of a special and supreme commission: 27th Feb. 1801, R.C.C. IV, page 199.
7 Ibid., page 99.
8 Ibid.
9 Ibid.

instance the group who killed an elephant.[10]

Trade fairs became regular events from 1824. The first seven months of that year drew 50 441 pounds of ivory, 16 800 pounds of gum and about 15 000 hides.[11] Xhosa from as far as the eastern side of the Kei River and Thembuland attended the fairs, which seem to have attracted two or three thousand people at a time.[12] The fairs were often accompanied by dancing and a beaded neck cascade, **istokfele,** derived its name from these stock fairs.[13] Less than two years after the trade fairs were instituted the colonists had, in return for beads, buttons and brass wire, received 112 943 pounds of ivory and 46 575 hides worth £74 620. By the 1830s Xhosa trade was valued at £40 000 a year.[14]

The colonial government abandoned trade fairs in 1830 and allowed traders to penetrate the interior, where they soon established regular stations.[15] They spread as far as Pondoland, establishing stations at which they resided for months at a time. This process was accelerated by the big traders who set up poor, white settlers in business as their agents. The settler trading network soon eliminated the Xhosa traders by virtue of its more efficient wagon transport and its control over the supply of trade goods.[16] Above all, once the supply of beads was made general throughout the interior their resale value was destroyed.[17] The Xhosa, who had been moving settler beads and buttons between the fairs and the interior, were unable to compete with these trading stations. As a result they lost the profits made as middlemen between the Colony and inland tribes.

Because the colonists placed no re-trading value on their own commodities but accepted only cattle, ivory, hides, gum or their own coins in barter, the Xhosa began losing spending power when ivory and hides became scarce through over-hunting. When this happened they were forced to purchase things from the colonists with the only 'money' they had - their cattle.

Without cattle the Xhosa were poor men, both in their own economic terms and in those of their colonisers. Their wealth was eroded, firstly, by loss of grazing lands which the colonial government confiscated and then by the depredations of the Frontier Wars when the colonial government killed and confiscated cattle as a military tactic. In addition, thousands of cattle died from lung sickness, a disease brought to South Africa from Europe in 1853 by a Dutch ship carrying Friesland bulls to

10 Ibid., quoting W.R.Thompson- J. Gregory, 30 April 1825, page 178.

11 Ibid., quoting Andrew Smith, Kaffir Notes, S.A. Museum, Cape Town.

12 Ibid., quoting various writers who give descriptions of trade fairs.

13 Dawn Costello, 1990, page 63: "The **istokfele** is a white neck cascade. While dancing the long streamers are thrown over the shoulder to hang over the buttocks where they sway in rhythm with body movement."

14 Ben Maclennan, 1986, page 230.

15 J.B. Peires 1981, page 99, quoting Ordinance 81 of 1830.

16 Ibid., page 102.

17 Ibid., quoting M.Donaldson, 1974, page 313.

Grahamstown, 1848

Mossel Bay.[18] Even though the Cape government hurriedly issued regulations to check the spread of the disease and the Xhosa took all the precautions they could to escape from it, lung sickness spread uncontrollably. Xhosa losses from lung sickness ran at about 5 000 cattle a month.[19] Finally, the desperate destruction of their herds in the Great Cattle Killing (1856-7) dealt the final blow to the wealth and independence of the Xhosa people. The resultant dependence of the Xhosa on their colonisers meant that eventually their own labour would become the only thing of value they had to trade.

18 J. B. Peires, 1989, page 70.
19 Ibid., page 71.

9 Names of towns and cities

"The word uQamata was used by some instead of uNkhulukhulu (to name God). I was told if any good fortune came to them they said, 'Qamata', and the name Qamata Poort originated in this way. The people in that part were lucky, fortunate above all others, so that they called that part of the country Qamata." [1]

In early times the Xhosa usually named places after some natural occurrence at the site, such as the type of mountain, the birds or animals which lived there, or the flowers and trees which grew in the vicinity. Places might also be named after famous chiefs or battles. Often a place name shared the same name as the river which ran through it because the Xhosa always settled near rivers or tributaries. Places which had many rivers and streams would be well populated by many communities. A large land area drained by a single river was likely to be occupied by a single community only. Usually a chiefdom had its own river and each sub-chiefdom had its own tributary.[2] Often the Xhosa used Khoi place and river names or adapted them into Xhosa. Some Xhosa and Khoi place names were retained by white settlers but most of them were replaced by English or Afrikaans names and these in turn were adapted phonologically by the Xhosa. Nowadays Xhosa speakers often know a place by two names, its English or Afrikaans name and its Xhosa name.

iMpofu	Seymour	Named after the elands which once roamed the area. [3] A military post called Eland's Post was built there in 1862. Seymour lies beneath the slopes of the Elandsberg mountain range.
iNqweba	Kirkwood	Perhaps from **umnqwebebana**, the Cape snowdrop. [4]
iDike	Alice	From **idike**, 'the deep pool' , or 'the lake'.

1 Joan Broster, 1967, page 68, quoting her grandfather, William John Clarke. Qamata is situated between Queenstown and Cofimvaba.
2 J.B.Peires, 1981, page 2.
3 Interview with Vuyiswa Totobela, Grahamstown, 1991.
4 Ibid.

iDaliwe	Cathcart	From **uDaliwe**, 'the place of paintings', referring to a cliff near the Thorn River on which San paintings are found. Cathcart's more common name, **iKathikati**, is a phonological adaptation of the English.
uBelekazana	Hogsback mountain	From **ukubeleka**, 'to carry a child on the back', from the mountain's fanciful appearance to a woman carrying a child or baby on her back.
iNyarha	Bedford	Derived from the Khoi, meaning 'river where many reeds grow'.
iLanga	Langa	Named after a chief.
Esikhaleni	Hole-in-the-wall	'At the place of the sound'. Heavy surf shoulders its way through this sea-cliff, making a deep rumble.
eGazini	The Kowie ditch	'Place of blood', where many Xhosa warriors died during the Battle of Grahamstown in 1819.[5]
iGoli	Johannesburg	From **igolide**, meaning 'gold' and adapted from the English.
iRawuthi	Johannesburg	From **irawuti**, meaning 'gold' and adapted from the Afrikaans, 'goud'.
iMonti	East London	From the Afrikaans 'mond', for the 'mouth' of the Buffalo River.
iBhayi	Port Elizabeth	Once called Algoa Bay. From the Afrikaans 'baai', meaning 'bay'.
inGxokolo	King William's Town	This was the first name given to King William's Town and means 'a vast number of things, men, cattle and houses, all together'.[6]

The following place names were not renamed by settlers but retained their beautiful Xhosa names.

Gonubie	Named after the brambleberries which once grew there.[7] From **uMqunube**, 'bramble bush', which is the Xhosa adaptation of the Khoi.
Lusikisiki	Takes its name from the sound of the wind blowing through marsh reeds in the evening.[8]
Mgwali	Named after a traditional harp.
Taleni	Named after a ledge of exposed rock.
Addo	Adapted from the Khoi, probably meaning 'euphorbia ravine'.
Engcobo	**Ingcobo** was the name of the long grass which grew on the hillside where Engcobo stands. Engcobo means 'at the place of the ingcobo grass'.[9]
Bizana	From **imbizana** meaning 'a small pot', referring to its situation in a hollow.

5 J.B. Peires, 1981, page 144.
6 Kropf-Godfrey, 1915, pages 114 and 500.
7 Interview with Lou Moore, Gonubie, 1983.
8 Interview with Nozizwe Mngqibisa, Tsakana, 1984.
9 Interview with Joan Broster, Gonubie, 1992.

Indwe	From the Xhosa name for the blue cranes, once found there in great numbers.
Komga (iQumrha)	Named after the red clay mines in the area. **Iqumrha** means 'red clay' or 'red ochre'.
Kasuka, Kasouga	Xhosa adaptation from the Khoi, meaning 'place of many leopards'.
Tarkastad	Adapted from the Xhosa, 'area of many birds'.
Xalanga	'The place of vultures' - the great sandstone cliffs of the Drakensburg range.
Umgazi Valley	Named after the Umgazi River, the 'blood' river. So many tribal fights broke out along this river that it was said to flow with blood.
Umtata	The town stands on the Umtata River. The name means 'the taker' and is derived from the phrase 'Take him, our Father', used in the river-burial ceremonies accorded to Mpondo chiefs.

Some places still have their Khoi names, although the clicks are no longer pronounced.

Keiskamma	'Large river'.
Cango	'Wet mountain'. It could also mean 'door' from the Xhosa **ucango**, and refer to the entrance to the large underground caves. [10]
Kareedouw	'Dry mountain pass'.
Goodhouse	'Gu-daos', meaning 'sheep pass'.
Tsitsikamma	'Clear sparkling water'.
Patensie	'Resting place for cattle'.

The names of cities are usually phonologically adapted from the English or Afrikaans.

iPitoli	Pretoria
iKapa	Cape Town
iBhofolo	Fort Beaufort
iTinara	Uitenhage

Black townships are usually named in Xhosa.

Emnyameni	Alexandria, 'Place of darkness'. Probably so-named because there was originally no electricity in Alexandria township. [11]
Khayelitsha	'New home', built as a new township for the squatter-residents of Old Crossroads in Cape Town .
Thembisa	'Promise'.
Guguletu	'Our pride'. (Also spelt Gugulethu.)

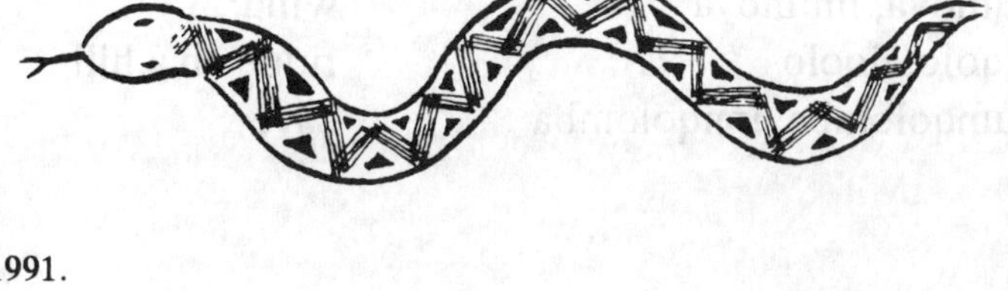

10 Interview with Vuyiswa Totobela, Grahamstown, 1991.
11 Ibid.

Vocabulary

umda, imida	a boundary
indawo, iindawo	a place
indlela, iindlela	a road
umendo (no plural)	a path
idolophu, iidolophu	a town/village
umzi, imizi	a homestead/ kraal/village
isixeko, izixeko	a city
ilizwe, amazwe	land/country
ukufika	to arrive/to reach
ukufuduka	to migrate/ to move to a new home
ukugoduka	to go home
ukuhamba	to travel/to walk
ukumka	to depart
ukusondela	to approach
ukusondeza	to bring near
ukuwela	to cross a river or sea

Geographical vocabulary

ihlabathi, amahlabathi	the world
ulwandle, iilwandle	the sea
unxweme, iinxweme	shore
isiqithi, iziqithi	island
intlango, iintlango	wilderness/desert
induli, iinduli	hill/kopje
isiduli, iziduli	ant-hill
umgxobhozo, imigxobhozo	swamp
isibhakabhaka, izibhakabhaka	sky/firmament
udonga, iindonga	washed out gully
umfula, imifula	valley
umlambo, imilambo	river
umlanjana, imilanjana	small river
ingxangxasi, iingxangxasi	waterfall
umhlaba, imihlaba	the earth/ground
ilanga, amalanga	sun
inyanga, iinyanga	moon
umoya, imimoya	wind
iqolo, iiqolo	ridge on a hill
umqolomba, imiqolomba	cave

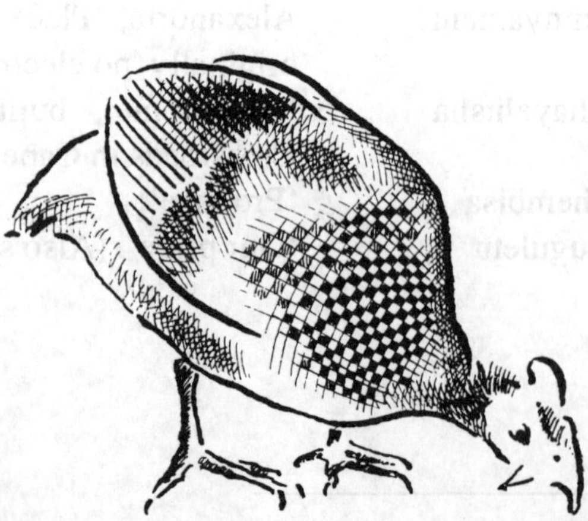

10 Travel, travellers and travellers' cairns

"The ancient Xhosa traveller fortified himself with charms and herbs such as **inyongwane** (*dicoma anomola*) which would enable him to vomit up poisoned food the instant he received it. For more visible dangers he carried a bundle of sticks and spears. Well-trodden footpaths guided him through dense woods of mimosa trees, punctuated with yellowwood, erythrina, spekboom, which the elephants ate, and sneezewood, the toughest of them all, which was hardened in fire to provide a substitute for iron. Emerging from the woods he might pass through long stretches of open plain covered with long **umqungu,** 'tambuki' grass, so high that it hid a man completely. If a river was too full to cross at the ford he might make a raft from reeds or simply hang onto the tail of his oxen." [1]

"On travels it is quite usual to use a bull for the moving of household articles and other requirements. A rounded piece of wood about six inches long and one inch thick is inserted diagonally through the gristle of the nose of the bull. Both sides of this small block of wood are pierced cross-wise by a peg and this controlling piece then remains permanently in the nose of the animal, so as to prevent the opening from closing up again, and when in use a rein is fastened to it. Such bulls are also often ridden, and actually carry their riders at galloping pace with all safety." [2]

A form of ritual centred around the **isivivane**, heaps of stones placed by travellers at certain steep or dangerous places. A person on a journey coming upon such a heap would throw a stone upon it and say a prayer for strength on the journey. When a group of travellers passed one, each person would throw a stone upon the pile.

The prominent Grahamstown landmark known in English as Makana's Kop and in Xhosa as **Intaba Izono,** 'the place of injuries', was made an isivivane site in 1952 by the ANC to give them strength in the

1 J.B. Peires, 1981, page 6.
2 L. Alberti, 1807, page 55.

A band of Xhosas travelling

Defiance Campaign which began in that year. The site is said to be the resting place of the soul of Nxele, also known as Chief Makana, who led an attack on Grahamstown in 1819.

The following is a quote from the writings of William John Clarke: "In 1880 I had occasion to leave my station to purchase some cattle at Cala Road, as it is now called. The chief, hearing that I wished to buy cattle, gave me a guide called Shume to conduct me there. We rode to Cala; there was no village there then, nor any roads, just bridle paths. We then proceeded through a gorge now called 'Cala Pass'. Whilst riding through this gorge my guide suddenly halted, dismounted, picked up a stone, removed his head-band of beads, and very reverently placed this stone upon a pile of stones lying to the side of our foot-path on the hillside, at the same time saying **'Unkhulukhulu maze sisigcine kolu hambo lwethu'**, 'May the Great One take care of us on this journey'. I questioned him as to what this pile of stones was, what they meant, and what his action meant. He was very loath to talk about it at first. Eventually he told me that this was one of their customs. When they come on one of these piles of stones they, too, in their turn must add one, remove their head-dress and ask the Great One to take care of them on their way, or ask for some special assistance they might be needing. We then went on our way. I have known Xhosas make special journeys of many miles to place a stone on one of these piles to make some special request. I know of only three such cairns, the one already mentioned, another near Clarkebury, a third on the way to Umtata. I have questioned many younger Xhosas with regard to these piles. They know nothing of them. The old men say the custom is dying out." [3]

3 Joan Broster, 1967, page 67, quoting from her grandfather's writings.

11 Patterns of a year

In pre-colonial times the agricultural cycle was closely bound to the passage of the year. It began in June when the cluster of seven stars called **isiLimela** (the Pleiades) signalled the start of ploughing and ended with the bright star **uCanzibe** (Canopus) seen rising before dawn during May.[1] In August and September the call of the hoopoe, **uboboyi**, signalled the end of winter and the croaking of the toad, **igogode**, welcomed spring. In September the flowering of **umsintsi** (lucky bean tree - *erythrina caffra*) and the ripening of **umbinza** (tree fuchsia - *halleria elliptica*) and other wild fruits announced that it was time to sow crops. The first rains of summer turned the sourveld green and the cows gave more milk. Milk was the main source of food until January, when the crops began to ripen, first maize and pumpkins, then sweetcorn and melons. Finally by mid-April the sorghum was harvested.

The distant past was expressed as a series of 'significant events', **iziganeko**, according to which a person could fix his or her age. These would be historical benchmarks such as a battle, a comet, a drought, disease, a great rain or the circumcision of a great chief. Although the Xhosa divided the year into four seasons, they made no divisions into weeks until the missionaries introduced the naming of the seven days.

In early times the Xhosa told the time by the sky. They fixed the hour by pointing to the sun's position at the time. Months were calculated according to the moon and were named after the stars which were visible, after seasonal weather patterns or after plants and flowers which grew during the time.[2] These beautiful names are seldom used now and have been replaced by new names formed from English.

eyomQungu	uJanuwari	The month of the tall grass; the ripening of the tambuki grass.
eyomDumba	uFebruwari	The month of the swelling grain; month of the pod; when pod-bearing trees are carrying pods.
eyoKwindla	uMatshi	The month of the first fruits; the harvest month.
Utshaz'iimpunzi	uApreli	The month of the withering pumpkins; when the pumpkins become frostbitten.
ekaCanzibe	uMeyi	The month of the star uCanzibe (Canopus) which is seen rising before daybreak in May.

1 J.B. Peires, 1981, page 7.
2 Ibid.

eyesiLimela	uJuni	The month of the **isiLimela** stars (Pleiades), the ploughing stars. This was the beginning of the Xhosa year.
eyeKhala	uJulayi	The month of aloes; when the red aloes burst into flower.
eyeThupha	uAgasti	The month of buds; when the trees begin to bud.
eyomSintsi	uSeptemba	The month when the *erythrina caffra* (lucky bean tree) blossoms.
eyeDwara	uOktobha	The month when *senecio latifolius* (small ragwort) blossoms.
eyeNkanga	uNovemba	The month when *senecio juniperinus* (large ragwort) blossoms.
eyomNga	uDisemba	The month when the *acacia karoo* (mimosa thorn) is in full bloom.

The four seasons

Intlak'ohlaza	Spring	The head of greenness; when the grass sprouts; green points of grass.
Ihlobo	Summer	Sameness; when all is of a kind, or all is green; the genial, friendly season.
Ukwindla	Autumn	The time of harvest; the time of eating the first ripe grain.
Ubusika	Winter	The time of cutting; when the corn is ripe for cutting.

Days of the week

uMvulo	Monday	The opening day.
uLwesibini	Tuesday	The second day.
uLwesithathu	Wednesday	The third day.
uLwesine	Thursday	The fourth day.
uLwesihlanu	Friday	The fifth day.
uMgqibelo	Saturday	The closing day.
iCawa	Sunday	The day for church.

On a certain day or in a certain month

If you want to say 'on' a certain day, or 'in' a certain month, use the prefix **nga-** in front of the name of the day or month.

nga + iCawa	ngeCawa	on Sunday
nga + uMvulo	ngoMvulo	on Monday
nga + uLwesibini	ngoLwesibini	on Tuesday
nga + uLwesithathu	ngoLwesithathu	on Wednesday

nga + uLwesine	ngoLwesine	on Thursday
nga + uLwesihlanu	ngoLwesihlanu	on Friday
nga + uMgqibelo	ngoMgqibelo	on Saturday
nga + uJanuwari	ngoJanuwari	
nga + uFebruwari	ngoFebruwari	
nga + uMatshi	ngoMatshi	
nga + uAprili	ngoAprili	
nga + uMeyi	ngoMeyi	
nga + uJuni	ngoJuni	
nga + uJulayi	ngoJulayi	
nga + uAgasti	ngoAgasti	
nga + uSeptemba	ngoSeptemba	
nga + uOktobha	ngoOktobha	
nga + uNovemba	ngoNovemba	
nga + uDisemba	ngoDisemba	

Eastern Cape flora by F.T. I'Ons

How to tell the time

To ask the time, say: **Ngubani ixesha?**

To ask at what time something will or did happen, say: **Ngabani ixesha?**

Time is now usually expressed using English and not Xhosa numbers.

If you want to say 'it is' six o'clock, use **ngu-6**.

If you want to say 'at' six o'clock, use **ngo-6**.

To express time 'how long' simply place the time-depicting noun after the verb.

Ndisebenza **imini yonke**.	I work the whole day long.
Ifilme ithathe **iiyure ezimbini**.	The film took two hours.

The phases of the moon

First quarter	Inyanga ithwasile.	The moon has commenced practice.
	Iceba lokuqala.	The first fragment.
Full moon	Inyanga ihlangene.	The moon has joined or rounded.
Third quarter	Inyanga iqhekekile.	The moon is broken.
	Inyanga liceba.	The moon is a piece.
Fourth quarter	Iceba lokugqibela.	The last fragment.
Waning moon	Inyanga iyaselwa.	The moon is a dried calabash.
	Inyanga eqhekekileyo.	The moon is a broken piece.
No moon	Inyanga ifile.	The moon is dead.
	Ukufa kwenyanga.	Death of the moon.
New moon	Ukuthwasa kwenyanga.	The appearance of the moon.
	Inyanga entsha.	The new moon.

Celestial bodies and natural phenomena

ilanga	the sun
inyanga	the moon
inkwenkwezi, iinkwenkwezi	star
iKhwezi	Venus as the morning star
uCel' izapholo	Venus as the evening star (the star of milking time - literally, the one who asks for a little milk from the teat)
imBal'ubusuku	Jupiter (the recorder of the night)
inGcand'ubusuku	Jupiter (the traverser of the night)
iSoka lasekunene	Sirius (the suitor on the right hand)
iSoka lasekhohlo	Canopus (Saturn - the suitor on the left hand)
uCanzibe	Canopus (Saturn when seen rising before dawn in May)
isiLimela	Pleiades (the ploughing cluster)

amaKroza	Orion (the stars in a row)
umNyele	Milky Way (literally, raised bristles along the back, as on an angry dog)
unomgca	a comet
inkwenkwezi entshotsholozi	a shooting star or meteor
umnyama	an eclipse
ithunzi lelanga	eclipse of the sun (a shadow on the sun)
ithunzi lenyanga	eclipse of the moon (a shadow on the moon)
inyikima lomhlaba	earthquake
ulwandle luzele	high tide (the sea is full)
ulwandle luvile	low tide (the sea has ebbed)
ulwandle luyalwa	stormy (fighting) sea

Some expressions about time

ngoku	now
ukuphuma kwelanga	at sunrise
ekuseni	at dawn
kusasa	in the morning
imini emaqanda	noon
emalanga	in the afternoon
emva kwemini	in the afternoon
ukutshona kwelanga	at sunset
ngoratya	at dusk
ebusuku	at night
ngokuhlwa	at night/in the evening
izolo	yesterday
ngomso	tomorrow
umzuzu, imizuzu	a minute/a time
emva komzuzu	after a time
kulo nyaka	this year
ixesha limkile	it is late (literally, time has left)
namhlanje	today
usuku	24 hour day
usuku olunye	one day
imini	the day time
emini	during the day
yonke imihla	every day
ngenye imini	the other day/ some day/ one day

12 The natural world of the Xhosa

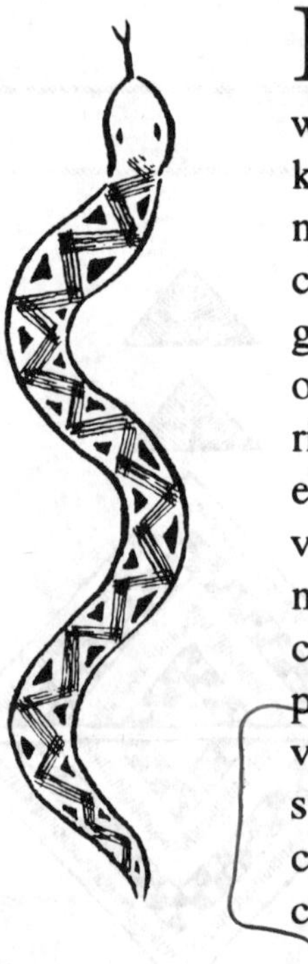

Before European colonisation the lands of the Xhosa were home to some of the most exotic flora and fauna that Africa could offer. There were prehistoric cycads, geraniums, lilies, proteas, euphorbias of every kind, strelitzias, plumbagos, arums, seashore pelargoniums, exotic forest mosses, parasitic creepers, orchids, gladioli, freesias, chincherinchee, cacti and aloes with their flaming red flowers.[1] All the continent's big game and wildlife roamed freely - wildebeest, rhino, lion, leopard, buck of every kind, eland, kudu and giraffe.[2] Hippos and crocodiles swam the rivers and basked at the waters' edge. Animals were in such plenty that elephants foraged in herds of hundreds. At times antelope covered the veld like a carpet. Herds of the now extinct quagga traversed the land in migratory patterns.[3] The Xhosa knew their land intimately and named the creatures and plants alongside them. Their language was filled with proverbs and idioms of birds and animals. They also knew the medicinal value of plants. The blue-flowered pelargonium warded off lightning and stopped up wounds. The aloe killed tapeworm and the star-like cluytia cured anthrax in men and cattle. Other plants cured the bites of spiders, cobras and adders.

It would be wrong to think that the pre-colonial Xhosa lived at one with their environment without harming it. All human societies have an impact on the earth and its living creatures. Like all human societies the Xhosa simply presumed that the veld and its creatures were for their use and sustenance. They grazed domestic animals, which led to veld degradation, and they seasonally burned large areas. They are likely to have persecuted wild grazers, which competed with their domestic livestock, and it is likely that their domestic stock introduced epizootic diseases to antelopes such as the roan and blue antelope.[4] However, the beginning of major environmental destruction in southern Africa can be

1 Noel Mostert, 1992, pages xxii - xxiii.
2 Ibid., page xxiv.
3 Bartle Bull, 1988, page 15.
4 Richard G. Klein: 'The Extinct Blue Antelope' in Sagittarius, September, 1987, page 20.

Scene at the Kareiga River by F.T. I'Ons

dated from the time of white settlement and the ruthless exploitation of natural resources that accompanied it.

Early European hunters in southern Africa, such as Captain William Cornwallis Harris, wrote of vast herds of game. Cornwallis Harris himself described the Magaliesburg Mountains (north-west of Johannesburg) as teeming with elephants: "The whole face of the landscape was actually covered with wild elephants. There could not have been fewer than three hundred within the scope of our vision. Every height and green knoll was dotted over with groups of them, whilst the bottom of the glen exhibited a dense and sable living mass, a picture soul-stirring and sublime." [5] He is reputed to be the first European to have seen these vast Transvaal herds and, although these were not the lands of the Xhosa, when his guns rang out their first terrible shots in November 1836, they prophesied that in less than a hundred years no wild herds would ever roam southern Africa again.

But the great elephant killing had begun far earlier. Jan Van Riebeek's journals tell of the difficulty he had in initiating the hunting of

5 Bartle Bull, 1988, pages 42-43.

elephant among the Khoisan and how he encouraged this by trading beads, copper wire and tobacco. Tusks began to have a commercial value for the Khoisan and their old, mutually respectful relationship with elephants was forever shattered. Previously the Khoisan only used the tusks of elephants which had died naturally. For centuries Khoikhoi cattle had shared the same feeding grounds as elephant and other big game. Elephants were so used to these little people and their herds that they had no fear of them. This lack of fear was commented on by Corporal Verbugh who wrote in October 1653: "Had met many elephants, once a herd of seven and another time a herd of eight elephants of which our men were rather afraid as they, like the rhinoceros, remained standing firm so that our men had to get out of their way." But firepower and an unprecedented slaughter instilled in elephants a terrible fear of humans. Those which were not killed, fled, eventually seeking refuge in the Tsitsikamma forest. John Barrow, the secretary of the government of the Cape, wrote in 1799: "However abundant this article (ivory) might once have been in the southern part of Africa, it has now become very scarce, and, in the nature of things, as population is extended, must progressively disappear. Except in the forest of Sitsikamma (sic) and the thickets in the neighbourhood of the Sunday's River, no elephants are to be found within the limits of the Colony." [6]

The sophisticated weaponry which white settlement brought with it spelt rapid extinction to many wild animals across southern Africa, not only in the lands occupied by the Xhosa. The blue antelope was the first large African mammal to become extinct in historic times. It was reported to be extremely rare as early as 1774 by the Swedish naturalist, Carl Thunberg, and the last one was reportedly seen in 1800.[7] By the same year elephants had been killed in such horrendous numbers that the southern African ivory trade was virtually at an end. The Cape lion was extinct by 1850 and the quagga by 1875.

Up until the end of the 19th century the Tsitsikamma Forest was completely impenetrable and her ageless trees, which had not known the destructive hand of man, formed a natural barrier between the Colony and the interior. An engineer, Baines, designed and built the first pass through the forest. He broke the first ground in November 1879, reaching Humansdorp in 1885. For the first time humans could travel through, instead of around, the vast forest to reach the interior from the Western Cape. The 'opening' of the Tsitsikamma spelt death to an estimated 500 elephants which had retreated to the forest. Majestic yellowwoods, spekboom, stinkwoods and other indigenous trees were felled by an insatiable need for hardwoods. The forest was sorely damaged by exploitation, fires and clearing for agriculture and

6 P. Schonstein Pinnock: The Trojan Elephant, unpublished.

7 Richard G. Klein: 'The Extinct Blue Antelope' in Sagittarius, September, 1987, page 20.

Fish River by unknown British soldier, 1822

plantations.[8] Even today the trees are felled for the furniture industry and alien pine plantations encroach into the remaining wild forest.

As the colonial juggernaut rolled north-east, the destruction of the natural environment engulfed the world of the Xhosa. Their lands were less populated and overgrazed than today. Their simple weaponry made hunting a skilful and not a wasteful operation. Their use of wood was limited as they were not boat builders, and the structure of their homes did not rely on the felling of mature, ancient trees. Today the wild, unfenced lands are gone, replaced by towns, cities and farms. Domestic animals graze the vast areas which once teemed with wildlife. Alien pine trees, Australian gums, wattle, hakea and other plants imported over the years grow in the African soil, embittering, acidifying or draining it so that indigenous trees and flora can no longer grow there. The land has not only been colonised by human settlers but by the seeds of another ecology.

Yet the Xhosa language still sings with the imagery of the old, beautiful and animal-filled world. Proverbs and sayings carry within them an exquisite picture of the natural world the Xhosa once lived in. And, far away from cities and human habitation, in isolated and remote valleys in Pondoland or the far reaches of the Eastern Cape, still grow ancient yellowwoods, stinkwoods, milkwoods and giant euphorbias which have never known the sound of an axe felling their companions but only the sounds of an earth still unharmed by human touch. It is in those places that the ancient language of the Xhosa resonates with the natural environment from which it drew much of its imagery.

8 Interview with C.F. Erasmus, Forestry Extension Officer of Southern Cape Forest Region, Knysna, 1992.

13 Birds

Early European travellers to the Eastern Cape described one of the most colourful bird populations the world has known. Herons, egrets, bitterns, storks, ducks, ibises, flamingoes, geese, vultures, eagles, kites, parrots, swallows, orioles, grouse, quail, guinea-fowl, hoopoes, hornbills, kingfishers, mouse-birds, ostriches and many others filled the hills and valleys with songs and colours. Sea birds of many kinds hovered over the beaches and hopped among the dunes.

Birds inspired the Xhosa and they were seen as messengers of death, harbingers of rain, and, in the case of the honey guide, even providers of food as the bird guided them to the nearest hive, sharing the contents with those who broke it open.[1] Xhosa is rich in proverbs and idioms which draw their inspiration and value from these birds. These proverbs refer to characteristics of particular species or to the possession of feathers and wings, to moulting, to nest building and to egg-hatching.

Many birds, particularly birds of prey, have become rare in modern times and are seldom seen, especially by city dwellers. The old proverbs and sayings are probably losing their relevance as fewer and fewer people see the birds which give the proverbs meaning. As birds succumb to loss of habitat, pollution of waterways and deforestation they also eventually lose their home in a language which once allowed them to nest in its idioms and colloquial latticing. The ecological changes occurring this century and their effect on birds and animals will, in time, no doubt be reflected in the modernisation of Xhosa. As we close in on the habitat of birds and other wild creatures we drive from our lives not only their actual beauty and song but also the linguistic plumage and wisdom handed down by past generations who knew birds and wild creatures intimately. Here are some examples of these flights of language.

Impundulu

SOME proverbs refer to a purely imaginary 'lightning bird' called **impundulu** or **intakezulu**. This awesome bird is unknown to ornithological science but is described as a white bird with red wings and red shanks. It is supposed to be the spirit of a dark cloud which assumes the shape of a bird. When it is thundering people say the lightning bird is clapping its red wings. The flapping of its wings causes the thunder, and

1 Noel Mostert, 1992, page xxiv.

lightning is produced by the **impundulu** rushing through the air to deposit its eggs in the ground. During thunderstorms the Xhosa hurled their assegais into the air hoping to kill the **impundulu** and prevent it from reaching the ground. When a person's nose is bleeding it is said **wanyiwa yimpundulu,** 'he has been sucked by impundulu'.[2]

Uthekwane

THE XHOSA name for the hammerhead is **uthekwane.** Its name can be used to describe a colour like that of the bird. "You may hear a woman, in buying a dark head-kerchief, say: **Ndiphe uthekwane**, 'Give me a thekwane', that is to say, one of the same colour as the bird."[3]

The hammerhead caught the imagination of the Xhosa because of its habit of remaining for hours at the edge of a pool, where it was thought to be admiring itself in the water and inwardly commenting on its personal appearance, bending its head first to the left and then to the right. It was supposed to be saying:

Ndimhle ngapha.	I am pretty here (while bending to the right side).
Ndimhle ngapha.	I am pretty here (while bending to the left side).
Ndoniwa yile ndawo.	But this crest spoils my beauty.[4]

It is said of a person who keeps staring at himself for a long time in a mirror: **Unguthekwane**, 'He is just a thekwane'.[5]

Ing'ang'ane

THE HADEDAH, **ing'ang'ane**, is a bird of good omen and is never intentionally harmed. Its call has given rise to the proverbial saying, **uthathisele amathole eng'ang'ane**, 'he has taken the hadedah's nestlings (and will consequently be kept mindful of it by the bird calling after him)'. It is a way of saying: 'He has offended a vindictive man.'[6]

Ixhalanga

THE CAPE vulture's name, **ixhalanga**, describes it as a glutton that eats everything. It is insulting to be likened to a vulture and any military person can be called a vulture. In early times it was seen as a curse to be likened to a vulture because the vulture, by eating even rotten meat, seemed to be declaring that nothing entering its stomach could kill it. The Benoni City Times reported an incident during January 1926 when about 500 vultures hovered over Germiston. Xhosa men watching this great assembly reportedly said that such an assemblage of vultures meant war and battle were imminent.[7]

2 Rev. R.Godfrey, 1941, page 2.
3 "Ungeva umfazi ethenga iqhiya emdaka athi: ndiphe uthekwane, oyiqhiya exela umbala wayo." Ibid ., page 11
4 Joan Broster, 1967, page 54.
5 Rev. R. Godfrey, 1941, pages 11 - 12.
6 Ibid., page 20.
7 Ibid., page 23.

Intambanane

INTAMBANANE is the name for the dancing kestrel, much loved by Xhosa girls. They thought of it as an expert dancer and, when they saw one hovering in the sky, began to sing and clap their hands, fancying that the bird would be encouraged by their song to continue its dance in the sky. Often at wedding dances young men and women formed a dancing circle, dancing in the centre of the circle one by one. Competition was keen and the best dancer was applauded with **akadlali yintambanane!** meaning, 'she is not simply dancing, she is **intambanane!**'.[8]

Ingqanga

INGQANGA is the name of the bateleur eagle. It is now such a rare bird and so seldom seen that its very name has a magic quality about it. It is held in great awe and thought to be a bird of omen, and this is enhanced by the fact that many people have never seen it. Nowadays should its call ever be heard it is considered very lucky and it is believed that something good will happen.[9] In the past it was known as **intaka yamadoda**, 'the bird of the men', **intaka yempi**, 'the bird of the army', and **intlaba mkhosi**, 'the raiser of the war cry'. Its cry, interpreted as **lof'ilizwe**, 'the country will die' (war is imminent) was thought to indicate trouble somewhere. The esteem in which the bateleur is held is echoed in the proverb, **ingqanga ifile**, 'the bateleur is dead', an expression used when a man of renown dies.[10]

Impangele

IMPANGELE is the onomatopoeic name of the guinea fowl. The name **impangele** can refer to anything with white spots or dots, alluding to the white spots on the guinea fowl's feathers.[11] When a baby who was brought up by his paternal grandparents returns to the home of his maternal grandparents, it is said **impangele izakubaba**, 'the guinea fowl will fly'.[12]

Igolomi

THE KNYSNA lourie is called **igolomi**, a name which developed from its cry. It is regarded by hunters as a bird of omen. It is said that the **igolomi** stays at the edge of the forest, making a peculiar cry when it foretells the death of a hunted buck, and remaining silent if the hunted animal will not die. Its bright red feathers have provided the name **ugolomi** for similarly coloured beads.[13]

8 Ibid., pages 25-26.
9 Interview with Vuyiswa Totobela, Grahamstown, 1992.
10 Rev. R. Godfrey, 1941, page 33.
11 Ibid., page 41.
12 Interview with Vuyiswa Totobela, Grahamstown, 1992.
13 Rev. R. Godfrey, 1941, page 55.

Intengu

INTENGU is the onomatopoeic name of the fork-tailed drongo. It is credited with a love of cattle. Herd boys believe that the cattle mistake the whistle of the drongo for their own whistle, and that on hearing it, they bunch together and feed together just as they would do to a boy's whistle. Herd boys often leave their herds under the care of a drongo while they sleep or smoke. Should a herd boy appear at home during herding hours, his parents say of him 'he is trusting to the assistance of intengu'. A similar meaning lies behind the proverb **indoda engu namalusi, iinkomo zayo zaluswa yintengu**, 'the cattle of the herdless man are herded by the drongo'.[14]

Umcelu

THE WAGTAIL has a number of names but its most common is **umcelu**. It is held in high regard as a bird of good omen. It is known as **yintaka yeenkomo,** ' the bird of the cattle', because its presence is said to assure an increase in stock. Children are warned that if they kill a wagtail the cattle will die, and anyone mischievous enough to kill a wagtail will never have cattle and will so be a poor man.[15]

Ingwangwa and unomyayi

THE PIED crow takes its name, **ingwangwa**, from its rough croak. It is sometimes nicknamed **umfundisi**, 'priest' or **inene**, 'gentleman' because of its white bib.

The black crow is called **unomyayi**. The proverb **uneyeza likanomyayi**, 'he has the black crow's medicine', is based on the bird's reputed ability to escape from difficulties.

Oonomyayi bezindada zaseAfrika	The black crows of the woods of Africa
Oonomyayi bezindada zaseAfrika	The black crows of the woods of Africa
Bathi ni? Bathi: Rwa!	What do they say? They say: Kwa!
Bathi: Rwa! xa balilayo	They say: Kwa! when they call out
Bathi: Rwa! xa balilayo	They say: Kwa! when they call out
Rwa! Rwa! Rwa!	Kwa! Kwa! Kwa!
Batsho, oonomyayi. Batsho, oonomyayi	They cry, the black crows. They cry, the black crows
Xa babejikela	When they circle around
Ngasetiyeni	In the maize fields
Xa babejikela	When they circle around
Ngasetiyeni	In the maize fields
Bathi: Rwa! Rwa! Rwa!	They say: Kwa! Kwa! Kwa!
Bathi: Rwa! Rwa! Rwa!	They say: Kwa! Kwa! Kwa![16]

14 Ibid., page 75.
15 Ibid., page 100.
16 Ibid., page 79.

Inkwili

THE SOMBRE bulbul is a bird of good omen for the traveller, who will always be happy to see the bird and hear its song and will feel that the journey is blessed. The bulbul knows no period of silence and even when all other forest birds have settled down at midday, it continues calling and singing. Its insistent song has been interpreted in many ways:

Wili! Ndikhumbula kwaNdatyana!	Wili! I'm thinking of Ndatyana!
Wili! Ukutya kumnandi ngantoni?	Wili! What makes the food nice?
Kumnandi ngetyuwa!	It's nice with salt![17]

A bird game to play

TWO PLAYERS sit together. The first player has a small pile of mealie grains or pebbles. She hands over a piece of grain to the other player and in a sing-song manner says: **Qobongo ntakani le?** 'What bird is this?'.

The second player takes up the refrain and sings **sisakwatsha,** 'it is a partridge', or **ngunomyayi,** 'it is a black crow' or **nguthekwane,** 'it is a hammerhead', or any other bird's name. As soon as the second player cannot name a bird when given a piece of grain, all the grain is given to him. He then becomes the questioner and his friend must try her skill at answering.

17 Rev. R. Godfrey, 1941, page 87.

14 Illnesses, remedies and medicinal plants

"Amongst these people the ordinary indications of colds or stomach upsets, such as sneezing, coughing, yawning and hic-coughing, are seldom observed, and one never sees skin diseases. Madness and craziness appear to be completely unknown. For the healing of wounds one uses certain herbs or roots with good results. I have seen scars from bullet-wounds, the healing of which would do honour to a skilful surgeon. The cause of internal illnesses is, on the other hand, mostly sought in magic and fought with charms. Against local pains, one usually applies blood-letting, which has a similarity to our bleeding." [1]

"The abundant health enjoyed by these people must undoubtedly be principally ascribed to the simple food on which they live: milk, the principle dish, which is supplied in abundance by numerous herds of cows; meat, mostly roasted, corn, millet and water melons, prepared in different ways appease hunger. Water quenches the thirst.

The milk is not drunk fresh, but is left to curdle and get sour, which is accomplished in a very short space of time in small baskets which have repeatedly served to bring about this transformation, and which are, therefore, already acid. Millet, as well as buck-wheat, are products which they owe to their own industry, as they cultivate these varieties of wheat themselves. Millet and buck-wheat are cooked whole with water and eaten without the addition of meat-broth or fat. One stamps and crushes these two sorts of wheat to meal with the assistance of a smooth stone, and it is then cooked with fresh milk. One also prepares a broth from this meal by crushing millet stalks, which have a very sweet sticky juice, thoroughly boiling some in water and then adding the necessary meal to the mixture. Finally bread is also made from both kinds of meal, for which the dough is prepared in the usual way with water, then forms a loaf of about three pounds weight, and bakes it in hot ashes (sic). Whole corn bushels are also roasted on coals and eaten in that way. Apart from these, honey and a number of kinds of wild onions, roots and berries serve as nourishment." [2]

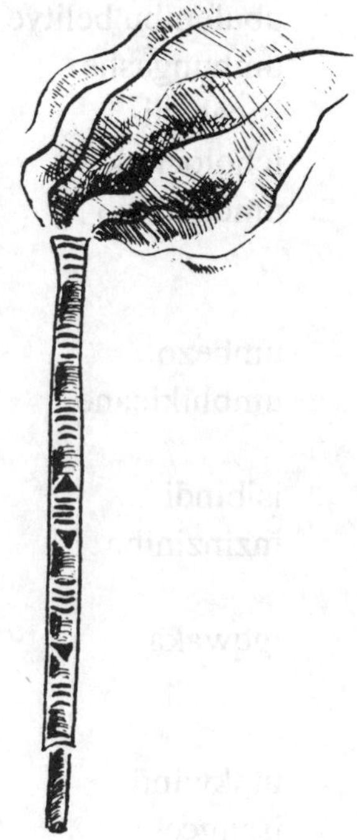

1 L. Alberti, 1807, pages 42-43.
2 Ibid., page 22-24.

Medicinal plants

Xhosa name	Scientific name	Medicinal use
idwara	*senecio latifolius*	Used for sores, especially on the backs of horses.
umfincafincane	*leonotis leonarus*	Used for colds, coughs and snakebites.
ubulembu belitye	unknown	Used for snakebite and syphilis.
umbungashe	*lichtensteinia interrupta*	Used for colds and coughs.
isicakadi	unknown	Used in childbirth.
icholocholo	*helichrysum nudifolium*	Used for colds and coughs.
umdambiso	*senecio concolor*	Used to heal wounds and sores.
umbezo	*crabbea cirsioides*	Used as an insecticide.
umbhikicane	*chenopodium ambrosioides*	Used to staunch bleeding; also used as an insecticide.
isibindi	unknown	Used for anaemia in cattle.
inzinziniba	*lippia asperifolia*	Used against measles, inflammation of lungs, coughs and colds.
igqwaka	*catha edulis*	Gives strength when chewed on a journey. Used for snakebite and chest disease.
umkwinti	*gazania pinnata*	Used to prevent miscarriage.
isangcete	*monsonia ovata*	Used for dysentery. Popularly called **gqita**, from the Khoi.
umnungumabele	*xanthoxylon capense*	An antidote to bite of tsetse fly.
umnquma	*olea verrucosa*	Used for tapeworm.

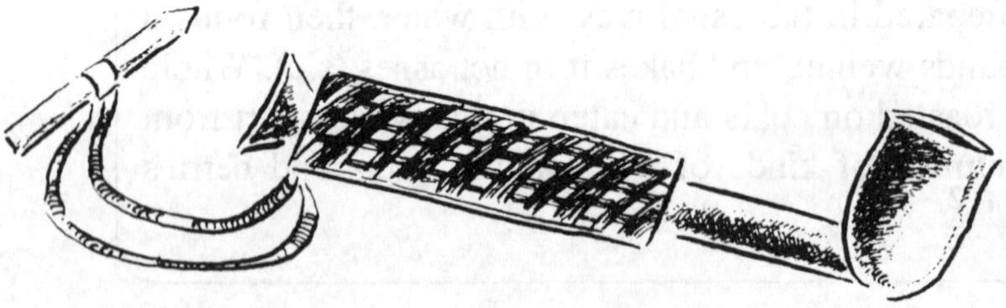

15 Ukuhlonipha, the court language

Traditional Xhosa customs are based on a code of sacred restraints and taboos called **amaconini**, which apply both to speech and to actions. There are many taboos restricting the course of daily life and their application is formal and inflexible.[1]

There are different taboos for men, boys, girls and married women. Most are associated with sex, the vital periods of life, the seasons of the year and food. All are held with superstitious awe and are observed with absolute loyalty. Failure to observe a taboo angers the ancestral spirits and the family.[2]

There is such a sense of awe surrounding taboos that they may not be named or discussed. This has led to the development of a special language called **ukuhlonipha**, or court language, used generally but not exclusively by women. It is made up of substitute words and is a polite and reverent language used only for taboos and the ancestral spirits.[3]

By this custom a daughter-in-law is required to **hlonipha** (revere) her father-in-law and all her husband's male relatives. She may not pronounce their names. When the emphatic syllable of either of their names occurs in any other word she must avoid it by substituting an entirely new word or another syllable in its place. Most women refer to their male-in-laws as the father of so-and-so, or the brother of so-and-so.[4] There are substitute names for everyday things as well. A similar language, called **isikhweta**, is used by young men during the period of circumcision rites. The custom of women of avoiding the cattle kraal by making a circuit in passing its gate is also called ukuhlonipha.

Hlonipha words can be derived through synonyms as well as from other languages. Many words are relics of the past and, except in their hlonipha use, are unknown.[5] Here are some examples of hlonipha words[6]:

1 Joan Broster, 1967, page 70.
2 Ibid.
3 Ibid.
4 Ibid.
5 Kropf-Godfrey, 1915, page 509.
6 Joan Broster, 1967, page 74.

English	Hlonipha	Xhosa
mealies/maize	utiya	umbona
sugar	intlabathi	iswekile
salt	imuncu	ityiwa
matches	umkhanyiso	umlilo/ imatshisi
bread	isiqhusheko	isonka
cotton-sheeting	iwayi	ibhayi

16 Early agriculture

"Next to cattle breeding, agriculture also provides them with a livelihood. A piece of land is fenced in, with thorn bushes dragged together, in an irregular shape, just depending on whether it is due to trees standing in the way, bushes or banks of rocks. The plants that are cultivated are a kind of millet, buckwheat, watermelon and tobacco. Also I have found potatoes, although these only very isolated and in insignificant quantities. Both the kind of millet, as well as the ordinary kind of watermelon, which is characterised by a bitter taste, are not grown in the Colony, from which it must be assumed that these plants must originate in some other part, as also that it does not seem to be open to the slightest doubt that these people had practised agriculture in earlier times, and before the founding of the Colony.

The tilling of the fields is not done in the usual way, but contrarily they are first sown and then dug over, whereby one first leaves the dug-up weeds lying on the surface of the tilled field to protect the sprouting shoots against the singeing (sic) rays of the sun. The digging is performed with spades, which are made of a very hard kind of wood, which goes by the name of sneezewood. As soon as the young plants have advanced to the stage that they can better resist the heat of the sun, the weeds which are now dry are removed and the fresh weeds growing up thrown out from time to time. At the time of ripening, one cuts the wheat ears off with the point of a javelin, assembles them in a heap and covers them with dry grass and thorns. Some time later these wheat ears are threshed with thin sticks and the fruit is tossed into the air with their hands, so as to rid them of the husks in this way. Finally a rounded pit is dug in the cattle enclosure, which is given greater width below than on top. The walls are hardened with a fire maintained in it for a time, whereafter the corn is brought for storage in it. This store room is first covered with dry grass and then with a large flat stone, which is finally completely sealed with dung. Buckwheat and tobacco are left to hang after reaping." [1]

1 L. Alberti, 1807, pages 56-57.

17 The Xhosa and their cattle

"His cattle is the foremost and practically the only subject of his care and occupation, in the possession of which he finds complete happiness. The bellowing or mooing of a cow is so pleasing in the ear that it can enchant it to the point where he will pay greatly in excess of its worth, and cannot rest until he has acquired it." [1]

Cattle were the focal point of Xhosa existence and their relationship was intimate and emotional. Life literally circled around cattle since the huts of an **umzi**, 'homestead', were grouped in a semi-circle around the cattle kraal, with their entrances facing it. The direction was eastwards, towards the sun. For a Xhosa, the first sight as he rose and emerged from his hut was of his beloved beasts, lowing in the rising light.[2]

The cattle kraal was sanctified because sacrifices to the ancestors took place there and because it was the future burial place of the chief. It was also the granary where corn was stored in bottle-shaped pits. Given this hallowed significance of the cattle kraal, it is easy to understand the outrage felt by Xhosas who had helped an English seaman, when he relieved himself in a cattle kraal. Poor William Hubberly had stumbled into an umzi in 1782, two months after his ship, the Grosvenor, had been wrecked on the Pondoland coast. A war with the Colony had recently been fought and Hubberly had been mistreated by most of the Xhosa-speakers he approached.[3] But when he finally found Xhosa hosts the richness of the milk and meat they gave him was too much for his empty stomach and, "being much troubled in my bowels I eased myself among the cows. When the natives came a-milking, they soon pointed out to me my indecency, at which they were highly offended. They instantly turned the cattle out, and refused giving me any milk". [4] He was driven away to continue his desperate, stumbling progress towards the Colony.

Women were not permitted to enter the cattle kraal except at their

1 L. Alberti, 1807, page 54.
2 Noel Mostert, 1992, page 189.
3 Ibid., page 191.
4 Ibid., quoting Kirby, Source Book 'Grosvenor' Van Riebeck Society, page 112.

marriage. On that occasion a bride presented herself to the chief and his counsellors, who admonished her to be a good wife.[5]

The Xhosa had twenty-five names to describe different cattle colours and skin patterns and seven different names for the shapes of their animals' horns, which they bent in a variety of fantastical forms by scraping almost to the quick the side of the horn towards which they wanted them to bend. Some horns were shaped to meet under the neck, others were shaped to stand straight up or point to the ground. Some had swept-back horns.[6] Some animals had large circular pieces cut out from the dewlap, while others had this part cut into strips so it hung like tassels.[7]

Cattle intricately bound the material and the sacred together. They were used in sacrifices to the ancestors and so linked the living and the dead. They represented the future because they served as the bride price, **lobola**, and sealed the marriage bond. They represented wealth and stability. In ordinary daily life they supplied the principal item of diet, milk, as well as the meat for feasting and leather for clothing.[8]

Even in a herd of 500 beasts a Xhosa could know instantly if one was missing and which. The aesthetics of their beasts were a source of endless delight and pleasure which 19th century missionaries used to their own advantage, as one Wesleyan missionary noted: "No sermon from a missionary is so popular to a Xhosa and so long retained by him in his memory, as one which draws all its illustrations from the cattle fold."[9]

Like the Khoikhoi, the Xhosa trained their cattle to a highly developed response. "No well-trained dog follows the command conveyed to him by a whistle more promptly than happens in the case of the cattle of those people," Ludwig Alberti wrote. "Following a piercing whistle, a whole herd will stand motionless. Upon a different signal, it again resumes its movement, assembles round its shepherd or follows him whether he leads them straight out or in a circle."[10]

Chiefs kept special bulls for their entertainment and these were taught to race or stampede. "When the bulls have been coached sufficiently in this way, they run, without being driven, with such impetuosity to the place, that the maker of the noise must save himself by timely flight, in order not to be trampled upon." Cattle were raced over a twelve-to-twenty mile course, and the glories of champion oxen were recited in praise poems for years after.[11]

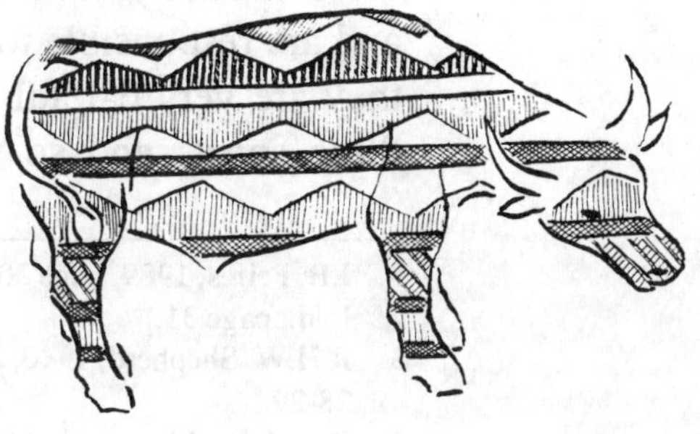

5 Ibid., page 191.
6 Ben Maclennan, 1986, page 44.
7 Ibid.
8 Noel Mostert, 1992, page 190.
9 London Missionary Society Archives, MS 309.
10 Noel Mostert, 1992, page 190, quoting L. Alberti, 1807, page 54.
11 Ibid., quoting L. Alberti, 1807, page 55.

18 Religion and the ancestral spirits

Early Xhosa religion was primarily a this-worldly religion, more concerned with guiding people's behaviour in the existing world than with the afterlife. They had no priests as such and their doctors, the **amagqirha**, dealt with practical matters such as omens, medicines, witchcraft and the relationship between people and their ancestors. It was believed that the ancestors rewarded those who venerated them and punished those who neglected them.[1]

Xhosa religion was deeply ambivalent about death and the question of the afterlife. On the one hand there was the feeling that the dead did not really die but remained with the living, that death was merely a transition from being human to being an ancestor. But there was also the feeling that death was not part of God's plan but something evil and unnatural.[2]

The traditional pre-Christian God of the Xhosa was known as **uNkhulukhulu**, 'the Great One' or **uQamata**. John Bennie recorded, in 1822, the name **Ruthlanga** for the creator of the sun, moon and stars.[3]

UThixo was the name adopted for God by the early missionaries, and used by the Christian churches. It is generally believed that the name does not properly belong to the Xhosa, but was derived from the Khoikhoi. The name **uThixo** literally means 'the wounded knee'. It is supposedly the name of a folk hero of the Namaquas (a Khoikhoi clan) who was held in high repute for extraordinary powers during his life. After death he continued to be invoked as one who could still relieve and protect. He had received some injury to his knee and was named by this injury.[4]

Today, traditional Xhosa people believe that God is the Supreme Being who made the world and all which exists in it. God lives in Heaven and although he rules the world does not concern himself with the everyday affairs of people. These he delegates to the ancestral spirits of each family. The spirits of the ancestors are subject directly to God and are responsible to him for the behaviour of their descendants, whom they are very careful to control and discipline. Contact is made through these spirits and so worship is offered indirectly to God through the

1 J.B. Peires, 1989, page 30.
2 Ibid., page 31.
3 R.H.W. Shepherd, 1940, page 55, quoting Glasgow Missionary Society Report, 1822, pages 28-29.
4 Rev. John Appleyard, 1850, page 13.

ancestors. The traditional way of approaching an ancestral spirit is through the sacrifice of an animal, an ox for major occasions and a goat for lesser ones. Thus the ancestor cult is dependent upon cattle and people have a religious attitude towards them.[5] A complex ritual of sacrifices, prayers, songs and dances maintains the link with the ancestral spirits. Ritual is strictly adhered to and the ancient ceremonies are celebrated with beauty and solemnity through tribal dress, beadwork, songs and dances. All social activities are utterly subordinated to the ancestral spirits in holding firmly to and preserving the truth as understood by previous generations.[6]

Ancestral chiefs and each family's departed relatives live in the spirit world. They keep in touch with the living and need the living to keep in touch with them. The tribe looks to them for protection and love. Both in ritual and in everyday life the people speak to their ancestors and address them quite naturally, communicating their needs.[7]

The rituals of worship support the social order and also give the individual a sense of awe and gratitude for his life. They guide him stage by stage through the crises of life, from childhood through adolescence, parenthood and old age.[8]

"In their worship of their ancestors each group reinforces itself by enacting its concept of the beauty of life. With perfect attention to detail their beadwork, songs and dances merge into one another. Thus movement and rhythm, form and colour, timbre and tone flow together, as with all their being the people reach out to the spirits of their ancestors. Their impressive ceremonies, which invoke an instant response, are their last defence against advancing civilisation. When the ancestral belief is discredited, their history, poetry and drama lose their impact. The strict guidelines fall away and the social structure disintegrates."[9]

5 Joan Broster, 1982, page 17.
6 Joan Broster, 1976, page 7.
7 Ibid.
8 Ibid., page 9.
9 Ibid., page 10.

19 Ubuntu - humanness

"I have noted repeatedly that the one who has obtained a small piece of meat or bread, has divided it with those surrounding him, whereby the portions became so small that they could hardly be tasted. "[1]

Xhosa society was closely knit, bound by intense ties of loyalty within the family, the chiefdom and the nation as a whole. These attitudes began with the family and extended upwards and outwards. The impoverished were never denied assistance. It was a duty to share food with others, whatever the circumstances.[2]

One of the most conspicuous examples of Xhosa hospitality was the consistently kind reception they gave to the survivors of shipwrecks. Only after the first war between white colonists and the Xhosa was there a change in attitude, and even then there were people still willing to assist. So many Europeans were cast in their midst that the Xhosa had a special word for them, **abelungu.**

These hospitable responses of the Xhosa were strongly affected by the emphasis they placed upon a value called **ubuntu**, 'humanness'. Its instinct was the preservation and stability of the whole. **Ubuntu** underlined the basis of Xhosa social laws and its workings within Xhosa codes of value was notable even in war, when women and children were never killed. In their wars with the Colony, the Xhosa ruthlessly slayed the white farmers and their grown sons at the feet of their wives and sisters, but no woman or child was deliberately killed in any of the nine wars that were fought with increasing bitterness and ferocity, despite the fact that the same chivalry was not always reciprocated by the other side.[3] To kill a woman or child, even if not deliberately, marked a man as a coward.

1 L.Alberti, 1807, page 79.
2 Mostert, 1992, page 196.
3 Ibid., page 197.

20 Numbers and counting

"Before the introduction of written numerals and the use of slates and paper, the Xhosa method of counting was upon the fingers, and by certain signs with the hands. In consequence their numeration is somewhat complex.

Even now, where written figures are not used, the method is by extending the fingers for the number intended to be expressed, and beginning with the little finger of one hand, mostly the right.

The number three would thus be expressed by three fingers extended, with the thumb and forefinger bent; four by thumb bent and four fingers extended.

Five would be represented by the whole hand extended. Six by the thumb extended, and all the fingers closed; or by the whole hand and thumb of the other hand extended.

Seven by the thumb and the forefinger extended, the others closed. Eight by the thumb and first fingers extended, the third and little finger remaining closed.

Nine is usually represented by bending the little finger; ten by clapping the palms of the hands together once; twenty by clapping twice; thirty, thrice, and so on.

Twenty-three would be represented by clapping the hands twice and extending the last three fingers of either hand, though generally the right. And any further combination of tens and units would be represented in the same way." [1]

1 James Stewart, 1901, page 129.

21 Song, dance and musical instruments

"I don't play uhadi anymore, now we have the FM radio."[1]

In traditional society, song and dance play an important role in cultural ceremonies. There are special songs sung at the **umtshotsho**, dance parties for boys and girls, the **intlombe**, dance parties for young men and women, and the **umngqungqo**, round dances performed by women at girls' initiation ceremonies. **Iingoma zotywala** are beer songs sung as part of the ancestor cult.[2] Although many Xhosa people have lost touch with their traditional music there is a strong culture of church music and song. An evocative and moving tradition has developed through the political struggle, particularly the **toyi-toyi** dance performed at rallies and marches.

Musical instruments

THE DESIGN of Xhosa instruments was influenced by Khoisan and western instruments. Traditional instruments are seldom seen in cities today, and in remote areas generally only old people play them.

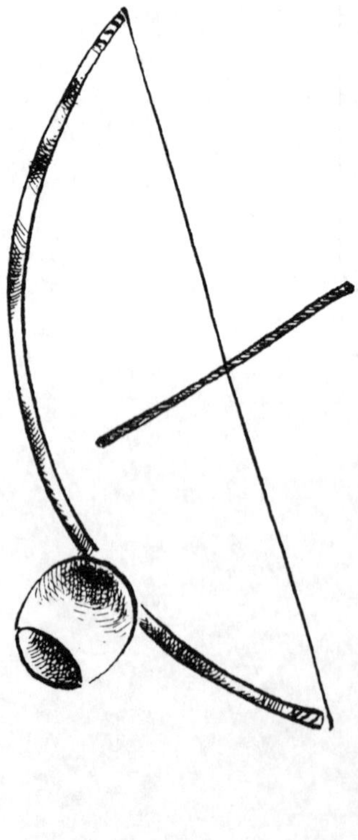

Of the string instruments, probably the **uhadi** has the most haunting and beautiful sound. It is a single-stringed instrument made from a hollowed out calabash which serves as a resonator, attached to a bent branch. Uhadi is played by holding the calabash against the breast and beating the wire with a stalk of thatch grass or reed. **Umrhubhe** is a mouth-resonated friction bow played with a scraped twig or reed to produce an evocative sound. **Inkinge** is a very rare, plucked mouth-bow which consists of a single string drawn tightly on a reed. Equally rare is the string-wind instrument **ugwali**, called **gora** by the Gonaqua Khoi and described in 1815 by Campbell as being "a bow with a piece of quill fixed near one end of the string on which they blow, which makes an agreeable sound". [3]**Igitali** takes its design and name from the guitar.[4] It is made of an oil tin and has three strings which are used to strum chords. **Ikatari** is also inspired by the guitar but consists of a five litre oil tin, a bent bow and only one string. Another string instrument is the

1 David Dargie, 1988, page 49, quoting an unnamed woman he interviewed in the Lumko district.
2 Ibid., page 33.
3 Ibid., page 42.
4 Ibid., pages 46-48.

utot'omdaka, 'dirty tin', which is made by flattening one end of a five litre tin so that viewed from the side it is triangular. A large hole is cut in the front of the tin and three rubber bands cut from car tyres are strung over the tin. The rubber bands are tapped with a twig.

Ingqongo is a drum made by fastening a dried ox-skin onto poles four or five metres above the ground, or held by performers while it is beaten. **Isigubu** is a bass drum made from a large tin drum and ox-skin. It is struck with short sticks which have rubber heads.[5]

Woman playing a jew's harp

Some traditional leg rattles are used by modern groups and street buskers. **Onokhenkce** are leg rattles made from bottle tops and **iirekene** are leg rattles made from the rubber of inner tubes. **Izinkunjane** are made of small tins and **ogesi** are leg rattles made from the insulation covering thick electric wire. **Iingcacu** are rattles worn by female diviners and diviners' apprentices. They are reeds which are wound around the legs when green and allowed to dry and remain in place, from ankle to the knee. **Izinkunjane** are ankle rattles made by encasing pebbles in small pieces of skin.

Different types of whistles are also used. The **impempe**, a double-fipple police-type whistle, is used for **umtshotsho** and **umngqungqo** dances. A smaller whistle used for these dances is called **umkhombe** or **ixilongo**, which is also the name of horn-type instruments. The referee's whistle is called **itywilitywili** or **ityorotyoro**. The siren whistle is called **isikhova**, because of its owl-like sound. **Ingcongolo**, a type of fipple whistle, is made from reeds and **utwitwitwi** is a whistle made from the stalk of a red-petalled flower. Whistles are often used at political rallies and funerals.

Isitolotolo, the jew's harp, once a very common instrument which traders sold, is now scarce although **ifleyithi**, the mouth organ, is still played in some areas.

5 Ibid., pages 43-44.

22 Orthography

The pre-colonial Xhosa did not write or read but relied instead on a rich oral tradition. The Xhosa language was first put to writing in the early part of the 19th century by Christian missionaries. These missionaries encountered sounds in Xhosa which did not exist in English and they had to create a way of capturing the new sound structures into written form. This was not an easy task but their efforts are laudable, particularly as the basic system they developed has not changed much to this day. The missionaries came across many dialects among the Xhosa and attempts were made as early as the 1830s to create some uniformity of language, as can be seen in the minutes of the Glasgow Missionary Society Report of 1831.[1] The need for uniformity was rooted in the missionaries' need to influence people and convert them to Christianity. It would have been impossible and impractical to translate and print scriptural texts into more than one dialect. The missionaries first settled among the amaNgqika and as a result of this their dialect, spoken around Alice in the Ciskei, was adopted as the standard form of literary Xhosa. It is still the version of Xhosa taught today in schools and heard over the radio and on television.

The copy of this reading sheet, *'All Cattle Come From God'*, was prepared by John Bennie in 1824 and printed by Lovedale Press. It is thought to be the first sheet printed in Xhosa, although there is not much certainty about this. Its subject matter would have appealed to the

---

1 "He (Mr John Bennie) is still going on with the printing of his Caffre Vocabulary. According to the last account he is now about the 100th page of his laborious work - collecting and arranging all the Caffre words - printing them in columns and giving their signification in English. This work when completed must be of immense advantage to all succeeding Missionaries. His progress during the year has been considerably retarded by a circumstance which has rendered, for the present, some of his labour useless, but which ultimately will facilitate the acquisition of the language, and cause all the Missionaries in Caffreland to speak with one tongue. In January 1830, the Rev. Messrs. Shaw and Young of the Wesleyan Society and the Rev. Messrs. Thompson, Ross, and Bennie, of the Glasgow Missionary Society, met with the Rev. Messrs. Brownlee and Keyser, of the London Missionary Society at Buffalo, for the purpose of fixing the rules for writing the language of the natives. They took Mr Bennie's system as the basis, but they made several alterations upon it, which Mr Bennie frankly says are improvements. For the time no doubt his vocabulary is considerably deranged, as his work is in the press, but as the measure agreed upon is highly important, we do not repine at the hindrance. It is pleasant in the extreme thus to hear of the members of different Societies, not only dwelling together in unity, but co-operating to carry on a plan for the general good." (Thirty-Sixth Year's Report of the Glasgow Missionary Society, 14th April, 1831.)

bum bi	**IN KO MO zon ke ze zi ka-Ti-**
pam bi	**xo: un gum ni ni zo ye na. Kun-**
dun ga	**ga bi ko nŭm tu o zi ci ta yo. I pi-**
tën da	**we gu ye i mi fi si, ne mi ti yon-**
gom so	**ke zi ya pi la ga yo; a pi we na-**
kam be	**man zi e zi wa së la yo. Yim vu-**
kan ti	**me yom ni ni zo u ku ba zi kon-**
vim ba	**ze ti na ’ban tu in ko mo; zi ya-**
fun da	**si kon za go ko. Za pi wa in ko-**
zem ka	**mo ku-No wa, na ku ti gu-Ti xo**
sën ga	**um ni ni zo, u ku ze si zi xë le, si-**
ham ba	**pi le ga zo; zi xë li we go ko. Zi-**
lin da	**xë li we in ko mo, go ku ba e vu-**
nam pa	**me le ne na zo um ni ni zo; go ko**
nan ga	**si na so i si xa so e si ku lu e si pi-**
wam bi	**la ga so. Zi ya ni ka i ma zi za-**
yim bi	**ko we tu lo ma si e si wa së la yo**
can da	**a da li we yo gu-Ti xo. Si nen gu-**
qon da	**bo, nem va ba, ne zin to e zi nin-**
tëm ba	**zi ge zi kum ba zen ko mo ze tu.**
jin ga	**Zi da li we in to e zi nin zi ga be-**
kan da	**lun gu ga ma tam bo en ko mo,**
kon xa	**nem pon do za zo. En zi we lo-**
tam ba	**ma ba la on ke e zi na wo in ko mo**
yon ke	**gu-Tixo um ni ni zo.**
4.	**J. B.**

All Cattle Come From God *by J. Bennie, 1824. Probably the first printed Xhosa reading sheet*

Xhosa as cattle were the focal point of their existence. The words in the main text and in the column alongside were divided into syllables, perhaps for ease of pronunciation. However, the writer was clearly guided by English pronunciation in dividing up the syllables and moved the nasal sounds **m** and **n**, which should occur before consonants, to the preceding syllable. Bennie thus wrote ‘bum bi’ instead of ‘bu mbi’, ‘pam bi' instead of 'pa mbi', 'dun ga' instead of 'du nga', etc. Some nasals were left off altogether. It is possible that the missionaries could not pronounce nasals before consonants, or possibly, because the sound of a nasal before a consonant was so strange to them, they simply could not hear it.[2] In this text aspirants also went unnoticed. The click sounds were depicted by **x**, **c** and **q**, as they still are today.

A great orthographic upheaval occurred in Africa in the 1930s as a result of the work of the International Institute of African Languages and Cultures founded in London in 1926 by D. Westermann and his colleagues.[3] A new and consistent African orthography was proposed and this sparked off a quest for language standardisation throughout the continent. Many African languages were severely mauled by ill-considered attempts at dialectical unification. By this stage the missionaries had already established the Ngqika dialect as the standard form of Xhosa to be used in schools and in print. In November 1926 the Central Orthography Committee met in Johannesburg under the chairmanship of Dr C. M. Doke to investigate the orthographies of the African languages spoken in the then Union of South Africa. Following their recommendations in July 1930, certain changes to the orthography were approved by the Union Government Committee.[4] The Xhosa orthography was revised in 1931 and became known as the 'new orthography', while the previous was called the 'old orthography'. The new orthography introduced far reaching changes with the introduction of three new letters, the creation of a number of two-letter consonants, the use of diacritic marks to indicate tone and stress, the practice of doubling vowels to indicate length and new rules for the division of words.

The use of new characters limited the printing of Xhosa to printing presses which had these characters and to modified typewriters. Often the new characters had to be handwritten over printed or typed text.

W.B. Bennie, the grandson of the founder of Lovedale Press, John Bennie, was Chief Inspector of Native Education in the Cape Province at the time. He became an enthusiastic convert and propagandist of the new orthography, and R.H.W. Shepherd, Director of Publications of Lovedale Press, supported him.

Although these changes may have seemed satisfactory from a linguistic point of view, their social implications were disastrous. The manner in which the regulations were imposed awakened deep

2 This error was acknowledged by Rev. Appleyard: "In writing (Xhosa), it has been a common custom to omit the initial **n** of particles and prefixes commencing with **nd**, **ng** or **nj**, and also of **nd** and **ng** as euphonic letters. No reason, however, can be assigned for such an omission, and the sooner, therefore, this orthographical anomaly ceases to occur, the better. The sound is universally acknowledged to be there, and why not then its representative?" Rev. J. Appleyard, 1850, page 80.

3 J.B. Peires, June, 1979.

4 Recommendations of the Union Government Advisory Committee on Bantu Studies and Research, 16th July, 1930.

resentment among educated Africans and brought many criticisms, particularly from Sol. T. Plaatje, who wrote numerous letters to the South African Outlook about the change. One of his strongest criticisms was that the changes were being made by academics, who ignored the "genuine indigenous point of view". The awesome effect of the new orthography was to turn every literate African into a functional illiterate and dealt a blow to Xhosa language, literature and history. [5] Many Xhosa manuscripts submitted to Lovedale Press for publication in the old orthography were rejected and their authors were told to rewrite them in the new orthography. The extra costs and delays in revising the orthographies of accepted manuscripts were to prove fatal in many cases. One such manuscript was the greatest historical work ever written in the Xhosa language, Tiyo Soga's *'Xhosa History'*. Soga had typed the manuscript in the old orthography and in single spacing and it had to be completely retyped. The task was never completed and the manuscript was never published. [6]

John Bennie, from a portrait painted in London two months before sailing to South Africa in 1821

In 1955 further modifications to the orthography were proposed and these were introduced in 1957. This became known as the 'standard spelling'. It is the orthography of all Xhosa text today and is the one taught in schools. The new letters introduced in 1931 were discarded. So, ironically, the 'standard spelling' used today is not too different to the old orthography used during the last century.

5 S.T. Plaatje: S.A.Outlook, May, 1931, pages 88-89; August, 1931, page 158.
6 J.B. Peires, June, 1979.

23 Missionaries and literacy

Because the Xhosa people had no method of writing, theirs was an oral culture and they carefully preserved their literature in their minds and memories through myths, legends, tales about people and animals, proverbs, songs, lyrics and praise poems. Every tribe had its own fables for the instruction and amusement of its children as well as for the explanation of natural and mythical phenomena. Eulogies and praise poems recorded the glories and worthy acts of heroes and renowned chiefs, and blame poems recorded their shortcomings.[1]

In order to preach Christianity and to spread the Gospel, the missionaries needed, soon after their arrival among the Xhosa people, to learn their language and then reduce it to writing. Since no group other than the missionaries undertook to educate the Xhosa, acceptance of Christianity remained the only means of access to literacy, which became exclusive to Christian converts and their families.

When the missionaries arrived among the Xhosa they settled initially among the amaNgqika, who were thus the first to be exposed to Christianity and to writing.[2] It was among these people that the writing of Xhosa originated and it was their dialect which came to dominate other dialects as the standard form of literary Xhosa.[3]

The first missionary to settle with the Xhosa was Dr Johannes Theodorus van der Kemp, a Dutch philosopher and medical doctor who was proficient in sixteen languages. His youth had been stormy and sensual and as a lieutenant in the Dutch dragoons he had led a fairly dissolute life of drinking and womanising. However, after the death of his wife and children in a boating accident near Rotterdam, he became a changed man and, at the age of 50, he offered his services to the London Missionary Society. He was ordained a minister of the Church of Scotland and sent out for missionary service at the Cape.[4] Although his first contact was with the Khoikhoi, his primary goal was to go

1 B.E.N. Mahlasela, 1973, page 1.
2 The British took over rule of the Cape from the Dutch in 1806. In 1818 Ndlambe, assisted by other Xhosa tribes, attacked and defeated Ngqika, who turned to the English for help. As a result Ndlambe was defeated and in his fury attacked Grahamstown, where he was again defeated and his power completely destroyed.
3 B.E.N. Mahlasela, 1973, page 2.
4 R.H.W. Shepherd, 1940, page 3.

further eastward and to try to establish a mission station among the Xhosa.

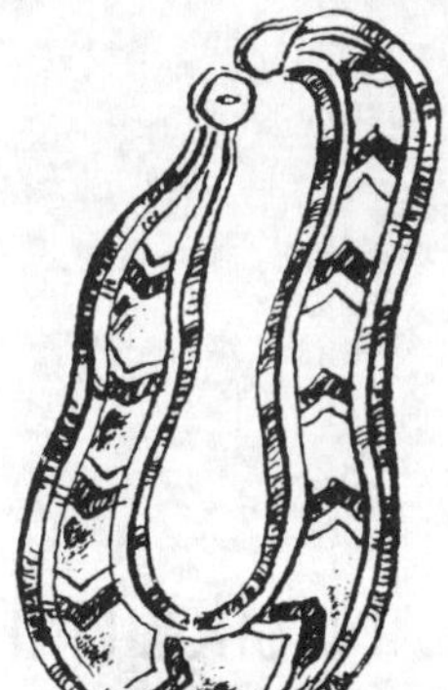

He penetrated Chief Ngqika's territory as far eastward as the Tyumie Valley and was named **uNyengana**, 'the one who has appeared as if by accident'.[5] Because of the unsettled state of the country he could not stay permanently in one place. The Xhosa language defeated him and, with rumours of tribal war in the air, he left the territory in 1800, two years after his arrival. He complained that the Xhosa "showed no desire for instruction in doctrines utterly strange to them".[6] He spent his remaining years working near Port Elizabeth with the Khoikhoi, who were by then an uprooted, insecure and unhappy people who welcomed Christianity as something stable and the mission itself as a refuge from the Boers.[7] As the years passed the gulf widened between him and the colonists, who detested him for taking up Khoi ways of living. In 1803 he greeted European visitors "without a hat, his venerable head exposed to the burning rays of the sun, dressed in a threadbare black coat, waistcoat and breeches, without shirt, neckcloth or stockings, and leather sandals bound upon his feet, the same as are worn by the Hottentots".[8] He created a scandal in the Colony when, at the age of 60, he married a young, freed Khoikhoi slave.[9] She bore him four children.[10]

Nobody followed up Dr Van der Kemp's missionary endeavours until April 1816 when Rev. Joseph Williams, also of the London Missionary Society, arrived. Williams crossed the Great Fish River and settled beside the Kat River about 48 kilometres inland from the Fish River boundary,[11] 24 kilometres from Ngqika's Great Place.[12] The mission station which Williams and his wife built gradually established the first white colonial presence within Xhosa territories east of the Great Fish River. Williams lived among the Xhosa people until his death in 1818, evangelising and teaching them the elements of reading and writing. He died after only two years, worn out and disheartened, believing he had failed in his missionary endeavours.

He was replaced by Rev. John Brownlee in 1820, who established his headquarters at Chumie, an outstation founded by Williams near the Kat River settlement.[13] This consisted of a primitive church and a missionary's house. The station was destroyed during the war of 1835 and the site later named Old Lovedale.[14] After three changes, the site

5 Kropf-Godfrey, 1915, page 505.
6 B. Maclennan, 1986, page 54.
7 Ibid., page 55.
8 Ibid.
9 R.H.W. Shepherd, 1940, page 11.
10 B. Maclennan, 1986, page 55.
11 R.H.W. Shepherd, 1940, page 15.
12 B. Maclennan, 1986, page 16.
13 Correctly spelt **Tyhume** and also called **Gwali**.
14 On the Old Lovedale site some ruined walls may be traced as well as a solitary tombstone standing in the veld. It marks the grave of Helen Ross, wife of the missionary John Ross, and their three children. The inscription is written entirely in Xhosa. It is the earliest Xhosa

presently occupied by Lovedale, near Alice, was chosen. It was named after an eminent member of the Glasgow Missionary Society, Dr John Love. He was one of the founders of the society and the first secretary of the London Missionary Society. Lovedale was formally opened by Rev. William Govan on July 21, 1841.[15] It was destined to become the focal point of the literate Christian culture among the Xhosa of the Eastern Cape.

Ntsikana

ONE OF the people inspired by Williams was Ntsikana, who became a flaming evangelist among his people. He survived his teacher by only two years but during that time made such a great impression that he became a figure of legendary proportions, credited with seeing visions and uttering prophecies that were fulfilled years later.[16] He composed one of the greatest Christian Xhosa hymns, *'Ulo Thixo omkhulu ngosezulwini'*.[17]

Ulo Thixo omkhulu ngosezulwini;[18]	Thou art the Great God - He who is in Heaven;
Unguwena wena khaka lenyaniso.	It is Thou, Thou shield of truth.
Unguwena wena nqaba yenyaniso.	It is Thou, Thou tower of truth.
Unguwena wena hlathi lenyaniso.	It is Thou, Thou bush of truth.
Unguwena wen'uhlel' enyangwaneni.	It is Thou, Thou who sittest in the highest.
Ulodal'ubomi, wadala phezulu.	Thou art the creator of life, Thou made the regions above.
Lo Mdali-dali wadala nezulu.	The Creator who made the heavens also.
Lo Menzi wenkwenkwezi nozilimela;	The Maker of the stars and the Pleiades;
Yabinza inkwenkwezi, isixelela.	The shooting stars declare it unto us.
Lo Menzi wemfama, uzenza ngabomi?	The maker of the blind, of thine own will didst thou make them?
Lathet' ixilongo, lisibizile.	The trumpet speaks, - for us it calls.
Ulonqin'izingel'imiphefumlo.	Thou art the hunter who hunts for souls.
Ulomkokheli wasikhokela thina.	Thou art the leader who goes before us.
Ulengub'enkulu siyambatha thina.	Thou art the great mantle which covers us.
Ozandhla zakho zinamanxeba wena.	Thou art he whose hands are with wounds.
Ulonyawo zakho zinamanxeba wena.	Thou art he whose feet are with wounds.
Ulogaz' lakho liyimikrozo - yinina?	Thou art he whose blood is a trickling stream - and why?
Ulogaz'lakho liphalelele thina.	Thou art he whose blood has spilt for us.
Lemali enkulu-na siyibizele?	For this great price we call?
Lomzi wakho-na-na siwubizile?	For thine own place we call?

inscription appearing on a tombstone erected to Europeans. R.H. W. Shepherd, 1940, page 69.

15 James Stewart, 1887, Introduction.

16 R.H.W. Shepherd, 1940, page 19.

17 Ibid., page 20.

18 Rev. John W. Appleyard, 1850, page 47-48.

John Bennie and the dawn of written literature

BROWNLEE was joined by Rev. John Bennie of the Glasgow Missionary Society, who arrived from Scotland in 1821 to live and work among the amaNgqika. He was a brilliant linguist and within a few months of his arrival he mastered Dutch in order to converse with and teach some of the Khoi and Xhosas who had learnt the language from Dutch settlers. He described Xhosa as a "fine, soft, agreeable language".[19] Within a year he had devised a Xhosa alphabet and orthography, wanting to "reduce to form and rule this language which hitherto floated in the wind".[20] In the same time he translated into Xhosa and was teaching the Lord's Prayer, a morning prayer, thirty short questions, a part of the Creed, a doxology and the Twenty-Third Psalm.[21]

In 1823 he was joined by Rev. John Ross, who brought with him a small Ruthven printing press, a supply of type, paper and ink. Bennie wrote to Dr Love on December 20 of that year: "On the 17th we got our press in order; on the 18th the alphabet was set up; and yesterday we threw off 50 copies. Through your instrumentality a new era has commenced in the history of the Xhosa nation."[22]

Perhaps the first major work printed in Xhosa and written by Bennie was *'All Cattle Come From God'*, an appropriate choice of topic because cattle were the focal point of Xhosa life. It was published at the Tyumie Mission Station in 1823. In 1824 Bennie printed *'Incwadi yokuqala ekuteteni ngokwamaXosa eTyume, Iliswe lamaXosa, yabadekwa lubadeko lwabatunywa eGlasco 1824'*, (*'The first book in the language of the amaXhosa at Tyumie, the land of the amaXhosa, and printed in the press of the messengers from Glasgow in 1824'*.)

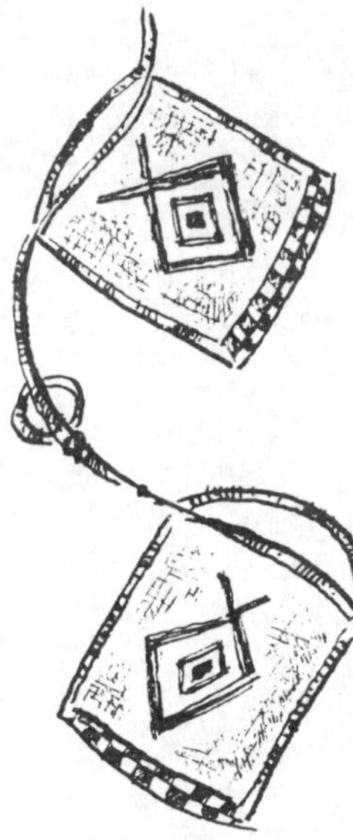

Over the years he translated several books of the Bible. He was also a prolific hymn writer and fifty one of his hymns were published in the Xhosa Presbyterian hymn book, *'Incwadi Amaculo Ase-Rabe'*. In 1829 he published the first *'Spelling Book'* and in 1839 two Xhosa readers. His most remarkable book was *'The Systematic Vocabulary of the Kaffrarian Language in Two Parts - To Which is Prefixed an Introduction to Kaffrarian Grammar'*. In addition to his printed works there exists a manuscript of grammar dated 1832, which is an elaborate treatise on the Xhosa alphabet and syllables with detailed discussions on the noun, the adjective, numerals, pronouns and verbs. Charles Brownlee, the first Secretary for Native Affairs in the Cape Colony, conferred on John Bennie the title 'The Father of Xhosa Literature'.

19 R.H.W. Shepherd, 1940, page 57.
20 Ibid., page 65.
21 Ibid., page 57.
22 Glasgow Missionary Report, 1824, page 27.

Breaking out of missionary constraints

THE LOVEDALE Press initially published books and pamphlets for the educational and evangelical work of the mission - grammars, dictionaries and eventually the complete Bible in Xhosa. It also ventured into serial publications in 1876, publishing *'The Lovedale News'*, *'The Healdtown Messenger'* and *'Isigidimi SamaXosa'*, which was the first African newspaper edited by Africans in southern Africa. Later Lovedale published more general literature, and in most cases these were simple narratives used as an aid to missionaries fighting superstition, witchcraft and 'vices of the flesh'. [23] But although the missionaries introduced literacy and the means of modern education, they severely constrained the birth of a free literature among the Xhosa. They made the written word a tool of evangelism to subdue a culture which they generally judged inferior to their own.

There was a large, potential reading audience among Christian converts drawn from missionary stations and outstations scattered throughout South Africa. By the 1870s and 1880s a discernible African Christian elite had begun to emerge from these communities which transcended differences in culture, language, geography and missionary heritage. [24] But members of this 'new elite' were well aware of their status and between the 1880s and the 1920s writers started to escape from the constraints of church publishing. Among them was John Tengo Jabavu, the editor of *'Isigidimi samaXosa'*. He pushed against the boundaries imposed on him, taking an increasingly political stance, raising secular issues and writing against segregation. He was eventually fired and, in November 1884, set up his own Xhosa/English weekly newspaper in King William's Town called *'Imvo zaBantsundu'*. It was the first African-owned and African-controlled newspaper and Jabavu used it on behalf of those without a political voice. He took a brave stand in going it alone as a journalist. His newspaper quickly became the most influential organ of African opinion in the Cape Colony and Jabavu himself became "perhaps the most widely known mission-educated African in southern Africa until 1910".[25]

The development of independent black writers alarmed the church, which saw itself losing control over the African Christian elite it had created. Lovedale Mission had to come to terms with something it could not control but it also recognised that publishing was lucrative. So by the early 1900s it was actively engaged in publishing the English and Xhosa works of African creative writers - novelists, poets, playwrights, composers and artists. By 1939, 238 books had been produced in Xhosa, more than in any African language except Swahili, and most were published at Lovedale. Under David Hunter (1901-1931) and especially R.H.W. Shepherd (1931-1964), Lovedale became one of the major

23 B.E.N. Mahlasela, 1973, page 8.
24 Switzer and Switzer, 1979, page 4.
25 Ibid., quoting Walshe, 1970, page 4.

Lovedale students, 1876

mission publishing centres for African literature in southern Africa.[26] Under the directorship of Shepherd, Lovedale monopolised the publishing of Xhosa works, with only a few titles being produced by Longmans Green, the S.P.C.K and the Witwatersrand University Press.

This was, however, a mixed blessing for Xhosa writers. Serious problems were caused by Xhosa literature being a virtual monopoly run by whites on religious grounds. Shepherd almost single-handedly controlled Lovedale Press and his motives and directives are frankly set out in his book *'Lovedale and Literature for the Bantu'.* He was concerned by the "danger that the missionary agencies, having in their schools taught vast numbers to read, should leave non-Christian and even anti-religious elements to supply the reading matter".[27]

Xhosa manuscripts were harshly appraised and writers forced to work within tight constraints. Shepherd looked upon the literate African as still being in an infancy of sorts, saying: "They are at an adolescent period, a period which, as in the life of individuals, is difficult for any people. A people at this stage is strong enough to feel its own strength, but sometimes not wise enough to be completely independent."[28] He could not speak Xhosa and manuscripts for consideration were given to a typesetter called I. Oldjohn or sent to Professor Davidson Don Tengo Jabavu at Fort Hare University, the son of John Tengo Jabavu. Oldjohn censored any reference to tribal customs such as polygamy, old religious ways and witchcraft. Jabavu was an Mfengu and was influenced by the age-old rivalries which existed between the Mfengu and the Xhosa proper. He rejected histories which took a pro-Xhosa line and favoured Mfengu manuscripts over those of other tribes. A Xhosa manuscript rejected by Lovedale had little hope of finding an alternative outlet and the world of Xhosa literature lost many fine works at this time.[29]

Indigenous writers increasingly put their efforts into the production of newspapers and in this way their writings became more accessible. As the emerging African elite sought a political place in the sun their

26 Ibid., page 3.
27 R.H.W. Shepherd, 1945, page 26.
28 Ibid., page 75.
29 J.B. Peires, 1979.

newspapers championed their own culture. But money remained a central problem. However, when by the 1930s there were enough literate Africans to make newspapers lucrative, whites like Bertram Paver and Charles Maggs stepped in and started the Bantu Press. Eventually the Argus Company took over the entire black independent press.

The missions as champions of the people

ALTHOUGH they had initially aided colonisation, by the mid-20th century the missions had become champions of the indigenous people against the ruthless administration of the Nationalist Party government. This shift was underpinned by a change in perceptions of their work, from saving souls to protector of the 'natives'. By the 1950s mission education was the best that Africans could get, and it produced writers of international standard like Henry Nxumalo, Can Themba, Todd Matshikiza, Nat Nakasa, Es'kia Mphahlele and many others, all of whom wrote in English.

But its opposition to apartheid was to be the downfall of mission education. From 1949 the government installed Christian National Education and in 'separate but equal' schools the battle began for the soul of the 'Bantu'. The Bantu Education Act of 1950 effectively destroyed the missions as centres of educational excellence and introduced 'Bantu Education'.[30] So-called 'smart Bantu' were not wanted, and the aim of this new education system was to educate Africans as "hewers of wood and drawers of water" and as labour units fit only to service the white-controlled economy.

Yet Bantu Education contained within it the seeds of its own destruction. Even though it offered a grossly inferior education, it placed African education on a broad national footing, drawing increasing numbers of pupils into the educational orbit. Between 1951 and 1970 African literacy rose from 23.8% to 49.5%.[31] As the missionaries had found, literacy and numeracy in any form were tools for broadening mental horizons and, ultimately, for rebellion. Education was at the heart of the struggles which exploded in Soweto in 1976 as pupils challenged the state's intention to teach in Afrikaans. The struggle continued through the political conflict of the 1980s and was not to die down until political freedom was gained in 1994.

Ironically, the effect of the mass politicisation of African culture, starting in 1912 with the formation of the ANC, was to have a damaging effect on the development of Xhosa literature. Segregation ghettoised African culture, using linguistic differences to divide and rule and to establish ethnically segregated 'bantustans'. African opposition to this was to proclaim the universality of African culture, but to do this it had to find a common language to unite the many African languages - and this was English. By the 1950s few 'black' newspapers were in an indigenous

30 Switzer and Switzer, 1979, page 14.
31 Ibid.

language, and the most prominent African writers, notably those who had passed through the dynamic newsroom of Drum magazine, wrote exclusively in English.

For the same reasons, much of the Black Consciousness protest writing after 1976 was also in the language of the old colonial masters. The year 1976 saw a birth of defiance not only in schools but also in protest poetry, literature and politics. A new crop of fiery African writers emerged who were bloodied in the battles of Soweto and fired by Black Consciousness. They wrote in English to build mass consciousness across race and language barriers. Much of their work was published through the journal *'Staffrider'*, which also resurrected the older writers of the 1950s. The effect of this wide use of English was to stunt the use of indigenous languages in contemporary literature. Even after liberation the top selling newspapers aimed at African culture are in English.

A new dawning of Xhosa literature

A GREAT challenge faces Xhosa literature today. Real openings have appeared which favour a return of Xhosa writing. During the apartheid years the publishing of Xhosa literature was not lucrative. Except for the limited production of educational material, publishers did not address the development of a Xhosa reading culture. An assessment of African families in Grahamstown during the 1980s, for example, showed that most children were growing up without books in their homes. Books were an unaffordable luxury. Black township schools suffered from a severe shortage of textbooks and had no libraries for general reading. Xhosa children attending private, English-medium schools only had access to books written in English or Afrikaans.[32]

There is now a tremendous potential for the rebirth of old traditions of story-telling and writing. It remains only for writers and publishers to realise this.

32 Rivendell Children's Centre Report on Books and Township Children, Grahamstown, 1988 - 92.

24 Traditional poetry

There is an important aspect of Xhosa literature which needs to be mentioned - the centuries old, orally transmitted and powerfully evocative tradition of inspirational poetry.

Xhosa poetry does not depend on a fixed metre and it has no fixed rhyme, but is naturally rhythmic because the Xhosa language, by its very structure and alliterative formations, begs for harmony. Much of the beauty of Xhosa poetry cannot be captured onto paper because a lot depends on voice presentation.

Imbongi by Noluthando Beyi

With the writing of hymns to fit English tunes and the spread of Western ideas of poetic diction, many Xhosa poets lost the original forms of Xhosa poetic construction.[1] But the tradition of the Xhosa praise poet or **imbongi** remains. This performer, whose origins are unknown, is indigenous to Xhosa culture and can be likened to the bard of old England. They are inspirational individuals who can compose and recite poems on the spot, using voice modulation, movement and dance in their presentations. They burst onto the international scene as performers of note, firstly in 1990 during the release from prison of Nelson Mandela, then in 1994 at his inauguration as State President, and again during the opening of South Africa's first democratic parliament.

The imbongi is both a composer and a public reciter, versed in history and lore, and is expected to know the traditional praises of certain species of animals and birds.[2] Praise poets have always been held in great esteem and hold positions of honour in the community.[3]

1 B.E.N. Mahlasela, 1973, page 10.
2 Prof. Peter Mtuze: Lecture, Rhodes University, July, 1992.
3 A.C.Jordan, 1973, page 21.

Traditionally the imbongi occupied the role of guardian of a society's values and practices, serving as the 'voice of the nation' and performing much the same role as newspapers in serving literate audiences.[4]

The imbongi could, traditionally, praise and criticise a chief, comment on current affairs and act as political commentator with impunity. His speeches took a particular form, involving a framework of poetic techniques within which his subject could be skilfully manipulated to meet the occasion. Subject matter would be derived spontaneously.[5]

Increasing literacy and education as well as the changing socio-economic and political scenario have not done away with the need for the imbongi. Instead their role is simply changing in order to accommodate new pressures. Poetry is now being produced not only in praise of chiefs and leaders but also in praise of trade unions and political organisations.[6]

And, although traditionally only males could be praise poets, today women **iimbongi** can also be heard.

The poet, Samuel E. Mqhayi, 'praised' the Prince of Wales on his visit to South Africa in 1925, as follows. It is a popularised version which now seems to exist in English only.

Ah, Britain! Great Britain!
Great Britain of the endless sunshine!
She has conquered the oceans and laid them low;
She hath drained the little rivers and lapped them dry;
She hath swept the little nations and wiped them away;
And now she is making for the open skies.
She sent us the Preacher; she sent us the bottle,
She sent us the Bible, and barrels of brandy;
She sent us the breechloader, she sent us the cannon;
O, Roaring Britain! Which must we embrace?
You sent us the truth, denied us the truth;
You sent us the life, deprived us of life;
You sent us the light, we sit in the dark,
Shivering, benighted in the bright noon-day sun.[7]

Bongani Sitole is an imbongi who lives in Ngangelizwe township in Umtata. He began praising in about 1954 while still at school in Transkei, praising at various functions such as school concerts. His poetry is mainly concerned with political leaders in Transkei and with the ANC. The following extract was taken from poems produced during Mandela's first visit to Transkei after his release from prison.[8]

4 Russell H. Kaschula, 1989, page 2.
5 Ibid.
6 Ibid.
7 A.C. Jordan, 1973, page 27.
8 Russell H. Kaschula, 1993, pages 66- 67 and 72.

Ziya ce-e-e-engwa izinto,	Things are approached with skill,
Ziyacengwa izinto xa zizakulunga,	Things are approached carefully if they are to succeed,
Azenziwa ngobuxhiliphothi,	They are not approached with vigour
Azenziwa ngokungxanyelwa,	They are not approached with speed,
Lithe Chu-u-u-u,	He is steady,
Umntaka Ngubengcuka kaNgangelizwe,	The son of Ngubengcuka of Ngangelizwe,
Uthe chu-u-u-u,	He is steady,
Uhambe nabafundi bakhe,	He is accompanied by his disciples,
NjengoYesu,	Like Jesus,
Uhamba noSisulu noMbeki,	He is accompanied by Sisulu and Mbeki,
Uhamba noMhlaba,	He is accompanied by Mhlaba,
Uhamba namadoda aphilileyo.	He is accompanied by healthy men.

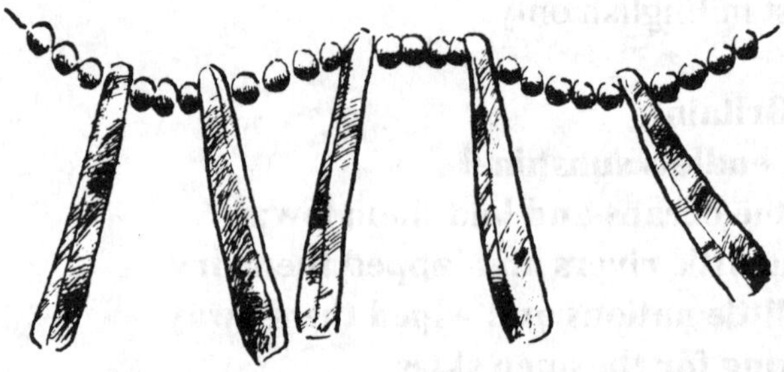

25 The Great Cattle Killing

Hayi uNongqawuse!	Oh Nongqawuse!
Intombi kaMhlakaza	The girl of Mhlakaza
Wasibulala isizwe sethu.	She killed our nation.
Yaxelela abantu yathi kubo bonke	She told the people, she told them all
Baya kuvuka abantu basemangcwabeni	That the dead will arise from their graves
Bazisa uvuyo kunye ubutyebi	Bringing joy and bringing wealth
Kanti uthetha ubuxoki.	But she was telling a lie.[1]

In 1856 a young Xhosa girl, Nongqawuse, saw two strangers standing among the reeds of the Gxarha River. They told her they had been sent by the ancestors with a message for the Xhosa people. They told her that the dead were preparing to rise again, with wonderful new cattle and that the Xhosa people stood on the threshold of an era of idyllic prosperity, free from their colonisers. For the prophecy to be fulfilled the Xhosa had to slaughter all their cattle. They should not cultivate in the new season, but should build great new cattle enclosures for the cattle which would rise, and dig deep grain pits for the corn which would miraculously appear. The prophecy would be fulfilled on an appointed day in August of that year, when the sun would not set, but would stand still in the noon sky.

The news of the prophecy was received with great rejoicing by many Xhosa people who were called **amaThamba**, Believers. They systematically killed their herds and destroyed their food stores. Their fields were left uncultivated as they waited for the miraculous resurrection of their ancestors and the fulfilment of all Nongqawuse's prophecies. Those who were not convinced by Nongqawuse's vision were known as **amaGogotya**, Unbelievers. They were blamed, when the appointed day came and went, for the failure of the prophecy. It had been necessary for all people to show faith by destroying their livelihood.

The prophetess set a new date in the coming February. "For a few days before the 18th, Believers slaughtered the remaining cattle and destroyed their food. They rethatched their huts and on the Wednesday, shut themselves up in the huts, waiting. On Thursday they came out, downcast, destitute and desperate."[2]

1 J.B. Peires, 1989, page xvi, acknowledging Mrs Beryl Wood for introducing the poem to him.
2 Gail Weldon, 1993, page 22 quoting Colonial Office 48/381 Grey's report in Despatch No.

Xhosas watching for the return of their dead warriors by F.T. l'Ons

Nongqawuse's fantastic prophecy lured tens of thousands of people to death by starvation, all pathetic victims of a beautiful but hopeless dream of the end of colonisation.[3] Those who survived the famine which followed became dependent upon the British for food. Their independence was completely broken and the only way they could find sustenance was through working for their colonisers.

Why did they take such desperate steps? What made them ransom everything they had against the wild stories of a young girl? Most official documents of the time contain references to a 'Chiefs' Plot', the theory that the cattle-killing was a conspiracy by the Xhosa chiefs to bring about war with the Cape Colony. Xhosa oral tradition gives a mirror image called 'Grey's Plot', the theory that the root of the cattle-killing was a trick by the Governor, Sir George Grey, to deceive the Xhosa into destroying themselves.[4]

According to the historian, Jeff Peires, there was no plot on either side. Rather, he believes, "the cattle-killing was a logical and rational response, perhaps even an inevitable response, of a nation driven to desperation by pressures that people of today can barely imagine". They were losing their lands to the British, whose military tactics were brutal and ruthless. Their cattle were dying in their thousands, infected with lung sickness which had been introduced by European herds. Perhaps their desperation found promise in the notion of the resurrection of the dead which the Christian missionaries had introduced them to. They were resorting to the ultimate sacrifice, rendering everything in the hope of renewal and replenishment. Perhaps it was their last great act of magic pitted against the guns of a culture which was engulfing their world. It failed, and the Xhosa were to lose their freedom and independence for more than a hundred years.

25 of 6/3/1857.

3 J.B. Peires, 1989, page ix.

4 Ibid.

26 Nkosi sikelel' iAfrika

Enoch Sontonga

The hymn, **Nkosi sikelel' iAfrika** was composed by Enoch Sontonga in 1897 to be sung by school children and church choirs. He was born in the Eastern Cape in 1873. He moved to Johannesburg where he became a teacher and taught in the then newly-founded township of Nancefield before the Anglo-Boer War. He composed songs for his pupils, including the original version of *Nkosi sikelel' iAfrika*. These he apparently recorded in an exercise book which, in later years, was lost after a friend borrowed it from his widow.

Nkosi sikelel' iAfrika was first sung at the ordination of one of the early Tsonga Methodist ministers. Later it was popularised by the Ohlange Institute Choir (under R.T. Caluza) on extensive fund-raising concert tours throughout South Africa. The original version consisted of one verse only. The poet, Samuel E. Mqhayi, later added seven more verses. These were first published in 1927 and appeared with the music in *'Incwadi yamaculo Aserabe', 'Presbyterian Xhosa Hymn Book'*, published by Lovedale Press in 1929.[1]

In 1925 it was adopted by the African National Congress to be the closing hymn at their meetings and became recognised as the national anthem of the people. It is often sung in a combination of Xhosa, Zulu and Sotho and versions of it are used as the national anthems in Zambia, Zimbabwe and Tanzania.

Many of the political leaders of Africa studied at Fort Hare College (later to be called Fort Hare University). *Nkosi sikelel' iAfrika* probably found its way into the rest of southern Africa through students who were influenced by the traditions of the South African ANC. Julius Nyerere of Tanzania studied at Fort Hare. So did Joshua Nkomo, who later founded the Rhodesian African National Congress. The hymn probably reached Namibia through the migrant workers at Cape Town docks who later formed the South West African People's Organisation, SWAPO.[2]

During the apartheid years, *Nkosi sikelel' iAfrika* was banned from the airwaves and from being played or sung in public. Since 1994 it serves, with *Die Stem*, as one of two national anthems. Here is the full Xhosa version.

1 Yvonne Huskisson, 1969, page 273.
2 Interview with Don Pinnock, Grahamstown, 1992.

Nkosi, sikelel' iAfrika	God bless Africa
Maluphakamis'uphondo lwayo	May her horn rise up [3]
Yiva nemithandazo yethu	Hear Thou our prayers
Ususikelele.	And bless us.

Yihla Moya, yihla Moya	Descend Oh Spirit
Yihla Oyingcwele.	Descend Oh Holy Spirit.

Sikelela iinkosi zethu	Bless our chiefs
Zikhumbule umDali wazo	May they remember their Creator
Zimoyika zezemhlonele.	Fear Him and revere Him.
Azisikelele.	And bless them.

Sikelel' amadoda esizwe	Bless the men of the nation
Sikelela kwanomlisele	Bless also the youth
Ulithwal'ilizwe ngomonde	That they carry the land with patience
Uwusikelele.	And bless them.

Sikelel' amakhosikazi	Bless the wives
Nawo onk'amanenekazi	And also all young women
Phakamisa wonk'umthinjana	Lift up all young girls
Uwusikelele.	And bless them.

Sikelela abefundisi	Bless the ministers
Bemvaba zonke zeli lizwe	Of all churches of this land
Ubathwese ngoMoya Wakho	Embue them with Thy Spirit
Ubasikelele.	And bless them.

Sikelel' ulimo nemfuyo	Bless agriculture and stock raising
Gxotha zonk' indlala nezifo	Banish all famine and diseases
Zalisa ilizwe ngempilo	Fill the land with good health
Ulisikelele.	And bless it.

Sikelel' amalinga ethu	Bless our efforts
Awimanyano nokuzakha	Of union and self upliftment
Awemfundo nemvisiswano	Of education and mutual understanding
Uwasikelele.	And bless them.

Nkosi sikelel' iAfrika	God bless Africa
Cima bonk'ubugwenxa bayo	Blot out all its wickedness
Nezigqitho nezono zayo	And its transgressions and sins
Uyisikelele.	And bless it.

3 **Uphondo - 'horn', 'tusk', 'steeple', 'the wing of an army'.**

27 War, resistance and liberation

The Xhosa were not a warlike people. They acquired a reputation under the Dutch administration of the 18th century as being a "very peaceful and timid people". Although every boy was trained from an early age to use a spear and a kierie, these were primarily employed for hunting.[1]

Xhosas fighting with kieries

Wars between Xhosa chiefs or with their neighbours were rarely bloody. They were conducted with an extraordinary amount of ceremony. An attacking army approached its enemy only after a complex ritual of purification by a war doctor, feasting, singing and dancing.[2] They sent ambassadors to give notice of an intended attack and would wait for word that the other chief and his warriors were ready. On the battlefield, warriors formed up in two lines, about 70 paces apart, hurling insults, shouting war cries and throwing their spears.[3]

The throwing assegai was not a very effective weapon and was not usually used with the intent to kill. Thrown from 20 paces it could pierce a man's body and could still be thrown with some accuracy from 60 paces. Beyond that a thrower had little hope of hitting his target.[4] Warriors concentrated their attention on trying to abduct the enemy's cattle and women, and the purpose of war was not the destruction of productive resources but their acquisition and absorption.[5]

European colonisers introduced total war which was a new and shattering experience for the Xhosa people. The havoc wrought by the colonial forces, who burned villages and destroyed food stores, was not only cruel but incomprehensible to African people. The Xhosa resisted their colonisers through nine Frontier Wars, which they fought bitterly and heroically. However, their military tactics were no match for the fire-power and ruthlessness of the British.

Weakened by war, their leaders killed or banished to Robben Island, the Xhosa's fighting power was finally destroyed as a result of the Great Cattle Killing which left them destitute and dependent. Increasingly, they became incorporated into the colonial world as labour where they were

1 Ben Maclennan, 1986, page 110.
2 Ibid.
3 Ibid.
4 Ibid., page 111.
5 Ibid.

deprived of the most basic civil rights. Unable to oppose the colonisers militarily, the Xhosa struggle for liberation eventually took political form. On January 8, 1912, there assembled in Bloemfontein several hundred of South Africa's most prominent African citizens: Professional men, chieftains, ministers, teachers, clerks, interpreters, landholders, businessmen, journalists, estate agents, building contractors and labour agents. These men, after singing Tiyo Soga's Xhosa hymn *Fulfil thy promise, God of truth,* unanimously resolved to form the South African Native National Congress, later known as the African National Congress. Although its prominent members were Xhosa, the ANC was nationalist and anti-tribal in character. One of the main factors which led to its formation was the 1910 Act of Union by which white domination was consolidated in South Africa. The new united state was based on the exploitation of cheap black labour which was controlled by a system of harsh laws. In 1913 African-owned land was expropriated by a Land Act which confined Africans to 17% of the land surface of South Africa. This devastated the peasantry.

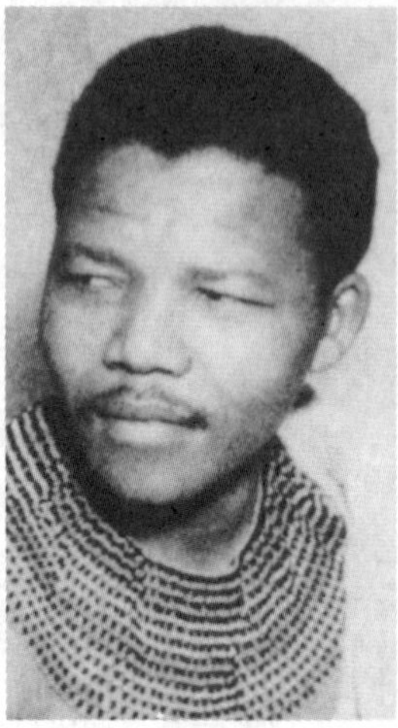

Nelson Mandela before his imprisonment

In 1914 an ANC delegation visited Britain to put their protest before the British government and public. But they were ignored. This galvanised mission-educated people into action and it was around them that the politics of resistance began in earnest.

African people continued to hope for whites to be reasonable and understanding of their plight. During World War One the ANC supported the Allies, hoping this would help end racial tyranny in South Africa. They were promised much when their labour and support were needed but were given almost nothing. A campaign against the pass laws was mounted in 1919 and another delegation was sent to Britain.

The post-war economic crisis and the world-wide revolutionary upsurge following the Russian revolution resulted in a wave of strikes in South Africa. These strikes led to an increase in membership of the ANC and, particularly, the Industrial Commercial Workers' Union (ICU) which had been set up in 1919. The leader of the ICU, Clements Kadalie, was a fiery speaker and his movement soon claimed a membership exceeding 100 000. He told members: "We natives have always given the game away, we are dealing with rascals, the Europeans are rascals. There is no native problem, but a European problem of weakness, greed and robbery."[6]

Another radicalising force was the Communist Party of South Africa which was formed in 1921. It supported and assisted the strike by mineworkers in 1922, known as the Rand Revolt, and showed its preparedness to work for African liberation. In 1928 it adopted a slogan which urged its members to work towards "an independent native republic as a stage towards a workers' and peasants' republic".

6 Carter and Karis, 1973, page 215.

Students protesting during the 1980s

These political movements drew increasing numbers of Africans into political opposition to white rule.

During the 1930s the Representation of Natives Act terminated the franchise for Africans in the Cape. This led to considerable resistance, but in general African political struggles decreased in the 1930s and both the ANC and ICU shed membership.

In contrast to this political lethargy, the 1940s was a period of ferment as political movements adjusted to the new pressures and opportunities created by the war. The period coincided with years of drought in the countryside and as the economy boomed around wartime demands, African people flooded into the cities - nearly doubling the urban African population between 1939 and 1952.

It was a decade marked by strikes, bus boycotts and squatter land invasions. The ANC, until then a middle class organisation, attracted fiery young men into its Youth League, which was formed in 1944. Under the guidance of Anton Lembedi, the League attracted men who no longer looked to the white government or to British intervention but to the burgeoning masses in the cities. A Youth League pamphlet called on its members to identify with the popular classes: "Every Youth Leaguer must go down to the masses. Brush aside all liberals - both white and black. No compromise is our motto. We recognise only one authority - the people, and our leader can only be he who is with the people."[7]

Into the League were drawn men who would shape the future of South Africa, including Walter Sisulu, Govan Mbeki, Oliver Tambo and Nelson Mandela. These young men demanded more militant action,

7 Tom Lodge, 1983 , page 22, quoting SA Institute of Race Relations papers, AD 1189, ANC 111, File 5, undated memo on provincial congress elections.

challenging the old guard of the ANC and finally taking over leadership positions in the movement from the early 1950s.

In 1952, after years of strikes and industrial action, the ANC joined with the South African Indian Congress, the Coloured People's Congress and the white Congress of Democrats to form the Congress Alliance.

The first big conflict between the newly radicalised ANC and the state was in the 1952 Defiance of Unjust Laws Campaign where thousands of Africans, in all major centres of the country, defied whites-only signs on benches, in post offices and at stations, voluntarily seeking arrest in a Ghandian display that was to startle the world. By then Nelson Mandela was president of the Transvaal ANC. He was arrested and tried, along with 18 others, for his part in the campaign. He received a nine month suspended sentence. The campaign ended in 1953 when the government introduced heavy sentences for lawbreakers and protesters. The politics which followed was one of confrontation with apartheid and was marked by the drafting of the Freedom Charter in 1955, which incorporated demands for equality and freedom for all people in South Africa.

In December 1956, 156 leaders of the Congress Alliance were arrested and charged with high treason. The Freedom Charter formed the basis of the charges against them. The marathon Treason Trial continued from 1956 to 1961. In this trial prominent leaders of the Congress Alliance were herded together in prison cells and were to become a virtual parliament of resistance in detention. Most of the accused were released. Meanwhile resistance to oppression continued on an ever-widening scale through bus boycotts and strikes.

A pass burning campaign began in 1960 which led to the Sharpeville massacre in which peaceful protesters were fired on by the police. A state of emergency was declared by the Nationalist government, 20 000 people were arrested and the ANC and PAC were banned. Turning its back on world opinion, South Africa entered an isolated and ruthless period of apartheid policy. Oppressive laws such as the Group Areas Act, the Immorality Act and the Separate Amenities Act were now heavily enforced. The 'homelands' were declared independent states and thousands of Africans were denied their South African birthright and forced to live in overpopulated and under-serviced areas.

Ignoring pressure from the Commonwealth, the Nationalist government proclaimed a republic in 1961. Repression intensified and all channels for peaceful protest were closed. In this year African patience with white politics finally ran out and the ANC and SACP launched **Umkhonto weSizwe**, 'the Spear of the Nation' with Mandela as its commander-in-chief. Umkhonto weSizwe (MK) opened its armed struggle against apartheid with a series of blasts which sent power lines crashing to the ground around the country.

But in 1963 Mandela and 10 others were arrested at Rivonia and tried for high treason. Many of those leaders not in jail fled the country while Mandela, Sisulu and others began terms of life imprisonment. It appeared as though all black resistance to apartheid had been stilled. Beyond the

UDF activists Gugile Nkwinti (left) and comrade at a political funeral in the 1980s

country's borders the ANC gathered strength. But resistance, when it emerged again, came from within the country during the early 1970s.

Black Consciousness emerged and was consolidated during the 1970s with the formation of the Black Consciousness Movement in Grahamstown under the leadership of Steve Biko. From 1972 strikes, boycotts and stayaways began to ripple through the urban areas of South Africa. These were followed in 1976 by the uprising of school children in Soweto who were objecting to the use of Afrikaans as the medium of instruction. The massacre which occurred when police opened fire on protesting children was to send shock waves around the world, strengthening resolve within the country to fight apartheid and raising the ANC's legitimacy abroad.

Many young people fled the country, brutalised and angry. They found ANC support structures and bases in the frontline states where they received a political education and where their anger was turned into armed resistance. Once trained, they re-entered South Africa and formed cells, spreading outwards from urban centres and securing on-ground support in African townships. The frequency of armed guerilla contacts increased. Coinciding with this was an upsurge of political activity within South Africa. Beginning with student uprisings in 1980, unrest led by politically active young people flashed through the cities. Under the slogan, "Make South Africa Ungovernable", the Congress of South African Students carried the ideas of the Freedom Charter and Congress Alliance from school to school and then into civics, street committees and universities. The state countered with mounting repression and a 'tricameral' parliament which satisfied nobody. This led to the formation of the United Democratic Front in 1983 which strategically revived the Congress policy of non-racism. Charismatic Eastern Cape leaders, like

Voting at farm
by Joel Sibisi

Gugile Nkwinti, Stone Sizani, Steve Tshwete, Michael Xego, Mkhuseli Jack, Wilson Fanti and the martyred Mathew Goniwe, instilled a sense of invincibility and hope in their people. From this point, apartheid became caught in a pincer movement between mass resistance at home and mounting international isolation and revulsion abroad.

Despite two declared states of emergency, the detention of thousands of political activists and the use of troops in the townships, the political temperature continued to rise. Then, in 1992, the Nationalist government finally succumbed to international pressure, economic sanctions and internal unrest. Nelson Mandela and other jailed leaders were released, the ANC, SACP and PAC were unbanned and they began negotiations for democratic elections. Voting took place in 1993 and Nelson Mandela, born a Prince of the Thembu royal house, became the first black president of South Africa.

It had been a long and terrible struggle from the Frontier Wars to freedom. But in those struggles the Xhosa people had always been in the forefront.

Part 2

Language

28 The poetry within Xhosa

> "The indigenous languages of South Africa are among the most beautiful in the world. They seem to resound always with the very nature, the poetic character of the lands where they are used. The cadences of the wild, of water and earth, rock and grass, roll onomatopoeically along the tongue." [1]

Xhosa is a rich and superbly textured language in which the sounds of words always seek to harmonise. It is melodious and rhythmic, rich in onomatopoeia and sound imitations and full of speech sounds called clicks. Its musical quality is further enhanced by changing tones of voice, stressed and lengthened syllables and sonorous vowels.

The important characteristic of Xhosa is that any word which has a relationship with a noun in a sentence shows that relationship through 'concordance' or matching. This concordance occurs essentially through sound. The words of sentences are made to match and agree with each other through alliterative sounds called concords. There are subject concords and object concords. Concords are also used with descriptive and possessive words as well as with adverbs.

Alliteration is the repetition of the same letter or syllable in any number of words immediately following each other or at short intervals in the same sentence. This is only moderately used in English. However, it weaves an underlying thread through Xhosa, applying precision to the structure of a sentence and harmony to its sound.

Agglutination

XHOSA is described as a 'glutinous' language. This means that syllables or different parts of words are joined or 'glued' into one word or into one sentence. Xhosa words and sentences are threaded together like beads on a string. A single word in Xhosa may, in translation, require between two and five words in English. These different words are frequently distinct parts of speech. This joining together of syllables and words facilitates the smooth flow of speech. [2]

1 Noel Mostert, 1992, page 35.

Speech clicks

CLICK sounds are universal but occur only as paralinguistic features in non-African languages and serve as gestures, such as 'Tsk! Tsk!'.[3]

The click sounds which Xhosa absorbed from the language of the Khoisan are a type of consonant produced by suction within the mouth. There are three basic clicks and each has a number of variants. They are represented by **x**, **c** and **q**. The **x** is pronounced with a strong snapping click of the tongue against the back palate (almost on the soft palate). The **c** is a short sucking click of the tongue against the two upper incisors. The **q** is a hard click of the tongue against the hard palate. Here are three rhymes, one for each click.[4]

Iqaqa laqikaqika kuqaqaqa.	The wild cat rolled on the turf.
Lixaben'ixoxo ngomxhaxha womxoxozi.	The bull frog is fighting over a meal of pig melon and mealie-meal.
Ndachol' itik' eQonce.	I picked up a tickey in King William's Town.[5]

The South African singer, Miriam Makeba, introduced Xhosa clicks to the world in her popular 'Click Song'. Here are a few of the lyrics.

Igqirha lendlela nguQongqothwane,	The witch doctor of the road is Qongqothwane,[6]
Ebeqabel'egqith'apha, aha! uQongqothwane.	He was passing over here, aha! Mr Qongqothwane.

2 "They all agree in this principle, that they keep the essential part of each word, the root, uncorrupted, while the other syllables may suffer more or less of change; and since these syllables can be added to or taken from the unchangeable core of the word, the languages are called 'agglutinative', that is, the languages which 'glue' or join on their varying elements to their permanent elements. They keep distinct the radical and the formative parts of their words." Professor Peile: Primer of Philology, Macmillan, quoted by W.G. Bennie, 1953, page 38.

3 There are roughly 20 million speakers of click languages in Africa today. There are no click languages outside Africa. Clicks occur in Ndebele, Southern Sotho and the 'Nguni' languages in Malawi. In Tanzania clicks are found in the Sandawe and Hatsha languages in which virtually all words have clicks. Clicks are a remnant of the time when most of the inhabitants of Africa were Khoisan. The clicks, together with Khoisan rock art, are a legacy of the first people of Africa.

4 These rhymes were taught to Joan Broster when she was a child by her grandfather, William John Clarke, a trader in the Engcobo district. Joan Broster, 1967, page 12.

5 **Itiki**, from the English 'tickey', an old three-penny coin.

6 **Uqongqothwane**, the dung beetle, is named after the sound it makes, which resembles someone knocking on a door. In English it is known as 'the knock beetle' and in Afrikaans as 'tok-tokkie'. "The unerring instinct of this insect in its search for food and then in its perseverance in pushing the ball of dung along rough terrain has earned it the name of **Doctor of the roads**, likening it to the witchdoctor's unending search for medicines." Joan Broster, 1976, page 100.

29 The Xhosa noun

In order to understand the workings of a Xhosa noun we need to first take a close look at prefixes, suffixes and infixes.

The prefix

A PREFIX is a letter or a group of letters which can be added to the beginning of a word in order to change the meaning of the word. The prefix becomes part of the word and through it we know whether a word is a noun, verb, adjective, etc. The following examples show how the meanings of the noun stems, **-ntu**, **-zwe** and **-ngcuka** can be changed by different prefixes.

umntu	a person/a human being
isintu	human race/species
uluntu	humanity/mankind
ubuntu	human quality/manhood
ilizwe	a country
isizwe	a people/nation/tribe
ingcuka	wolf/hyena
ubungcuka	fierceness/ ferocity

The suffix

A SUFFIX is a letter or a group of letters added to the end of a word. The suffix becomes part of the word and it adds to or changes the meaning of the word.

intombi	girl	intomb**azana**	a small girl
ukubetha	to hit	ukubeth**isa**	cause to be hit
inja	a dog	inj**ana**	a small dog
inkosi	a king	inkosi**kazi**	a queen

The infix

AN INFIX is a letter or group of letters added inside a word. The infix becomes part of the word and it adds to or changes the meaning of the word.

Akafiki.	He doesn't arrive.	Aka**ka**fiki.	He does not **yet** arrive.
Uyathetha.	He is speaking.	Uya**wa**thetha.	He is **always** speaking.
Uyasebenza.	He is working.	Us**a**sebenza.	He is **still** working.

The Xhosa noun and its importance

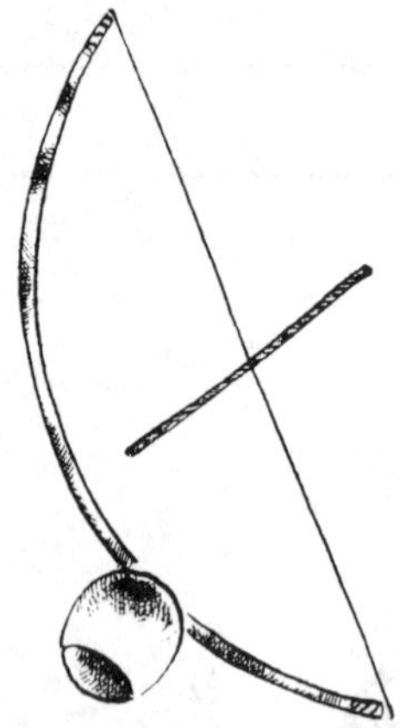

THE XHOSA noun is a fluid, dancing, moving word. It is made up of two parts - a prefix and a basic stem. The basic stem of a noun never changes, but the prefix changes according to how the noun is used in a sentence and to show singular and plural.

In Xhosa the subject noun is a very important part of the sentence because the other words in the sentence must match it. They do so by means of small linking affixes called concords.

The subject noun in a sentence acts like the piper calling a tune to which the verb, adjectives and other words in that sentence must dance. The 'music' of the sentence comes from the concords. 'Concord' means agreement. [1]

Xhosa nouns are grouped into families

DURING the last century missionaries and grammarians who analysed the underlying structure of Xhosa recognised that different nouns were identified by different prefixes and that, originally, like-nouns shared the same types of prefixes. Each person or thing, concrete or abstract, was recognised as belonging to a particular group. They identified eight 'groupings' or 'classes' of nouns which they numbered from one to eight. All early grammar books used this numbering method.

Modern grammarians further divided these groupings by giving singular and plural forms of each noun a class of their own. This created a group of 14 classes plus two sub-classes. It can be cumbersome and daunting for beginners to use 14 classes and in this grammar outline we have reverted to the original classification system of eight classes, with

1 "The language of the Congos and others of Negro lands is not founded, nor forms its rules, upon the declension of words, but upon their principiation." (i.e. their beginnings) Brusciotto: A Grammar of the Congo Language, 1659. (Quoted by W.G. Bennie, 1953, page 39.)

the addition of one sub-class. Using the eight classes makes it much easier to understand the patterning of the language.

A closer look at the prefix of the Xhosa noun

ALL XHOSA nouns begin with a prefix. The prefix:

- ☐ begins with a vowel.
- ☐ identifies to which class (family) a noun belongs.
- ☐ can change the meaning of the noun.
- ☐ indicates whether the noun is singular or plural.
- ☐ only has a capital letter when it is at the beginning of a sentence. The stem of the noun carries the necessary capital letter.

There are no articles in Xhosa

THE PREFIX should not be confused with the small words in English called articles. In Xhosa there are no equivalents for the English articles 'the', 'an' or 'a'.

Umntu can mean 'a person' or 'the person' or 'person'.

Itafile can mean 'a table' or 'the table' or 'table'.

Strong and weak prefixes

THE SOUNDS of Xhosa prefixes are described as being either 'weak' or 'strong'. All prefixes which are formed by a vowel-consonant-vowel are called 'strong' prefixes and noun classes which have 'strong' prefixes are called 'strong' classes. These are **aba-**, **o(b)o-**, **ili-**, **isi-**, **izi-**, **izin-**, **ulu-**, **ubu-** and **uku-**.

The prefixes **um-**, **in-**, **im-**, **imi-** and **ama-** are called 'weak' prefixes. This is because the letters **m** and **n** are not considered to be true consonants. They are known as nasals. Noun classes which have 'weak' prefixes are called 'weak' classes.

Memorising nouns

THE BEST way to learn new nouns is to memorise the singular and plural together. This makes it easy to discern changes to prefixes when they function in sentences. It also makes class identification easier.

30 The noun classes

As explained in the previous chapter, Xhosa nouns are grouped into eight noun classes and one sub-class. They are grouped alliteratively, that is, words which begin with the same prefix belong to the same group, or noun class. There is also a 'loose' gathering of like-nouns within each noun class, summarised in the next chapter.

The noun classes form the foundation of Xhosa and need to be learnt thoroughly. In this initial introduction of the classes, a hyphen is placed between the prefix and the noun stem for ease of understanding, although this is not how nouns are normally written.

Class 1

THESE nouns all refer to people. The singular nouns in this class begin with the prefix **um-**.

The prefix of class 1 words was originally **umu-**. In time and through use the second **-u-** fell away. It is important to remember that the prefix was once **umu-** because the vowel which fell away still has an effect, as will be explained later. The plural nouns in this class begin with the prefix **aba-**. Singular nouns in class 1 are 'weak' because of the **-m-** in the prefix **um-**. Plural nouns in class 1 are 'strong' because the prefix is formed by a vowel-consonant-vowel.

Singular		**Plural**	
um-ntu	person	**aba**-ntu	people
um-ntwana	child	**aba**-ntwana	children
um-fazi	woman	**aba**-fazi	women
um-limi	farmer	**aba**-limi	farmers

In some exceptions the plural prefix changes from **aba-** to **abe-**, as in **abe**-lungu, 'white people'.

Class 1a

THIS IS known as a 'sub-class' because its nouns are closely related to those in class 1 and because they share the same concord forms. Class 1a nouns are also 'people' nouns and include proper names, family names, names of relations, kinship terms and titles. A few names of non-human living things are also found in this class. These non-human living things have cultural importance and are known as 'familiars'. Some nouns are also included when there is a concept of personification, as in 'doll', 'machine' or 'radio'. Class 1a also includes a few foreign words which have been absorbed into Xhosa.

The prefix of singular class 1a nouns is **u-**. The prefix is 'weak' because it has no consonant. The prefix of plural class 1a nouns is **oo-**. Double vowels do not usually occur in Xhosa. **Oo-** is contracted from the original prefix of this class, **abo-**.

Oo- indicates a lengthening in pronunciation. Whenever a vowel is 'swallowed up' through language usage, its 'place' is still acknowledged by a lengthening in pronunciation.

Plural prefixes of class 1a are 'strong' because they originally contained a consonant. The plurals of class 1a nouns can be used in two ways:

- ☐ As a regular plural indicating two or more of a kind.
- ☐ To indicate a person and the people grouped with him, such as his family, his companions or his associates.

Singular		**Plural**	
u-mama	our mother	**oo**-mama	our mothers
u-nina	their mother	**oo**-nina	their mothers
u-nyoko	your mother	**oo**-nyoko	your mothers
u-Mary	Mary	**oo**-Mary	Mary and the others
u-John	John	**oo**-John	John and the others
u-nonkala	crab	**oo**-nonkala	crabs
u-nomadudwane	scorpion	**oo**-nomadudwane	scorpions
u-nomyayi	a crow	**oo**-nomyayi	crows
u-titshala	teacher	**oo**-titshala	teachers
u-loliwe	train	**oo**-loliwe	trains
u-nomathotholo	radio	**oo**- nomathotholo	radios[1]
u- matshini	a machine	**oo**- matshini	machines
u- nopopi	doll	**oo**-nopopi	dolls

1 "Certain traditional healers may have spirits manifest in themselves as voices, whistles, etc. This is regarded as both rare and singular and an honour from the ancestors. Thus the derivation of the Xhosa word for 'radio' comes from the association between the disembodied voices of the traditional healers, **oonomathotholo**, and the radio - a box from which voices are heard." Kirsh and Skorge, 1990, page 38.

Class 2

THE singular prefix of class 2 nouns is **um-**. Class 2 nouns generally refer to non-humans and include parts of the body, rivers, trees and objects in the natural environment. Both singular and plural prefixes are 'weak'.

Singular		**Plural**	
um-lambo	a river	**imi**- lambo	rivers
um-zi	a homestead	**imi**-zi	homesteads
um-lenze	a leg	**imi**-lenze	legs
um-lomo	a mouth	**imi**-lomo	mouths

Class 3

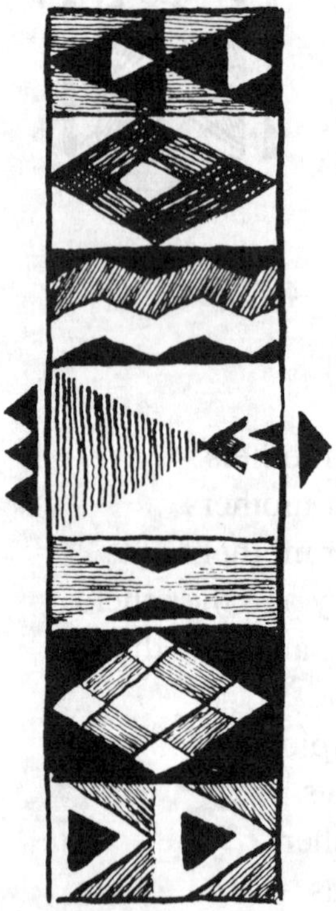

THESE are miscellaneous nouns. The singular prefix of class 3 nouns is either **ili-** or **i-.** If the noun stem has only one syllable, the prefix is **ili-.** If a noun has more than one syllable, the **-li-** falls away and the prefix is shortened to **i-**. You need to be aware of the full prefix, however. An important thing to note is that Xhosa often lengthens short words and shortens long words.

The plural prefix of all class 3 nouns is **ama-**. Both **ili-** and **i-** take the prefix **ama-** in the plural. Singular prefixes of nouns in class 3 are 'strong' because of their consonant. Plural prefixes are 'weak' because they contain a nasal, **-m-**, which is not considered a true consonant.

Singular		**Plural**	
ili-tye	stone	**ama**-tye	stones
ili-fu	cloud	**ama**-fu	clouds
ili-zwe	a country	**ama**-zwe	countries
i-sela	frog	**ama**-sela	frogs
i-qanda	an egg	**ama**-qanda	eggs

Class 3 also contains some 'borrowed' words which probably should belong to class 5. These are:

Singular		**Plural**	
i-planga	a plank	**ama**-planga	planks
i-polisa	policeman	**ama**-polisa	policemen
i-khaphetshu	cabbage	**ama**-khaphetshu	cabbages

The plural prefix of class 3 is shared by certain words which have their singular forms in other classes. These are the plural forms of tribal names such as **ama**-Xhosa (**um**-Xhosa, class 1) and words like **ama**-ntombazana (**in**-tombazana, class 5).

In some exceptions the plural prefix changes from **ama-** to **ame-**.

Singular		**Plural**	
ili- va	a thorn	**ame-** va	thorns
ili- so	an eye	**ame-** hlo	eyes

Class 4

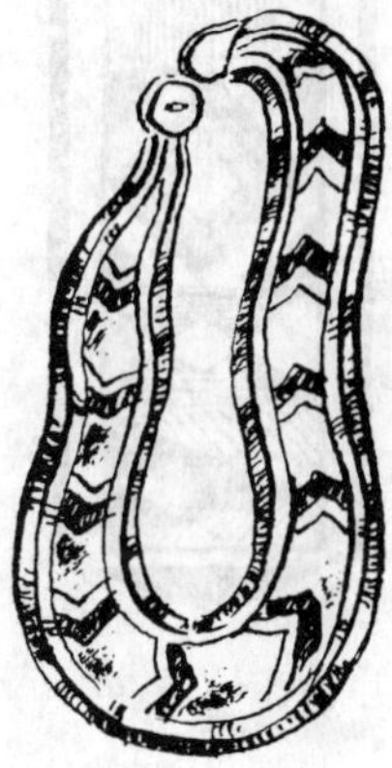

THESE are miscellaneous nouns which include many words borrowed from English or Afrikaans. The singular prefix of nouns in class 4 is **isi-**. Some nouns do not use this full prefix, but drop the second **-i-**. This happens when the **-i-** is dropped before a noun stem which begins with a vowel, as in **is(i)-onka**, bread, and will be explained in detail in a later chapter. However you will still see from the shortened prefix **is-** that the noun belongs to class 4.

If a borrowed word begins with the letter **s** in its original language (school, stool, etc.) it will be found in class 4. If a borrowed word begins with **sk**, **st**, **sp** the **s** becomes part of the prefix **isi-** and the consonant (**s**, **k** or **p**) is used as the first letter of the noun stem, as in **isi**-kolo, 'a school'.

The plural prefix for all class 4 nouns is **izi-**, even nouns whose singular prefix has been shortened to **is-**. There is only one exception and that is **iz-** onka, 'breads'. Singular and plural prefixes of class 4 nouns are 'strong' because the prefix is formed by a vowel-consonant-vowel.

Singular		**Plural**	
isi-xeko	city	**izi**-xeko	cities
isi-tulo	stool/ chair	**izi**-tulo	stools/ chairs
isi-tya	a dish	**izi**-tya	dishes

Class 5

MANY nouns of this class are the names of animals so it is sometimes called 'the animal class'. The singular prefix is **in-**, although it changes under certain circumstances. Words which have been absorbed from Afrikaans or English and which do not start with the letter **s** in their original language, are found in class 5. Here their singular prefix is simply **i-**. If the stem of a noun in class 5 begins with a sound made by the lips (**f** or **p**, **b** or **v**), the prefix becomes **im-**. This is simply for ease of pronunciation.[2] Even though there are these variations in the singular

prefix, the prefix is still considered to be **in-** and it is a 'weak' prefix because **-n-** is not considered to be a true consonant. The plural prefix is **izin-**. If the stem of the noun has more than one syllable, the **-z-** falls away and the prefix becomes **iin-**.

Because Xhosa often lengthens monosyllabic nouns and shortens long nouns, in this class we find that the **in-** of short nouns is lengthened to **izin-** in the plural and longer nouns take the prefix **iin-** to keep them shorter. All borrowed words use the prefix **ii-** and never **iin-** in their plural forms. The plural prefix of class 5 is 'strong', even in its contracted form, because the full form contains a consonant.

Singular		**Plural**	
im- pempe	a whistle	**iim**-pempe	whistles
im- vumi	singer	**iim**-vumi	singers
im-babala	bushbuck	**iim**-babala	bushbucks
im-beko	respect	**iim**-beko	respects
in-yoka	snake	**iin**-yoka	snakes
in-yosi	bee	**iin**-yosi	bees
i-tafile	table	**ii**-tafile	tables
i-mali	money	**ii**- mali	monies

In class 5 we also find short, single syllable nouns.

in-ja	a dog	**izin**-ja	dogs
in-to	a thing	**izin**-to	things

Class 6

THIS CLASS contains nouns which indicate long objects and high things as well as some abstract nouns. The singular prefix of class 6 nouns is **ulu-**. If the noun stem has more than one syllable, the **-lu-** falls away and the prefix is shortened to **u-**. The plural prefix of class 6 nouns is **izin-**. (The same as the plural prefix of class 5.) Monosyllabic nouns use a long prefix, **izin-**, in the plural, and long nouns take the shortened plural prefix **iin-**. Both singular and plural prefixes are 'strong', because of their consonants, even in their contracted forms.

2 A similar process exists in English phonology. The prefix **'in-'** meaning 'not' is **'in-'** before t but **'im-'** before p, e.g. **in**tolerable, **in**tact, but **im**possible, **im**perfect.

Singular		Plural	
ulu-vo	opinion	**izim**-vo	opinions
ulu-su	human skin	**izin**-tsu	skin
u-cango	door	**iin**-gcango	doors
u-lwimi	tongue/ language	**ii**- lwimi	tongues/languages
u-sapho	family	**iin**-tsapho	families
u-lwandle	sea	**ii**-lwandle	seas
u-fudo	tortoise	**iim**-fudo	tortoises
u-nyawo	foot	**ii**- nyawo	feet

Class 7

MOST of the nouns in this class are abstract nouns. The prefix of class 7 nouns is **ubu-**. There is no plural form for class 7 nouns. Many of these nouns have developed from other parts of speech such as adjectives, relatives and verbs.

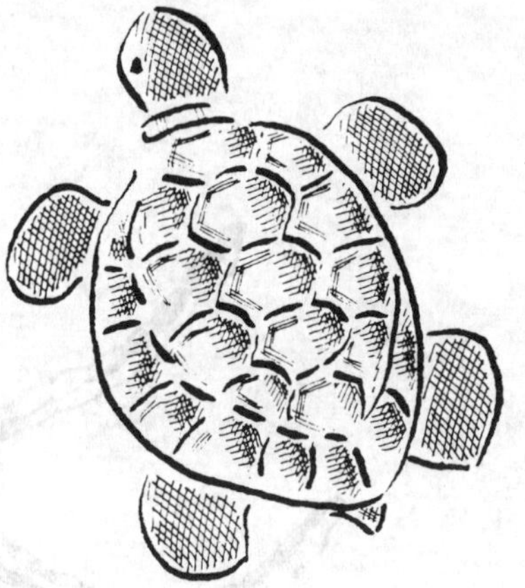

ubu-lumko	wisdom
ubu-hle	beauty
ubu-bi	evil
ubu-thongo	slumber/sleep/weariness
ubu-lawu	sweet-smelling ointment

Some class 7 nouns do not begin with the prefix **ubu-**.

u-tywala	beer
u-bomi	life
u-boya	wool
u-tyani	pasturage

Although this class does not have a plural form, two of its nouns may take a plural.

u-buhlanti, **ii**ntlanti	kraal
u-tywala, **ii**ntywala	beer/beer drinks/parties

Some class 7 nouns are derived from nouns of other classes by merely changing the prefix.

Noun		Abstract noun	
imfama	a blind man	**ubu**-mfama	blindness
ihlwempu	a pauper	**ubu**-hlwempu	poverty
isidenge	a fool	**ubu**-denge	foolishness
umntu	a person	**ubu**-ntu	human attributes
izibele	acts of feeling or affection	**ubu**-bele	kindness

Class 8

IN XHOSA the infinitive consists of the prefix **uku-** plus a verb root. This form of the verb is found in class 8 and is described in a later chapter. For the moment it is sufficient to know that the infinitive is recognised by the word 'to' in English, as in 'to run', 'to laugh', 'to sing', etc. Verbal nouns take the same form as the infinitive and are also found in this class. There is no plural form in class 8.

uku-mamela	to lisen/listening
uku-thetha	to speak/speaking
uku-bulisa	to greet/greeting

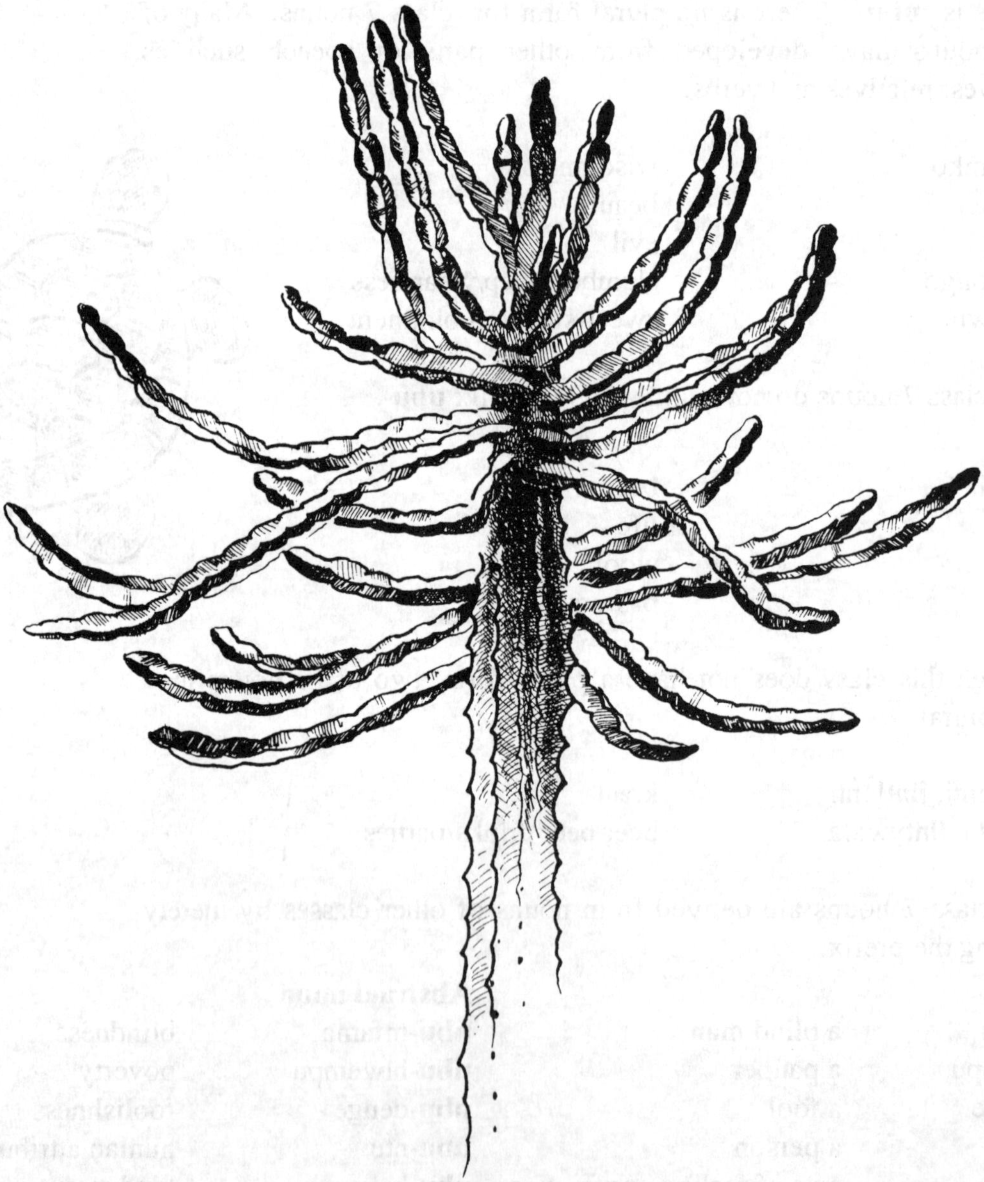

31 Summary of noun classes

This chapter lists the types of words found in each class. Xhosa nouns are listed in their singular and plural forms.

Class 1

Personal designations of a general nature
umntu, abantu - person
umfo, abafo - a chap
umfazi, abafazi - woman

Personal designations of a tribe
umXhosa, amaXhosa
umPondo, amaMpondo
umZulu, amaZulu

Occupations
umfundi, abafundi - student
umpheki, abapheki - a cook
umthungi, abathungi - a tailor

Nouns derived from verbs which denote the doer of an action
umhambi, abahambi - a traveller
umqhubi, abaqhubi - a driver
umbhali, ababhali - a writer

Class 1 a

Names of persons
uSandile, ooSandile
uNomsa, ooNomsa

Titles or relationships
ubawo, oobawo - father
udade, oodade - sister

Words which have become compounded with '**-so-**' and '**-no-**'
uSomandla - the Almighty
usombawo, oosombawo - an ancestor
unobhala, oonobhala - a secretary
unocanda, oonocanda - a surveyor

Some personified words, usually the names of animals
unziphonde, oonziphonde - a spring hare
undlebende, oondlebende - a mule
uxam, ooxam - a lizard
ukrebe, ookrebe - a shark
ukhetshe, ookhetshe - a hawk
uxomoyi, ooxomoyi - a kingfisher

Class 2

Names of trees and plants
umthi, imithi - a tree
umkhoba, imikhoba - yellowwood tree
umnga, iminga - a thorn tree
umkhiwane, imikhiwane - wild fig tree
umhlaba, imihlaba - aloe/ earth/ soil

Names of living or moving things other than animal or human
umZimvubu - Umzimvubu River
umoya, imimoya - wind
umlilo, imililo - fire
umbane, imibane - lightning

Some body parts
umzimba, imizimba - body
umqolo, imiqolo - the spine
umhlana, imihlana - the back
umlenze, imilenze - leg
umqala, imiqala - the throat
umlomo, imilomo - the mouth

Names which describe locality or position, especially on or near the earth
umendo, imendo - a way or path
umjelo, imijelo - a water-furrow
umhadi, imihadi - an ant-bear hole
umsele, imisele - a ditch
umqolomba, imiqolomba - a cave
umda, imida - a boundary

Abstract nouns derived from words usually expressing the result of an action
umboniso, imiboniso - an exhibition
umbuliso, imibuliso - a salutation
umbulelo, imibulelo - a thanksgiving
umdlalo, imidlalo - a game
umthetho, imithetho - a law

Names denoting periods of time
umhla, imihla - a day or date
umnyaka, iminyaka - a year
umso, imiso - the morning
umzuzu, imizuzu - a moment
umVulo - Monday

Class 3

Hard objects
iliwa, amawa - a precipice
ithala, amathala - an exposed rock
iphoba, amaphoba - the skull
iligxa, amagxa - the shoulder
izembe, amazembe - an axe
ikhuba, amakhuba - a hoe

Names of fruits
ikhiwane, amakhiwane - a fig
ithuma, amathuma - a Cape gooseberry
iqokolo, amaqokolo - a Kei apple
ithungula, amathungula - a Natal plum

Names of voracious or dangerous animals
iphimpi, amaphimpi - a cobra
iramba, amaramba - puffadder
ifoli, amafoli - a python
iramncwa, amaramncwa - a beast of prey
ixhalanga, amaxhalanga - a vulture

Names of diseases
iphika, amaphika - asthma
iqhenqa - leprosy (no plural)
ihlaba, amahlaba - a pain in the side

Personal designations expressive of character
ibawa, amabawa - a greedy person
igora, amagora - a hero
igwala, amagwala - a coward
igcisa, amagcisa - a skilful person
iciko, amaciko - an eloquent speaker
iqabane, amaqabane - comrade
ikhalipha, amakhalipha - a brave person
isoka, amasoka - a bachelor

Some words of Khoisan origin
icala, amacala - a side
icephe, amacephe - a spoon
icici, amacici - an ear ring
iculo, amaculo - a song
iqela, amaqela - a company
iqudu, amaqudu - a koodoo
ixhama, amaxhama - a hartebeest
ixolo, amaxolo - bark, peel or fish scales
ixina, amaxina - brass
iQonce - the Buffalo River
iNciba - the Great Kei River

Certain parts of the body
ibele, amabele - breast
ithambo, amathambo - bone
igazi, amagazi - blood
izinyo, amazinyo - teeth

Additional plural forms in class 3

The plural of proper names which have the prefix **um-** in class 1
amaXhosa; amaMpondo; amaBaca; amaZulu; amaGcaleka

The plurals of nouns of class 5 which have diminutive or feminine suffixes
amantombazana - girls
amankazana - young married women
amakosikazi - women
amankonyana - young calf or foal

Names of things occurring in pairs or in quantity
amathatha - the nostrils
amasini - the gums
amaKroza - the constellation of Orion
ameva - thorns
amanya- wrinkles

Names of liquid or viscid substances
amanzi - water
amasi - fermented milk
amathe - spittle

Classes of persons having a certain character in common

amachithi - those who cause discord
amadladla - vagabonds
amanyange - the old people

Some words denoting place or locality

amantloko - the upper parts
amaphandle - the outer parts
amalengelenge - the firmament
amalandalahla - nowhere/ Utopia

Words denoting mental feelings or impressions

amathandabuzo - doubts
amayana - disdain
amabenya - subterfuges
amanga - lies
amarethurethu - rumours
amanqabanqaba - difficulties
amaqajiqaji - guesses

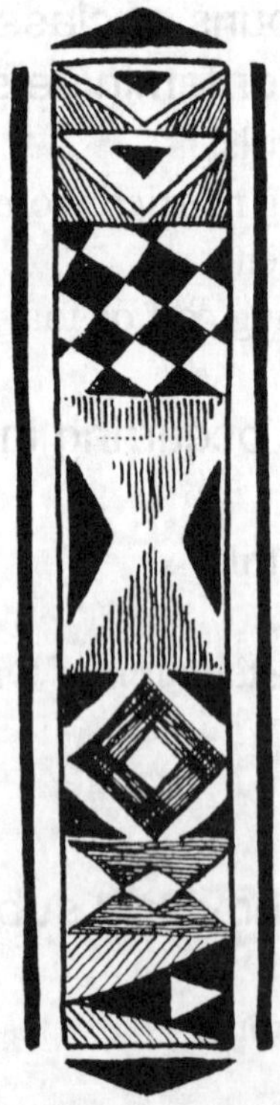

Class 4

Names of useful things

isiphatho, iziphatho - a handle
isisulu, izisulu - a bargain
isixholo, izixholo - a chisel
isitya, izitya - a vessel or plate

Names of persons possessing some quality in a high degree

isibadama, izibadama -a great 'stupid'
isibadubadu, izibadubadu - a great vagabond
isibovubovu, izibovubovu - a great blusterer
isilumko, izilumko - a wise, prudent person
isazi, izazi - a sage

Names of languages

isiXhosa
isiZulu
isiNgesi - English
isiJamani - German
isiPutukezi -Portuguese
isiBhulu - Afrikaans

Collective nouns and some human characteristics

isinga, izinga - a clump of thorn trees
isikhoba , izikhoba - a clump of yellowwoods
isihlaba, izihlaba - a clump of aloes
isintu, izintu - mankind
isifazi, izifazi - woman-kind
isinqanawa, izinqanawa - a fleet
isiLimela - the constellation Pleiades

Abstract nouns derived from verbs, especially from monosyllabic and vowel verbs, mostly denoting things done

isakhiwo, izakhiwo - building
isaziso, izaziso - a notice
isenzo, izenzo - a deed
isiphatho, iziphatho - treatment

Words formed from Dutch, Afrikaans and English words beginning with 's' followed by a consonant

isikolo, izikolo - school
isitalato, izitalato - street
isitovu, izitovu - stove

A few collective nouns

izibidi - dregs
izibilini - intestines
izikhohlela - phlegm
izixhobo - weapons

A number of class 4 nouns are formed from verbs by prefixing the verb with **isi-** and replacing the final **-a** with **-i** to denote a person, or **-o** to denote a non-person

isithethi - a speaker
isithetho - a speech

Some parts of the body

isihlahla, izihlahla - wrist
isifuba, izifuba - chest
isidlele, izidlele - cheek

Ordinal numbers

isibini - second
isithathu - third
isine - fourth
isihlanu - fifth

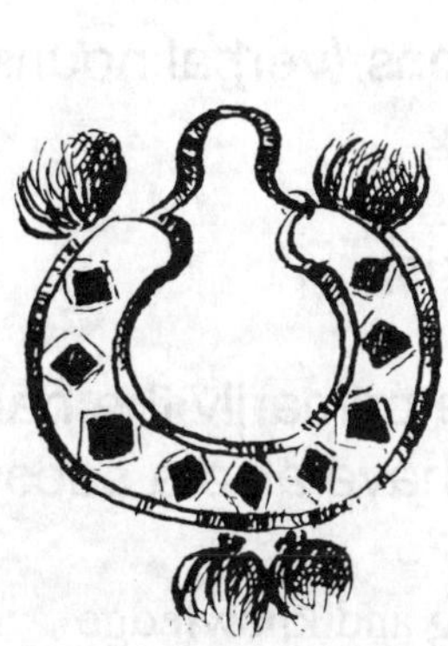

Class 5

Names of animals

ingwe, izingwe - leopard
indlovu, iindlovu - elephant
ingonyama, iingonyama - lion
imfene, iimfene - baboon
inyamakazi, iinyamakazi - antelope
imvubu, iimvubu - hippopotamus

Common objects

into, izinto - a thing
indlela, iindlela - way or a road
intloko, iintloko - head
inqwelo, iinqwelo - wagon
indlu, izindlu - house

Personal designations mostly denoting the agent or doer

imbaleki, iimbaleki - a runner
imbali, iimbali - an expert writer
inkosi, iinkosi - a chief
intombi, iintombi - a girl

Abstract nouns derived from verbs denoting things done

intando, iintando - will
ingcelo, iingcelo - a report
ingxolo, iingxolo - noise
imfundo, iimfundo - learning

Nouns derived from other languages which have a single vowel for the singular form of the prefix

ibokhwe, iibokhwe - a goat
ilokhwe, iilokhwe - a dress
ihempe, iihempe - shirt
isepha, iisepha - soap
ikomityi, iikomityi - a cup

Class 6

Things that are long or high

ubambo, iimbambo - a rib
unyawo, iinyawo - a foot
uphakathi, iimpakathi - the middle finger
ucingo, iingcingo - wire
ulundi (no plural) - the horizon
uphondo, iimpondo - a horn

Names of things long in a metaphorical sense

uluhlu, izintlu - a row or line of things
uluntu - the human race
uwangawanga, iinwangawanga - an endless thing

Words with a depreciatory sense

uthuthu, iintuthu - ashes
udaka, iindaka - mud

Abstract nouns usually expressing a state, derived from verbs

ubabalo, iimbabalo - a favour
uncedo, iincedo - a help
uphatho, iimpatho - conduct
uluvo, izimvo - an opinion
uthando - love
uxolo - peace
ulonwabo - happiness

Class 7

Names denoting quality

ubuntu - human quality
ubuntwana - childhood
ubugqi - magic
ubulungisa - righteousness
ubumhlophe - whiteness
ubumnyama - blackness

Names of common objects, especially soft ones

ubulembu - lichen
ubusi - honey
ubuzele - mucus
ububovu - pus
ubuchopho - the brain
ubulongo - cow dung
ubulawu - incense
utyani - pasture grass

Some designations of time or place

ubusuku - night
ubusika - winter
ubuhlanti - kraal

Class 8

Infinitive form of verbs

ukumamela - to listen
ukuthanda - to love

Names of actions (verbal nouns)

ukuhamba - going
ukubhala - writing
ukuthetha - speaking

Words that are primarily the names of actions but have also a secondary meaning

ukwazi - knowing and knowledge
ukufa - dying and death
ukutya - eating and food
ukukhanya - shining and light

32 The subject concord

In a Xhosa sentence, whenever an action is being performed by a subject noun or subject pronoun, agreement must be shown between the subject and its verb. The subject and its verb must match each other in order to function correctly. The agreement or matching between subject and verb is done by using a linking formative called a subject concord. It is called a formative because it is not a word in itself and cannot function on its own but needs to be attached to a verb.

Subject concords for 1st, 2nd and 3rd persons

IN ENGLISH the first, second and third persons, 'I', 'we', 'you' (singular and plural), 'he', 'she' and 'they' are called personal pronouns. They can stand alone as separate words. Their Xhosa equivalents are not words as such and cannot function as separate words. They are subject concords and must be prefixed to a verb or to the part of speech which forms the predicate in a sentence. Subject concords for the 1st and 2nd persons, singular and plural, are not derived from any noun form. Those of the 3rd person are derived from class 1.

1st person singular	ndi-	I
1st person plural	si-	we
2nd person singular	u-	you
2nd person plural	ni-	you
3rd person singular	u-	he/she
3rd person plural	ba-	they

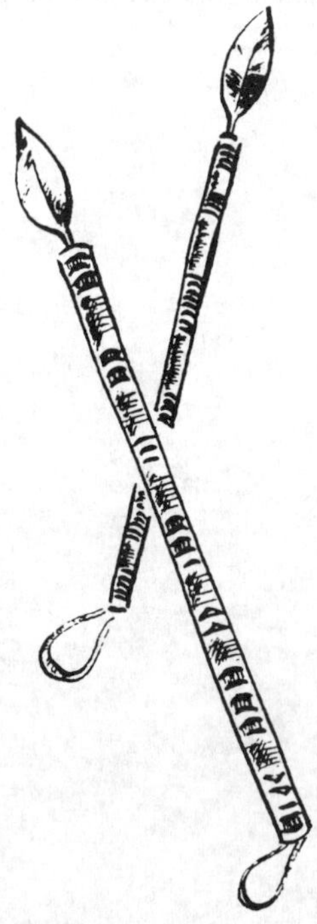

The following examples show how personal subject concords are prefixed to verbs.

Ndifuna isonka.	I want bread.
Sifuna isonka.	We want bread.
Ufuna isonka.	You (singular) want bread.
Nifuna isonka.	You (plural) want bread.
Ufuna isonka.	She wants bread.
Bafuna isonka.	They want bread.
Usela amanzi.	You (singular) drink water.
Nisela amanzi.	You (plural) drink water.

The subject concords of nouns

THE NOUNS in each noun class share the same kind of prefix and they also therefore share the same kind of subject concord. The exception to this is class 1a in singular and plural. Nouns in this class do not form subject concords of their own, but share the subject concords of class 1. For this reason class 1a is not regarded as an independent class but as a sub-class.

As already explained, Xhosa nouns and their prefixes are described as being either 'strong' or 'weak'. 'Strong' and 'weak' nouns form their subject concords in different ways, and these concords are also identified as being 'strong' or 'weak'.

A 'strong' prefix consists of a vowel-consonant-vowel. To form a subject concord from a 'strong' prefix the first vowel is dropped and the remaining consonant-vowel serves as the subject concord. A 'strong' subject concord contains a consonant.

A 'weak' prefix consists either of just a vowel or of a vowel and a nasal, **m** or **n.** The nasals **m** and **n** are not true consonants. The subject concord of a 'weak' prefix is formed from the vowel of the prefix. In other words the **m** or **n** is dropped. A 'weak' subject concord consists only of a vowel.

Although 'bits' of the subject noun's prefix are used to form the subject concord, they are not actually 'removed' from the subject noun. The subject noun and its prefix remain intact in a sentence. They merely guide the formation of the subject concord.

More than one subject

IF A SENTENCE has more than one subject, and the subjects are all people, the subject concord is **ba-**. If the subjects are animals or inanimate objects, the subject concord is **zi-**. However, in colloquial speech the class of the first noun, or the last one, determines the subject concord.

Amadoda nabafazi **a**yahamba.	The men and women go.
Amadoda na**ba**fazi **ba**yahamba.	The men and women go.
Amahashe ne**zi**nja **zi**yabaleka.	The horses and the dogs run.

Table of the subject concords

ALL XHOSA nouns are considered to be in the 3rd person and each noun class has its own distinctive singular and plural subject concords.

Class	Noun	Prefix	Subject concord
Class 1	umntu	um-	u-
plural	abantu	aba-	ba-
Class 1a	uMeri	u-	u-
plural	ooMeri	oo-	ba-
Class 2	umlambo	um-	u-
plural	imilambo	imi-	i-
Class 3	ilifu	ili-	li-
plural	amafu	ama-	a-
Class 4	isikolo	isi-	si-
plural	izikolo	izi-	zi-
Class 5	inja	in-	i-
plural	izinja	izin-	zi-
Class 6	uluvo	ulu-	lu-
plural	izimvo	izim-	zi-
Class 7	ubulumko	ubu-	bu-
Class 8	ukufunda	uku-	ku-

Some easy sentences

Umntu **u**bona inja.	The person sees the dog.
Abantu **ba**bona inja.	The people see the dog.
Umntwana **u**bona inja.	The child sees the dog.
Abantwana **ba**bona inja.	The children see the dog.
UMeri **u**bona inja.	Mary sees the dog.
OoMeri **ba**bona inja.	Mary and the others see the dog.
UMeri **u**funa isonka.	Mary wants bread.
OoMeri **ba**funa isonka.	Mary and the others want bread.
Umntu **u**funa isonka.	The person wants bread.
Abantu **ba**funa isonka.	The people want bread.
Umntwana **u**funa isonka.	The child wants bread.
Abantwana **ba**funa isonka.	The children want bread.
Umlambo **u**hamba apha.	The river goes here.
Imilambo **i**hamba apha.	The rivers go here.
Umthi **u**mila amasebe.	The tree grows branches.
Imithi **i**mila amasebe.	The trees grow branches.

Ilifu **li**zisa umthunzi.	The cloud brings shade.
Amafu **a**zisa umthunzi.	The clouds bring shade.
Ihashe **li**tya iziqhamo.	The horse eats the fruit.
Amahashe **a**tya iziqhamo.	The horses eat the fruit.
Isikolo **si**fundisa abantwana.	The school teaches children.
Izikolo **zi**fundisa abantwana.	The schools teach children.
Imoto **i**betha umthi.	The car hits a tree.
Iimoto **zi**betha umthi.	The cars hit a tree.
Intombi **i**thenga isonka.	The girl buys bread.
Iintombi zithenga isonka.	The girls buy bread.
Inja **i**sukela ikati.	The dog chases the cat.
Izinja **zi**sukela ikati.	The dogs chase the cat.
Imvula **i**zalisa umlambo.	The rain fills the river.
Iimvula **zi**zalisa umlambo.	The rains fill the river.
Uluvo **lu**nika amandla.	The opinion gives strength.
Izimvo **zi**nika amandla.	The opinions give strength.
Unyawo **lu**bamba isihlangu.	The foot holds the shoe.
Iinyawo **zi**bamba izihlangu.	The feet hold the shoes.
Ucango **lu**misa isela.	The door stops the thief.
Iingcango **zi**misa isela.	The doors stop the thief.
Usana **lu**funa ubisi.	The baby wants milk.
Iintsana **zi**funa ubisi.	The babies want milk.
Ubuhle **bu**nika uvuyo.	Beauty gives joy.
Ukucula **ku**nika uyolo.	To sing gives pleasure.

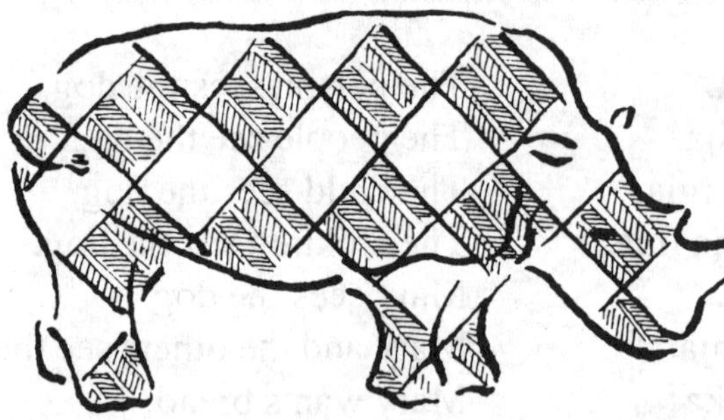

33 Vowel changes

Language is like a river. It rounds and softens sharp turns and sounds. In Xhosa you will hear much of this smoothing out of sounds. This is an important chapter and you will often need to refer back to it because it deals with these slight changes within the spoken language.

Hiatus is the sounding of two vowels in close succession. In Xhosa this is usually avoided but it is not always possible, particularly with some words of foreign origin such as **i-orenji**, 'orange' and **ama-apile**, 'apples'.

In some cases two vowels standing together merely indicate a lengthening of sound, as in **oobani.** There would originally have been a consonant between these two vowels, o(**b**)obani. Through language usage this consonant was 'swallowed up' but its presence is acknowledged by the lengthened vowel sound. Usually when two vowels come together one of them is discarded in some way. There are different ways of discarding vowels in nouns and in verbs.

Vowel changes within verbs

Vowel elision

THIS IS the dropping of a sound. The final vowel of the prefix falls away completely and the first vowel of the verb root remains. The vowel of the verb root never falls away because the verb root itself should not be changed.

ndi + azi	Ndazi.	I know.
ndi + onwaba	Ndonwaba.	I am happy.
ba + azi	Bazi.	They know.
ba + onwaba	Bonwaba.	They are happy.

Consonantalisation of the first vowel

THE VOWEL is pronounced with such intensity and closeness that it becomes a semi-vowel. A **w** or a **y** sound is formed. The rule is simply that:

i- becomes **y-** before a vowel

u- becomes **w-** before a vowel

u + **o**yika izinja	**Wo**yika izinja.	You fear dogs.
ikati **i** + **o**yika inja	Ikati **yo**yika inja.	The cat fears the dog.

Vowel changes within nouns

WHEN two vowels come together in nouns they form a new vowel sound. This is called **vowel coalescence**. The new vowel is called a secondary vowel. It is 'stronger' than the vowels it was formed from and always takes precedence. Vowel coalescence happens as follows.

a + a = a   a + i = e   a + u = o   a + ii = ee

Abazali na **a**bantwana *becomes* abazali n**a**bantwana.	Parents and child.
Abantwana na **i**kati *becomes* abantwana nekati.	Children and cat.
Abantwana na **u**tata *becomes* abantwana notata.	Children and father.
Abantwana na **ii**kati *becomes* abantwana neekati.	Children and cats.

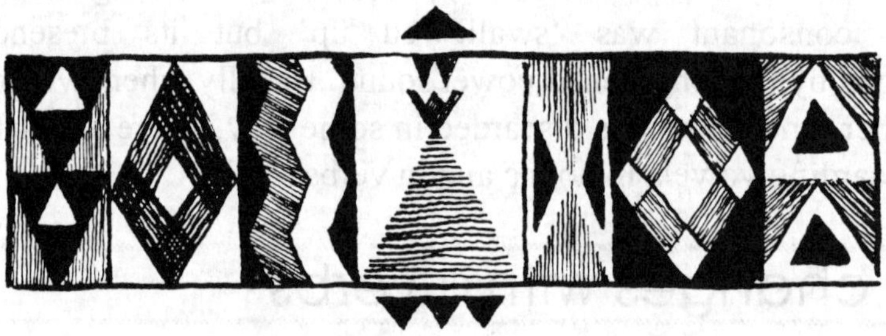

34 The infinitive verb

The infinitive mood names the action of a verb. In English an infinitive verb is often recognised by the word 'to' in front of it. In Xhosa the infinitive verb has the prefix **uku-** which means 'to'. All infinitives belong to class 8.

The following infinitive verbs have been written with a hyphen between the infinitive prefix **uku-** and the root of the verb for ease of understanding, although they are normally written as one word.

uku- hamba	to go
uku- thanda	to love
uku- funda	to learn
uku- baleka	to run
uku- thetha	to speak

Xhosa infinitives can also be used as verbal nouns (gerunds).

Ukufunda isiXhosa kumnandi.	To learn/learning Xhosa is fun.
Ukudanisa kunika uvuyo.	To dance/dancing gives joy.
Ukupheka kakuhle kumnandi.	To cook/cooking well is a pleasure.
Ukudanisa kumnandi.	To dance/dancing is fun.

The negative of the infinitive verb

THE negative of the infinitive verb is formed by placing **-nga-** after the prefix **uku-** and by changing the final **-a** to **-i.**

uku**nga**boni	not to see
uku**nga**baleki	not to run
uku**nga**thethi	not to speak
uku**nga**mameli	not to listen

35 The present tense

The present tense is used for any action which takes place in the here and now. The present tense in Xhosa expresses the present continuous, 'I go', and the present habitual, 'I am going'. Subject concords do not express gender, so **uhamba** can mean 'she goes', 'he goes' or 'it goes'.

subject concord	verb root	-a

Ndithanda uPiwe. — I love/I am loving Piwe.
Sifunda isiXhosa. — We study/we are studying Xhosa.
Upheka inyama. — You (singular) cook/are cooking meat.

The long form of the present tense

XHOSA often seeks to lengthen short sounds and shorten long sounds. If a present tense sentence has no object, the sound of the verb is stretched out by putting the infix **-ya-** between the subject concord and the verb. This is the long form of the present tense and it is used when there is no object or adverb following a verb. The infix **-ya-** is only used in the present tense and there is no English equivalent.

subject concord	-ya-	verb root	-a

Ndi**ya**funa. — I want/ I am wanting.
Umama u**ya**pheka. — Mother cooks/Mother is cooking.
Abazali ba**ya**thetha. — The parents speak/The parents are speaking.
Abantwana ba**ya**hamba. — The children walk/ are walking.
Ihashe li**ya**baleka. — The horse runs/is running.
Inja i**ya**lala. — The dog sleeps/is sleeping.

The long form of the present tense can be used to throw special emphasis on the verb when an adverb follows the verb.

Ndi**ya**baleka ngokukhawuleza. — I am running quickly.
Ndi**ya**thunga kakuhle. — I am sewing beautifully.
Abazali ba**ya**thetha ngolumko. — The parents are speaking wisely.
Abantwana ba**ya**hamba ngoku. — The children are going now.

The long form of the present tense can also be used to throw special emphasis on a verb, even though an object follows.

Ndiyafuna isonka.	**I want** the bread.
Ndiyathanda abantwana.	**I love** the children.
Abantwana **bayathanda** imidlalo.	The children **like** the toys.

When not to use the infix -ya-

THE INFIX **-ya-** is not used in the negative or with the imperative, two verbal constructions which will be taught in later chapters. All infinitive verb roots end in **-a**, except the following, which never use the infix **-ya-**.

ukwazi	to know	Ndazi.	I know.
ukuthi	to say	Uthi.	She says.
ukutsho	to say so	Nditsho.	I say so.

The short form of the present tense

THE SHORT form of the present tense occurs when an object or an adverb, or both, follow a verb. If this occurs in a sentence the verb does not use the infix **-ya-**. However, as explained earlier, if you ever want to emphasise the verb in a sentence you use the long form, even if the verb is followed by an object or adverb.

Ndifuna incwadi.	I want the book.
Umama upheka isidudu.	Mother cooks porridge.
Umama ubilisa amanzi.	Mother boils the water.
Ndibona umfazi.	I see the woman.

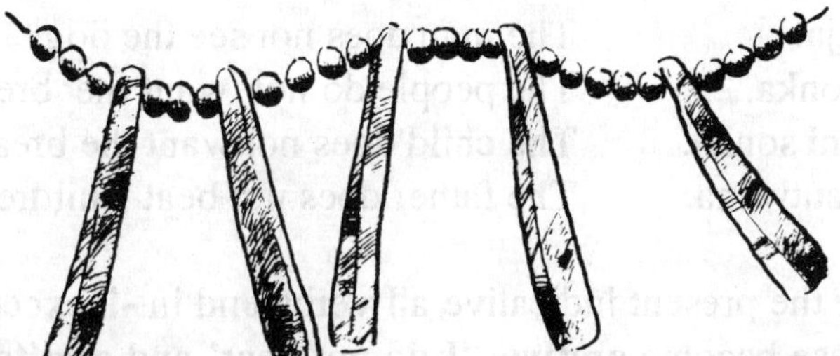

36 The negative of the present tense

The negative of the present tense is formed by prefixing **a-** to the subject concord and suffixing **-i** to the verb root. The **-ya-** of the long form does not occur in the negative.

a-	subject concord	verb root	- i-

If two vowels come together when the **a-** is prefixed, **-k-** or **-w-** or **-y-** is inserted between the two vowels, as follows:

2nd person singular	a + u = **aku-**
class 1 singular	a + u = **aka-**
class 2 singular	a + u = **awu-**
class 2 plural	a + i = **ayi-**
class 3 plural	a + a = **aka-**

Positive		**Negative**	
Ndiyafuna.	I want.	**Andifuni.**	I don't want.
Siyafunda.	We learn.	**Asifundi.**	We don't learn.
Uyabiza.	You call.	**Akubizi.**	You don't call.
Uyathanda.	You love.	**Akuthandi.**	You don't love.

If an object follows the verb in a complete statement, the first vowel of the object noun falls away. Such a negative sentence would be 'he does not eat bread'. If the negative statement is incomplete, such as 'he does not eat bread but likes cake', the vowel of the object is retained. The following are examples of complete negative sentences.

Umntu **akaboni** nja.	The man does not see the dog.
Abantu **abafuni** sonka.	The people do not want the bread.
Umntwana **akafuni** sonka.	The child does not want the bread.
Utata **akabethi** bantwana.	The father does not beat children.

In the negative of the present indicative all verbs end in **-i** except **ukuva** and **ukutsho**. These become **andiva**, 'I do not hear' and **anditsho**, 'I do not say so'.

37 Vowel verbs and latent (i) verbs

Verbs which begin with e-, a- and o-

MOST Xhosa verb roots begin with a consonant and those which begin with a vowel are called 'vowel verbs'. When a verb root begins with a vowel, the infinitive prefix modifies in the following way. If a verb begins with the vowel **e-** or **a-** its infinitive prefix is **ukw-** and not **uku-**. This is because the final **-u-** of **uku-** becomes the semi-vowel **-w-** as it joins the vowel of the verb. For example:

uku-enza becomes uk**w**enza, 'to make/ to do'
uku-akha becomes uk**w**akha, 'to build'

If a verb begins with the vowel **o-**, the final vowel of **uku-** elides.
uku-oja becomes ukoja, 'to roast/ to bake'

The subject concord contracts before vowel roots. **Ndi-** becomes **nd-**; **si-** becomes **s-**; **u-** becomes **w-**; **ni-** becomes **n-**.

Ndenza (ndi- enza) ntoni?	What am I doing?
Senza (si-enza) ntoni ?	What are we doing?
Wenza (u-enza) ntoni?	What are you (singular) doing?
Nenza (ni-enza) ntoni?	What are you (plural) doing?

Verbs which begin with a latent (i)

A SMALL group of commonly used verbs known as 'latent (i) verbs' have a hidden (latent) initial vowel, **i-**. This only reveals its presence when it is preceded by the vowel **a-** of a subject concord or of an infix. It then changes the immediately preceding vowel to **e-** .

This latent (i) does not always occur in the verb and cannot be considered an integral part of the verb root, but rather as a 'loosely attached' vowel. All latent (i) verbs are monosyllabic.

ukufa	to die
ukuhla	to go down
ukukha	to scoop
ukuma	to stand/ stop/ wait

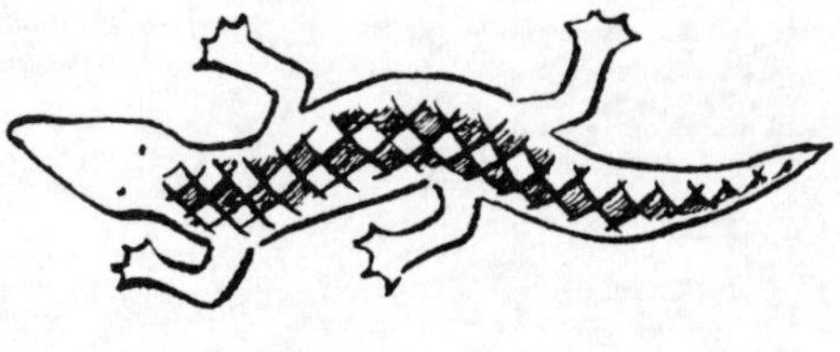

ukumba	to dig
ukumka	to leave
ukuva	to hear
ukuwa	to fall
ukuza	to come

Latent (i) and vowel verbs in the long form

IN THE case of these latent (i) verbs and all verbs which begin with a vowel, vowel elision takes place when the infix **-ya-** is used in the long form of the present tense. That is, the **-ya-** drops its **-a-** when joined to the verb, or changes to **- e-** when **-a-** and **- i-** come together.

ndi-**ya**-akha	Ndiyakha.	I am building.
u-**ya**-azi	Uyazi.	You know.
ndi-**ya**-oyika	Ndiyoyika.	I fear.
ndi-**ya**-iva,	Ndiyeva.	I hear.
ndi-**ya**-iza	Ndiyeza.	I am coming.

Latent (i) and vowel verbs in the negative infinitive

THE NEGATIVE infinitive is characterised by the negative infix **-nga-** and the suffix **-i**. When forming negative infinitives with vowel verbs, the **-a-** of **-nga-** elides. Before latent (i) verbs, the **-a-** of **-nga-** becomes **-e-**.

Positive		**Negative**		
ukwakha	to build	ukungakhi	(uku-nga-akh-i)	not to build
ukwenza	to do	ukungenzi	(uku-nga-enz-i)	not to do
ukuza	to come	ukungezi	(uku-nga-iz-i)	not to come
ukuma	to stand	ukungemi	(uku-nga-im-i)	not to stand

38 The progressive tense

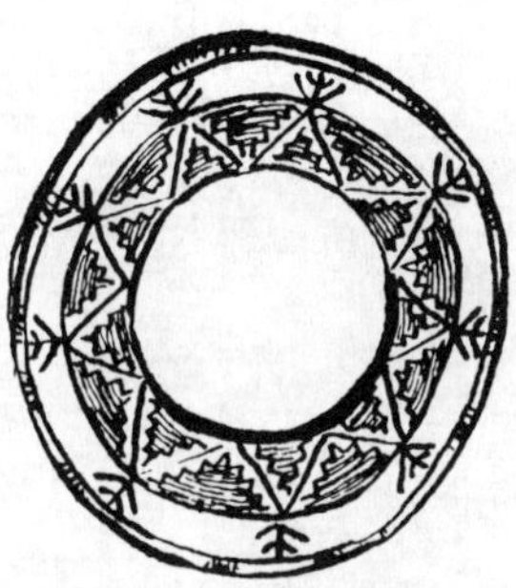

The progressive tense is used to express an action which is still in progress. If you want to say 'I am still talking', the word 'still' is translated by **-sa-**, ndi**sa**thetha.

subject concord	-sa-	verb root	-a

Ndi**sa**pheka. I am still cooking.
Abazali ba**sa**funda. The parents are still learning.
Inja i**sa**baleka. The dog is still running.

Using the progressive **-sa-** in the negative

THE INFIX **-sa-** can be used in a negative sentence to translate the English 'no longer' and 'anymore'. This is done by taking the negative form of the present tense and placing the infix **-sa-** between the negative prefix and the verb root.

negative prefix a-	subject concord	-sa-	verb root	-i

Andi**sa**fundi. I am no longer learning.
Aba**sa**thethi. They are no longer talking.
Inja ayi**sa**baleki. The dog is no longer running.

Using **-ka-** to express 'not yet'

IN THE same way that **-sa-** is used to express 'still', the infix **-ka-** is used to express 'not yet' in a negative sentence. The negative prefix **a-** is placed in front of the subject concord and the negative suffix **-i** is placed at the end of the verb root.

negative prefix a-	subject concord	-ka-	verb root	-i

Andi**ka**fundi. I have not yet studied.
Aba**ka**thethi. They have not yet spoken.
Inja ayi**ka**baleki. The dog is not running yet.

39 Gender

Gender has no influence on the grammatical construction of Xhosa. However, a feminine noun can be distinguished by using the suffix **-kazi**. This suffix serves the same way as in English when we form count**ess** from the noun count, hero**ine** from the noun hero, duch**ess** from the noun duke and priest**ess** from the noun priest. Here are some examples:

inkosi	a chief/lord	inkosi**kazi**	chieftainess/lady
ukumkani	a king	ukumkani**kazi**	queen
isicaka	man-servant	isicaka**kazi**	woman-servant
imvu	a sheep	imvu**kazi**	a ewe
inja	a dog	inja**kazi**	a female dog

Not all feminine forms of a noun are formed in this way. The feminine is sometimes a completely different word.

indoda	a man/husband	**umfazi**	a woman/wife
uyise	his father	**unina**	his mother
unyana	son	**intombi**	daughter

Male and female animals

THERE is usually a general name which does not tell the sex of the animal, such as in English we have horse, cattle, sheep, etc. There are two ways to distinguish male from female animals using their general names:

☐ By placing the word **inkunzi** for male and the word **imazi** for female before the general name of the animal. In this way we are literally saying 'the male of a horse', 'the female of a horse', etc.

inkunzi yenkomo	bull	imazi yenkomo	cow
inkunzi yehashe	stallion	imazi yehashe	mare

☐ By placing the words **iduna** or **induna** for male and **imazi** or **-kazi** for female after the general name of the animal.

ingwe induna	male leopard	ingwekazi	female leopard
ithol'iduna	bull-calf	ithol'imazi	heifer-calf

To show that an animal has been castrated the word **inkabi** is placed in front of the general name.

inkabi yehagu	neutered pig
inkabi yenkomo	an ox

40 Asking questions

When you are learning a new language it is essential to ask questions. In doing this both the words and the tone are important. The simplest way to ask a question is to raise the tone of your voice at the end of a sentence. Normally a sentence which is a statement ends in a low tone. A statement can also be turned into a question by adding **na** to the end of a sentence, after the verb. **Na** is known as a particle of a question and can be used to turn a single word into a question.

Sisonka **na**?	Is it bread?
Ngumama **na**?	Is it mother ?
Indlu inkulu **na**?	Is the house large?
Uyandibiza **na**?	Are you calling me?

The word order does not change in a question.

Uya edolophini.	He goes to town.
Uya edolophini?	Is he going to town?

Questions can also be formed by using question words such as 'why', 'when' and 'what'. Many Xhosa question words end in **-ni**.

-bani?	who or whom?
nabani?	with whom?
kabani?	whose?
ngubani?	who is it?
ntoni?	what?
nini?	when?
njani?	how?
yantoni?	of what?
ngantoni?	by means of what?
yintoni le?	what is this?
phi?	where?
ngaphi?	which way/ how many?
kangaphi?	how often?
kutheni?	why?
kwakutheni?	why? (used in the past tense)
ngoba?	why?
ngakanani?	how big/ how much?

The question word bani? - 'who?'or 'what?'

The subject concord is used to show the relationship between subject and question word.

Ufuna ubani?	Who do you want?
Ngoobani?	Who (plural) are they?
Yinja kabani?	Whose dog is it?
Uthetha nobani?	With whom are you talking?

The question word ntoni? - 'what?'

Ufuna ntoni?	What do you want?
Uthetha ngantoni?	What are you talking about?
Yintoni le nto?	What is this thing?
Bafuna ntoni?	What do they want?

The question word njani? - 'how?'

Banjani abazali?	How are the parents?
Zinjani iintombi?	How are the girls?
Wazi njani?	How do you know?
Injani ijezi?	What is the jersey like?
Kunjani ukutya?	What is the food like?

The question word phi? - 'where?'

Uya phi?	Where are you going?
Uvela phi?	Where do you come from?
Uhlala phi?	Where do you stay?
Ufunda phi isiXhosa?	Where do you study Xhosa?
Uphi umama?	Where is mother?

The question word nini? - 'when?'

Ufike nini apha?	When did you arrive here?
Isikolo sivula nini?	When does school open?
Ufunde nini eyunivesiti?	When did you study at university?
Uza kuya nini edolophini?	When are you going to town?

The question word ngaphi? - 'how many?' or 'which way?'

Bangaphi abafundi?	How many students are there?
Zingaphi izinja?	How many dogs are there?
Umoya uvela ngaphi?	From which direction is the wind blowing?
Uhlala ngaphi?	In which direction do you live?
Isikolo singaphi?	In which direction is the school?

The question word ngakanani? - 'how big?'

Indlu yakho ingakanani?	How big is your house?
Ingakanani ikhabhathi?	How big is the cupboard?

The question word ngantoni? - 'by means of what?'

Uza kuhamba ngantoni?	With what will you go?
Uza kuziphatha ngantoni iincwadi?	What will you carry the books with?
Uza kuwuvuthisa ngantoni umlilo?	What will you light the fire with?

The question word kutheni? - 'why?'

All question words, with one exception, are placed immediately after the verb. The exception is **kutheni**, 'why'. It is placed at the beginning of a question.

Kutheni ufunda isiXhosa?	Why are you learning Xhosa?
Kutheni umama elila?	Why is mother crying?
Kutheni abantwana becula?	Why are the children singing?

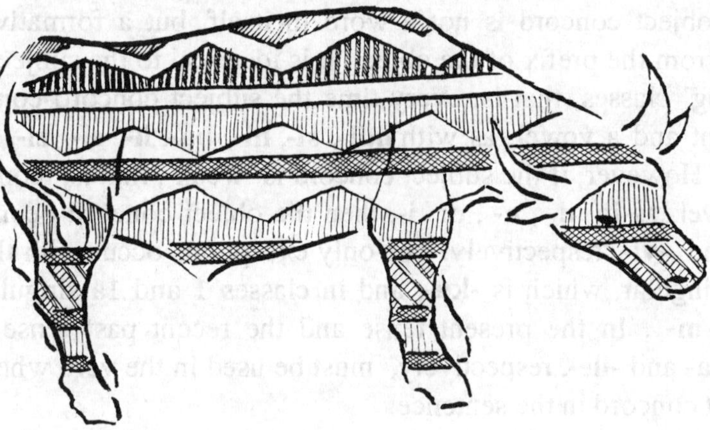

41 The object concord

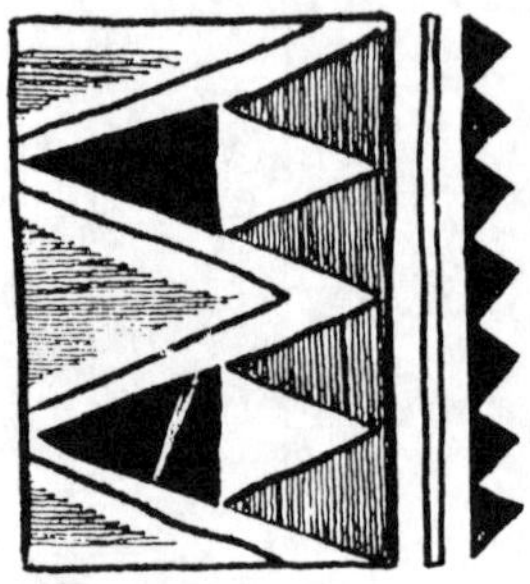

Just as subject concords are used to bring verbs into a relationship with their governing nouns, so can the relationship between the object and verb of a sentence be indicated with a concord. This kind of concord is called the object concord.

The object concord represents the object in a sentence and can even replace the object noun. It is often used in a sentence to refer to an object which is omitted, but known.

The object concord is not a word in itself, but a formative, and is derived from the prefix of the object. It is identical to the subject concord of 'strong' classes, that is, every time the subject concord consists of a consonant and a vowel, as with **ndi-**, **si-**, **ni-**, **ba-**, **li-**, **si-**, **zi-**, **lu-**, **bu-**, and **ku-**. However, if the subject concord is 'weak', that is, consists only of a vowel, as in **u-** , **a-** , or **i-**, then the object concord beomes **-wu-**, **-wa-** and **-yi-** respectively. The only exceptions occur with the second person singular, which is **-ku-**, and in classes 1 and 1a singular, which become **-m-** . In the present tense and the recent past tense the long forms **-ya-** and **-ile-**, respectively, must be used in the verb when there is an object concord in the sentence.

The object concord is always placed immediately before the verb root and two object concords never precede the same verb.

subject concord	-ya-	object concord	verb root	-a

Easy sentences using subject and object concords

Inkwenkwe iya**zi**phatha iinkuni.	The boy carries wood.
Indoda iya**ba**thanda abantwana.	The man loves the children.
Umntwana uya**li**thatha iapile.	The child takes an apple.
Ndiya**si**tya isonka.	I eat the bread.
Umthi uya**wu**nika umthunzi.	The tree gives shade.
Umlambo uya**wa**nika amanzi.	The river gives water.
Utata uya**ba**biza abantwana.	Father calls the children.

If there is more than one object and they are not of the same noun class, the object concord is formed either from the noun nearest the verb, or **-zi-** is used for animals and **-ba-** for people. If a sentence has more than one subject, this has no effect on the object concord.

Utata uya**yi**thenga imifumo neziqhamo.	Father buys vegetables and fruit.
USipho uya**yi**tyala iitapile nombona.	Sipho plants potatoes and maize.
Ihashe liya**yi**tya ingca nombona.	The horse eats the grass and the mealies.
Amafu aya**wu**zisa imvula nomthunzi.	The clouds bring rain and shade.

The object concord with questions

IF THE object concord is used in an interrogative sentence, the short form is used. In other words, the long form **-ya-** is never used with an object concord in an interrogative sentence.

Abantwana ba**yi**thanda ipudini na?	Do the children like pudding?
Ba**yi**phunga iti uSipho noPiwe?	Do Sipho and Piwe drink tea?

The object concord in negative sentences

WHEN there is an object concord as well as an object noun in a negative sentence, the initial vowel of the object's prefix is retained. Normally in negative sentences the initial vowel of the object falls away.

Umama notata aba**yi**thengi **i**mifuno.	Father and mother do not buy vegetables.
Amahashe neenkomo azi**wa**seli **a**manzi.	The horses and cows do not drink the water.
Umntwana aka**ku**tyi **u**kutya.	The child does not eat the food.

The object concord with vowel verbs

VERBS which begin with vowels cause the object concord to change because two vowels cannot stand side by side. It is important to remember that the root of the verb never changes, it is the vowel of the object concord which modifies. It modifies either by falling away or, in the case of 'weak' classes, becoming a semi-vowel **-y-** or **-w-**.

Akayenzi iti.	She is not making the tea.
Abayoyiki inyoka.	They do not fear the snake.
Amadoda ayakha indlu.	The men are building a house.
Ndiwaphula umthetho.	I break the law.

42 The reflexive

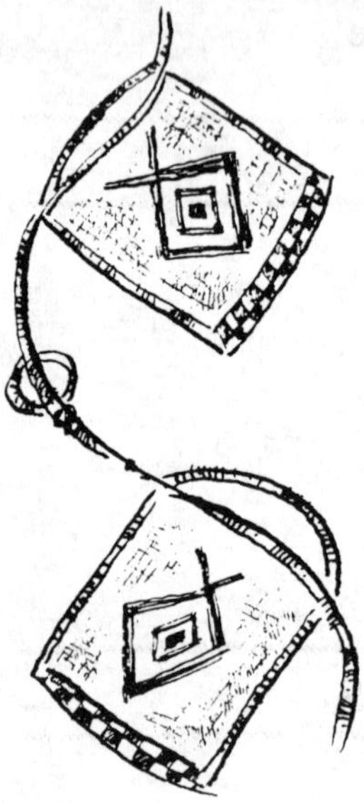

In Xhosa the reflexive particle **-zi-** is used to express 'myself', 'yourself', 'himself' and 'ourselves'. The particle **-zi-** is placed before the verb root and is used to show that the subject and the object of an action are the same. It is used exactly like an object concord, but it is not a concord because it is constant and never changes within a sentence, irrespective of class, person, or number.

Although the reflexive particle **-zi-** is the same as the objectival concords of plural nouns in classes 4, 5 and 6, they are not easily confused because the sense of the sentence makes the meaning of **-zi-** clear. In negative sentences **-zi-** is placed after the negative subject concord and before the verb root.

positive

subject concord	-ya-	-zi-	verb root	no object

subject concord	-zi-	verb root	object

negative

negative subject concord	-zi-	verb root	-i

Ndiya**zi**fundisa.	I teach myself.
Andi**zi**fundisi.	I do not teach myself.
Baya**zi**hlamba.	They wash themselves.
Aba**zi**hlambi.	They do not wash themselves.
Umfana uyazihlamba.	The youth washes himself.
Umfana akazihlambi.	The youth does not wash himself.

The verbal extension **-ela-** gives a sense of doing something for oneself.

positive

subject concord	-ya-	-zi-	verb root	-ela	no object

subject concord	-zi-	verb root	-ela	object

negative

negative subject concord	-zi-	verb root	-eli

Umfana uya**zi**hlamb**ela**.	The youth washes for himself.
Umfana aka**zi**hlamb**eli**.	The youth does not wash for himself.
Inja **izi**fuman**ela** ithambo.	The dog finds himself a bone.

43 The identifying copulative

A verb gives a sentence complete meaning by expressing the action played by the subject. In Xhosa, verbal action can be expressed without a verb by using certain prefixes which function as verbs. These prefixes are called copulatives. Copulative prefixes serve to translate the English verb 'to be'.

The copulative of nouns starting with um-, aba- and ama-

For all nouns which begin with the prefixes **um-** , **aba-** and **ama-** , the prefix **ng-** is used to say 'it is' or 'they are'.

Ngumlenze.	It is a leg.
Ngamahashe.	They are horses.
Ngumakhulu.	It is grandmother.
Ngabafundi.	They are students.

The copulative of nouns beginning with imi- and in-

For all nouns which begin with the prefixes **imi-** and **in-** , the prefix **y-** is used to say 'it is' or 'they are'.

Yinja.	It is a dog.
Yindlu.	It is a house.
Yimithi.	They are trees.
Yimilomo.	They are mouths.

Other copulatives

The copulative prefixes for all other words are easy to remember. The consonant of the noun prefix serves as a copulative prefix.

isitya	a dish	**Sisitya.**	It is a dish.
izikolo	schools	**Zizikolo.**	They are schools.
uluvo	an opinion	**Luluvo.**	It is an opinion.
ubusi	honey	**Bubusi.**	It is honey.
ilitye	a stone	**Lilitye.**	It is a stone.
ilifu	a cloud	**Lilifu.**	It is a cloud.

The copulatives of adapted prefixes

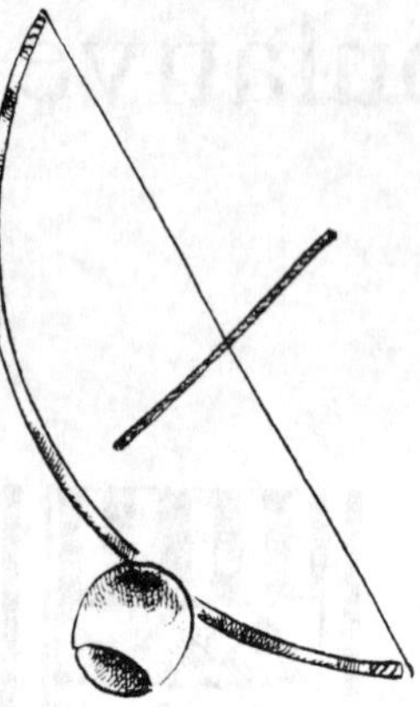

Some prefixes change and become shortened through time and usage. The original form of the prefix, and not the shortened form, is used to form the copulative. The following examples of words with contracted prefixes show how the original prefix influences the copulative prefix.

Noun with original prefix	Copulative prefix	
i(z)inkomo	**Zi**inkomo.	They are cows.
u(lu)donga	**Lu**donga.	It is a wall.
i(li)gama	**Li**gama.	It is a name.
i(li)hashe	**Li**hashe.	It is a horse.

Personalising the copulative

All the above examples show you how to say 'it is' or 'they are' something. To personalise the sentence by saying 'she is', or 'he is' or 'they are', the appropriate personal subject concord is used before the copulative.

Ngumntwana.	It is a child.	**Ungu**mntwana.	She is a child.
Ngabantwana.	It is children.	**Banga**bantwana.	They are children.
Ngabantu.	It is people.	**Banga**bantu.	They are people.
Ngumfazi.	It is a woman.	**Ungu**mfazi.	She is a woman.
Ngabafazi.	It is women.	**Banga**bafazi.	They are women.

Identifying yourself by profession

You identify yourself by profession with the copulative.

Ndingumfundisi.	I am a teacher.
Singabafundi.	We are students.
Ungutitshala.	She is a teacher.
Bangootitshala.	They are teachers.

The negative copulative

The prefix **asi-** is used to express 'it is not'. The letter immediately following the copulative prefix, which is the first vowel of the noun, changes to **-o-** for ease of pronunciation.

asi -	copulative prefix	-o-	noun

They are not students.	**Asingo**bafundi.
They are not trees.	**Asiyo**mithi.
It is not a car.	**Asiyo**moto.
They are not cars.	**Asizo**moto.

The impersonal ku-

When 'it is' is expressed in an impersonal sense to describe a condition or situation such as 'it is nice', 'it is pleasant', 'it is warm', etc., **ku-** is prefixed to adjectives, parts of verbs, certain adverbs and conjunctions. It is never used before a noun or pronoun. We can say **kulungile**, 'it is good', but we cannot say **kumntwana**, 'it is a child'. 'It is not' is expressed by **aku-**. Some of these constructions stand alone, others do not, as in **kukho umoya**, 'there is wind'.

Kulungile.	It is fine/ it is good.
Kunjalo.	It is so.
Akunjalo.	It is not so.
Kumnandi/ **ku**myoli.	It is nice.
Kunzima.	It is heavy/difficult.
Kungokuba...	It is because...
Akungokuba...	It is not because...
Kukho...	There is/there are...

Weather conditions are also expressed with the prefix **ku-**.

Kuyabanda.	It is cold.
Kuyafafaza.	It is drizzling.
Kuyatshisa.	It is very hot (causing one to burn).
Kushushu.	It is hot.
Akubandi.	It is not cold.
Akuni.	It is not raining.
Akufafazi.	It is not drizzling.

You can use the negative to imply an extreme in weather conditions.

Akubandi!	It is not cold, but it is extremely cold!

44 The locative

The locative is used to express all relationships of place out of which an action occurs and which in English are expressed by the prepositions 'in', 'on', 'to', 'from', 'into','among', 'out', etc. Sometimes the Xhosa locative can also tell the time in which an action takes place. There are a number of ways to express the locative in Xhosa.

The locative with the prefix '**e-**'

MANY nouns simply take the prefix **-e** to express position. These are some parts of the body, the geographical names of places, the four seasons and the cardinal points, north, south, east and west. All the other nouns which use the prefix **e-** should be memorised as there is no rule to identify them. There are many possible translations of **e-** .

Noun	**Locative**	
intshonalanga	entshonalanga	in the west
impumalanga	empumalanga	in the east
ilintla	e(li)ntla	in the north
umzantsi	emzantsi	in the south
ubusika	ebusika	in the winter
ukwindla	ekwindla	in autumn
intlakohlaza	entlakohlaza	in the spring
ihlobo	ehlotyeni	during summer
iGoli	eGoli	in Johannesburg
iKapa	eKapa	in Cape Town
iPitoli	ePitoli	in Pretoria
iBhayi	eBhayi	in Port Elizabeth
iQonce	eQonce	in King William's Town
iMonti	eMonti	from East London
ubuhlanti	ebuhlanti	at the kraal
ibhayoskophu	ebhayoskophu	at the bioscope
ihotele	ehotele	in the hotel
ihostele	ehostele	at the hostel
irestyu	erestyu	from the restaurant
isibhedlele	esibhedlele	at the hospital
intloko	entloko	on the head
ibunzi	ebunzi	on the forehead

umhlana	emhlana	on the back (upper)
umqolo	emqolo	on the back (lower)
iziko	eziko	on the hearth
imini	emini	during the day/at noon
ubusuku	ebusuku	during the night
ulwandle	elwandle	in the sea
indle	endle	in the veld/outside
ikhaya	ekhaya	at home
umnyango	emnyango	in the doorway

The locative with **e-** and **-ini**

A GENERAL way of expressing the locative is to prefix a noun stem with **e-** and suffix it with **-ini**. A few place names in which their original meaning is still clearly recognisable take **e-** plus **-ini**. An example is **eRawuthini**, in Johannesburg, formed from **irawuti**, from 'goud', the Afrikaans for 'gold'. Because of the different vowel endings, vowel changes occur. Here is a short summary of final vowel changes:

Words ending in **-a**, such as **intaba**, take **-eni** (**entabeni**, 'on the mountain').
Words ending in **-e**, such as **itafile**, take **-eni** (**etafileni**, 'at the table').
Words ending in **-i**, such as **amanzi**, take **-ini** (**emanzini**, 'in the water')
Words ending in **-o**, such as **imoto**, take **-weni** (**emotweni**, 'in the car').
Words ending in **-u**, such as **indlu**, take **-wini** (**endlwini**, 'in the house').

Some examples

Noun	Locative	
inja	**enjeni**	on the dog
intaka	**entakeni**	on the bird
intaba	**entabeni**	from the mountain
isitya	**esityeni**	in the dish
ihashe	**ehasheni**	on the horse
isikolo	**esikolweni**	to the school
imoto	**emotweni**	in the car
isitulo	**esitulweni**	on the chair
ubuso	**ebusweni**	on the face
indlu	**endlwini**	to the house
umntu	**emntwini**	to the person
idolophu	**edolophini**	in the town
ilifu	**elifini**	from the cloud
umthi	**emthini**	to the tree
amanzi	**emanzini**	to the water
incwadi	**encwadini**	in the book

Uhlala **endlwini.**	He lives in the house.
Ungena **endlwini.**	He enters the house.
Utata ufika **emini** emaqanda.	Father comes home at noon.
Ihlosi lihlala **entabeni.**	The leopard lives on the mountain.

The locative with **kwa-**

Kwa- is a formative used to express 'to', 'from', 'in' or 'at' the residence or property belonging to someone. **Kwa-** is also used if a town, settlement or place is named after a person or tribe. It is used to signify the domain of a tribe, nation, race or community. **Kwa-** is used with people-nouns which occur in classes other than class 1 and class 1a, such as **ipolisa**, **intombazana**, etc. **Kwa-** remains intact when it joins a person-noun.

Ndiya **kwa**Lunga.	I am going to Lunga's place.
Ndivela **kwa**malume.	I come from uncle's place.
Ndiya **kwa**Langa.	I am going to Langa.[1]
Ndivela **kwa**mapolisa.	I come from the police.

The following words are followed by **kwa-** to indicate a place. In such cases, vowel elision occurs when **kwa-** joins a vowel. (Unlike when it joins a person-noun and remains intact.)

phambi	in the front/before
phantsi	the ground side/down
phezulu	the sky side/up
phandle	outside
phesheya	the farther side/beyond
phakathi	inside
emva	at the back
endle	in the open

Amaxhego ahlala **phambi kwe**nkosi.	The old men sit before the chief.
Utata ubeka ubisi **phezu kwe**tafile.	Father puts the milk on the table.
Iinkwenkwezi zikhanyisa **phezu kwe**sibakabaka.	The stars shine above the sky.

1 Langa is a suburb of Cape Town, named after Chief Langa (Inkosi uLanga). It is thus prefixed by **kwa-** and should not be confused with **ilanga** (the sun).

The locative with **ku-**

Ku- is also used with people-nouns or kinship terms, but there is a slight distinction between **kwa-** and **ku-**. **Kwa-** refers to a place and is only used if a place belongs to a person or is named after a person. **Ku-** refers to a person. **Ku-** also translates as 'from', 'to' or 'of'. It can be used with a pronoun as well as with a noun. The difference between **kwa-** and **ku-** is illustrated in the following two sentences:

Ngeholide ndiza kuya **kwa**malume.	In the holidays I'm going **to my uncle's house.**
Ngeholide ndiza kuya **ku**malume.	In the holidays I'm going **to my uncle.**

The locative with **kulo-**

Kulo- is used with proper names to indicate 'at the home of someone's parents'. It indicates the person's place of residence and not ownership.

KuloZodwa.	At Zodwa's parents' home.
KuloPiwe.	At Piwe's parents' home.

Verbal locatives

THE locative can be expressed without using a verb by simply placing **-s-** between the subject concord and the locative form of the noun.

Li**se**Rhini.	It is in Grahamstown.
U**se**dolophini.	He is in town.
Ndi**se**khaya.	I am at home.
Ba**se**fama.	They are on the farm.

Locked in the locative

SOME expressions have become 'locked in the locative'. They cannot function unless they are used in a locative way.

endle	the open veld
entla	above/north
ezantsi	below/south
ele/ese (+ kwa-)	out of sight

Ndigawula inkuni endle.	I chop wood in the veld.
Kuhle endle.	It is beautiful in the veld.

Some exceptions

NOUNS in class 5 and class 6 keep the full prefix when forming the locative prefix.

iintombi	**ezin**tombini	to the girls
izinja	**ezin**jeni	to the dogs
iikati	**ezi**katini	to the cats
usana	**elu**saneni	to the baby
udaka	**elu**dakeni	in the mud

Sound changes

SOME sound changes occur for ease of pronunciation.

-bh- becomes **-j-**	isigubhu	esigujini	in the drum
-b- becomes **-ty-**	ihlobo	ehlotyeni	in the summer
-m- becomes **-ny-**	umlomo	emlonyeni	in the mouth
-mb- becomes **-nj-**	umlambo	emlanjeni	in the river
-ph- becomes **-tsh-**	usapho	elusatsheni	in the family
-mp- becomes **-ntsh-**	ihlwempu	ehlwentshini	to the poor person

Where is it?

Aphi amasele?	Where are the frogs?
Asemlanjeni!	They are in the river!
Aphi amahashe?	Where are the horses?
Asentabeni!	They are in the mountains!
Ziphi iintaka?	Where are the birds?
Zisehlathini!	They are in the forest!
Ziphi iinkomo?	Where are the cattle?
Zisedlelweni!	They are in the pasture!
Baphi abafundi?	Where are the pupils?
Basesikolweni!	They are at school!
Baphi abazali?	Where are the parents?
Basecaweni!	They are at church! [2]

2 By Nomakomani Zinnia Baai.

45 Using verbs in different ways

In this chapter we look at different verbs used in different situations.

ukuthwala	to carry on the head
ukupatha	to carry in the hands
ukubeleka	to carry a child on the back
ukuphunga	to drink something hot
ukusela	to drink something cold
ukudada	to swim (an animal or bird)
ukuqubha	to swim (a person)
ukuqgiba	to finish a task
ukuphela	to finish something up/to consume something/to terminate
ukuxhentsa	to dance traditionally
ukujiva/ ukudanisa	to dance western style
ukufaka	to put in
ukubeka	to put on top
ukuphangela	to work specifically to earn money
ukusebenza	to work in general or to earn money
ukubanda	to be cold (inanimate objects)
ukugodola	to be cold (humans and animals)
ukubuza	to ask a question
ukucela	to ask for something
ukusweleka/ ukubhubha	to die (human)
ukufa	to die (animal)

Although **ukufa** is generally used to express the death of animals, it can be used to express the death of humans when they die without dignity in mass kiilings, wars or genocides. **Ukufa** would also be used if a person dies alone, or is not given a correct burial.

There are also differences in the verbs **ukuya** and **ukuhamba**. **Ukuya** means 'to go to' or 'to travel' and must always be followed by the locative. It is used when a destination is named. However, **ukugoduka** specifically means 'to come home' or 'to go home'.

Ndiya eKapa.	I am going to Cape Town.
USipho uya edolophini.	Sipho is going to town.

The verb **ukuhamba** means 'to go', 'to depart' or 'to walk'. It is used when you do not name a destination.

Ndiyahamba.	I am going.
Abantwana bayahamba.	The children are leaving.
USindiswa uyahamba.	Sindiswa is walking.

There are a number of different verbs used to express 'to look'. **Ukukroba** means 'to look through something' or 'to peep'.

Abazali bakroba ngefestile.	The parents look through the window.
Umntwana ukroba emnyango.	The child looks through the doorway.
Umama ukroba ngefestile.	The mother peeps through the window.

Ukujonga means 'to look at something', 'to look fixedly' or 'to stare'. It is used to tell someone to look at something.

Jonga le nja.	Look at this dog.
Umama ujonga usana.	Mother is looking at the baby.

Ukubuka means 'to admire' or 'to look at something with pleasure' and can also be used to express looking at books or watching television and the cinema.

Sithanda ukubuka iTV.	We like to watch TV.
La mfazi uyabukeka.	That woman is 'lookable' - nice to look at.

Ukukhangela means 'to check something', like a rain-gauge, or 'to look intensely at something', like a set of figures or a map.

Ndikhangela umntwana.	I am looking for the child.
Ndikhangela imaphu.	I am looking at the map.

46 Giving direct instructions and commands

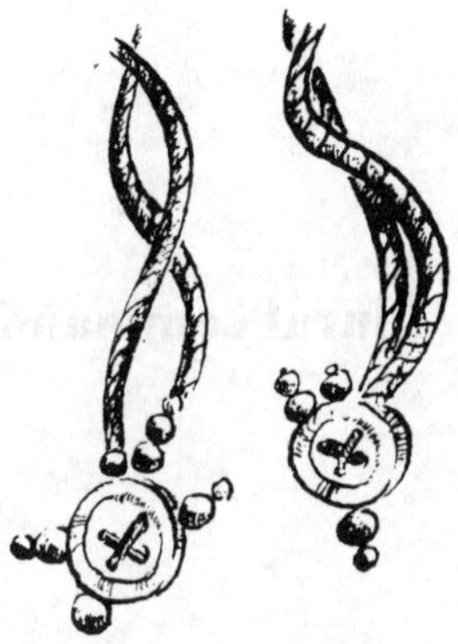

The imperative is a verb mood which carries a command or instruction. It is only expressed in the present tense and can be used either in the positive or negative, singular or plural. To give one person a direct instruction, or a command, the verb root is suffixed with **-a**. To give more than one person a direct instruction, or a command, the verb root is suffixed with **-ani**.

Because a verb in the imperative has no subject concord, it is not considered a complete verb. The imperative is usually written with an exclamation mark.

Only direct commands are expressed in the imperative. To 'soften' an instruction by saying 'please' or 'won't you do something' the subjunctive mood is used. This will be explained in a later chapter.

Singular commands

THE FOLLOWING commands are made with verbs of two or more syllables.

Sebenza!	Work!
Jonga!	Look!
Hamba!	Go!
Hlala!	Stay! (or sit!)
Thatha!	Take!
Hamba kakuhle!	Go well!

Plural commands

THE FOLLOWING commands are made with verbs of two or more syllables.

Sebenzani!	Work!
Jongani!	Look!
Hambani!	Go!
Hlalani!	Stay! (or sit!)
Thathani!	Take!

Commands using verbs of one syllable

IF A VERB has one syllable, **yi-** is prefixed to the root to lengthen the verb. **Yi-** is not used with verbs of more than one syllable. The verb root remains suffixed with **-a** in singular commands and with **-ani** in plural commands.

Singular commands

Yidla (or **yi**tya!)	Eat!
Yitsho!	Say so!
Yithi!	Say!
Yima!	Stop!/Stand!/Wait!
Yiza!	Come!

Plural commands

Yidlani! (or yityani!)	Eat!
Yitshoni!	Say so!
Yithini!	Say!
Yimani!	Stop!/Stand!/Wait!
Yizani!	Come!

The imperative with vowel verbs

IF A VERB root begins with a vowel, **y-** is placed in front of the vowel.

-enza becomes **Yenza!/Yenzani!**	Make!
-akha becomes **Yakha!/Yakhani!**	Build!
-oja becomes **Yoja!/Yojani!**	Bake!
-ala becomes **Yala!/Yalani!**	Refuse!

The negative command (singular)

THE NEGATIVE singular of the imperative is formed by **musa,** followed by the infinitive form of the verb. **Musa uku-** means 'do not'. It is not a prefix. In colloquial speech, the negative command is usually shortened by contracting **musa + uku** to **suku-** which means 'don't'.

Musa ukubaleka!/Sukubaleka!	Do not/don't run!
Musa ukuba!/Sukuba!	Do not/don't steal!
Musa ukutya!/Sukutya!	Do not/don't eat!
Musa ukuhamba!/Sukuhamba!	Do not/don't go!

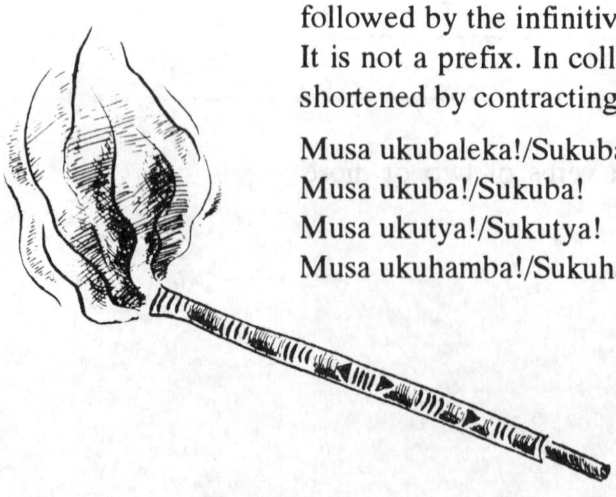

The negative command (plural)

THE PLURAL of a negative command is formed by suffixing **-ni** to **musa** followed by the infinitive of the verb. **Musani** is usually contracted to **sanuku-**.

Musani ukubaleka!/Sanukubaleka !	Do not/don't run!
Musani ukuba!/Sanukuba !	Do not/don't steal!
Musani ukutya!/Sanukutya !	Do not/don't eat!
Musani ukuhamba!/Sanukuhamba !	Do not/ don't go!

The usual rules for vowel changes occur with verbs which begin with a vowel:

u + o = o

u + e = we

u + a = wa

Musa ukoyika! or sukoyika!

Musa ukwenza iti! or sukwenza iti!

Musani ukwakha apha! or sanukwakha apha!

Commands with the object concord and the reflexive -zi-

THE OBJECT concord is always placed in front of the commanding verb. The reflexive **-zi-** is also placed before the commanding verb. The final vowel of the verb changes from **-a** to **-e** . This is actually a subjunctive ending, and will be fully explained in a later chapter.

Yithenge inyama!	Buy (it) the meat!
Libalekiseni ihashe!	Make (it) the horse run!
Mbethe!	Smack him!
Ziphathe kakuhle!	Behave yourself! (literally, hold yourself well!)
Zihlambe!	Wash yourself!

Some expressions

Lumka!	Look out!/Be careful!
Lumkela inja!	Look out for the dog!
Sukungxola!	Don't make noise!
Kahle!	Carefully!/Gently!
Misa!	Stop!
Yimise!	Stop it!
Yimise imoto!	Stop the car!
Yeka!	Leave off!/ Let go!
Myeke!	Leave him!
Yiza apha!/Yiz'apha!	Come here!
Bazise apha!	Bring them here!

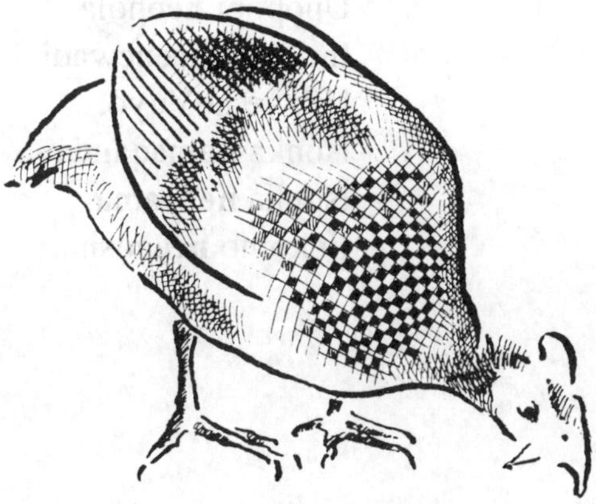

47 Formatives and prepositions

Prepositions do not exist in Xhosa as separate words the way they do in English. Instead of prepositions, Xhosa uses particles which join with the nouns or pronouns they relate to. These 'particles' are called formatives and they carry a variety of meanings.

A formative cannot stand alone. It must be joined to a word in order to function. Formatives may be added to the stems of nouns, adjectives, pronouns and the roots of verbs. They can change the meaning of a word or show a connection with other words in a sentence. The concords which are placed before verbs to link them up with the nouns to which they refer, are all formatives. So are the prefixes of nouns.

The formative **na-**

IN ENGLISH the word 'and' is a joining word known as a conjunction. In Xhosa, **na-** is used to express 'and' or 'with'. It is used to join nouns, adverbs and adjectives together but is never used to join sentences or actions together. The vowel of **na-** coalesces with other vowels.

na + a = na-

na + i = ne-

na + u = no-

na + ii = nee-

Some examples

Abazali **na**bantwana.	Parents and children.
Unopopi **ne**bhola.	The doll and the ball.
Imidlalo **nee**ncwadi	Games and books.
UPiwe **no**Vuyo.	Piwe and Vuyo.
Isonka **na**maqanda.	Bread and eggs.
Isonka **ne**nyama.	The bread and meat.
Iinkomo **nee**gusha.	Cattle and sheep.

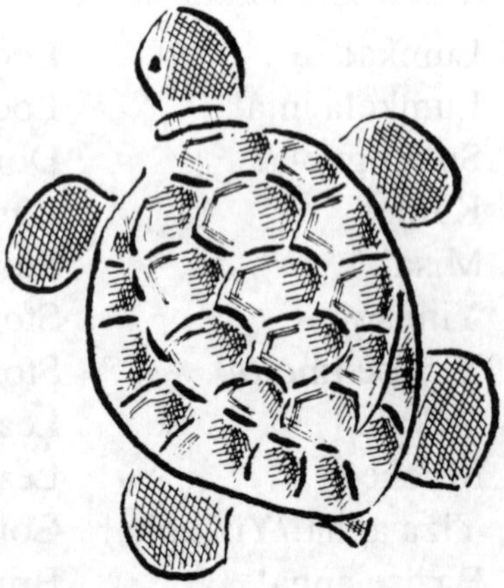

Different classes joined by **na-**

WHEN NOUNS of different classes are joined by **na-** to function together as a joint subject, the subject concord of the last mentioned noun is prefixed to the verb. However, if one of the nouns belongs to either class 1 or class 1a, the subject concord of class 1 is used.

Abafundi **na**maNgesi bayathetha.	The students and the English people speak.
Inja **na**mahashe ayabaleka.	The dog and the horses run.
Umntwana **na**bazali bayacula.	The child and the parents sing.

Verbs commonly associated with **na-**

SOME verbs are commonly associated with **na-**. Here the **na-** is joined to the following word.

ukudibana **na-**	to meet with
ukuhlangana **na-**	to meet together
ukulwa **na-**	to fight with
ukuthigaga **na-**	to bump up against
ukuthetha **na-**	to speak with/ to
Iintombi zidibana **na**makhwenkwe.	The girls meet with the boys.
Utata uthetha **na**bantwana.	Father speaks to the children.

All verbs with the reciprocal suffix **-ana** (each other) use **na-**.

Ndithand**ana** noMeri.	Mary and I love each other.
UPiwe usebenz**ana** noVuyo.	Piwe and Vuyo work with one another.

Other uses of **na-**

The formative **na-** has a number of other uses.

☐ **Na-** can be used to express 'together with'.

Yiza **no**mntwana.	Come with the child.
Ndihlala **na**bahlobo.	I live with friends.
Ndihamba **no**Peter.	I travel with Peter.

☐ **Na-** can be used to mean 'also', 'too' and 'as well'.

Biza **na**bantwana.	Call the children as well.
Thenga **ne**phephandaba.	Buy the newspaper too.
Mamela **no**nomathotholo/ **ne**radiyo.	Listen to the radio as well.

☐ **Na-** can be used to express 'having' or 'possessing'. In Xhosa there is no verb for 'to have'. Instead, use is made of the formative **na-** which literally means 'to be with'.

Ndi**ne**mali.	I have money. (literally, I am with money)
Ndi**na**bantwana.	I have children.
UJohn **une**sithuthuthu.	John has a motorbike.

☐ **Na-** can also mean 'to be in love with'.

UThemba **uno**Princess.	Themba loves Princess.
UThandile **uno**Nwabisa.	Thandile loves Nwabisa.

☐ **Na-** can mean 'be like' when placed after **ukufana**.

Umntu ufana **ne**ngonyama.	The man is like a lion.
Isiqhamo sifana **no**mfuno.	The fruit is like a vegetable.
Unopopi ufana **ne**ntombi.	The doll is like a girl.

☐ When **na-** is prefixed to the infinitive of a verb, it indicates an ability or willingness to act.

Ndi**no**kusebenza kakuhle.	I am able/willing to work well.
U**no**kuphatha izinto.	He is able to carry the things.

To use **na-** in the negative, the negative subject concord is prefixed to **na-**. The noun it is attached to loses its first vowel. The vowel of **na-** does not coalesce in the negative, therefore **na-** does not change.

Andinamali.	I have no money at all.
Akanabantwana.	She has no children at all.
UPeter **akana**moto.	Peter has no car.

The formative **kunye**

KUNYE is a conjunction which also means 'and', 'as well as' or 'together with'. It functions together with **na-** as follows.

Ndinxiba idyasi **kunye ne**jezi.	I wear a jacket and a jersey.
Ndinotata **kunye no**mama.	I have a father and a mother.
Abazali baphunga iti **kunye ne**kofu.	The parents drink tea and coffee.

The formative **nga-**

THE formative **nga-** has many meanings.

☐ **Nga-** is used to express 'with', 'by' and 'by means of'.

Ndihamba **nge**enyawo.	I go by foot. (literally, I walk by means of feet)
UMeri uya eKapa **ngo**loliwe.	Mary goes to Cape Town by train.

☐ **Nga-** can mean 'on', 'in' or 'at' when used before words expressing time.

Fika **ng**exesha!	Arrive on time!
Isikolo siqala **ng**entsimbi yesibini.	School starts at two o'clock.

☐ **Nga-** can mean 'about'.

Ndifunda **ng**engozi kwiphephandaba.	I read about the accident in the newspaper.
Siva **ng**omntwana kaThambo.	We hear about Thambo's child.
Ndithetha **nga**bantwana.	I talk about the children.

☐ **Nga-** is used with adverbs to express vagueness of locality.

Uhlala **nga**pha.	He stays this side.
Bahlala **nga**phaya.	They stay over there.

☐ **Nga-** is used with numerals to mean 'one by one' or 'two by two' or 'three by three', etc. It can also mean 'each'.

Izinto **nga**bini.	Things are two by two.
Itakane **nga**linye.	Each lamb.

☐ **Nga-** can be used to say 'each' in a sense of 'different types of'.

Ilizwe **ng**elinye alifani.	Each country is not the same.
Inja **ng**enye ayifani nenye.	Each dog doesn't look like another.

☐ **Nga-** can be used to mean 'nearby' when it is prefixed to a locative and joined by **-s-**.

Uhlala **nga**seKapa.	She lives near Cape Town.

☐ **Nga-** can be used to mean 'may' or 'can' in the sense of 'would you mind if?'.

Ndi**nga**hamba?	May I go?
Ewe, u**nga**hamba.	Yes, you may go.

The formative **njenga-**

Njenga- expresses 'like' or 'just as'.

Ubhala **njengo**titshala.	He writes just like a teacher.
Utya **njengo**mntwana.	He eats just like a baby.
Ubaleka **njengo**mvundla.	He runs just like a hare.

48 The recent past tense

The recent past tense is also known as the perfect past. In Xhosa it indicates an action which has just taken place or which has taken place sometime today or yesterday. The perfect tense has a long form and a short form, in the same way that the present tense has. It translates into English as either 'I have come' or 'I came' and indicates a completed action.

The long form of the past tense

IF THERE is no object in the sentence, **-ile** is suffixed to the verb root. As with the long form of the present tense, the long form of the past serves to 'lengthen' the sound of a sentence.

subject concord	verb root	-ile	no object in sentence

Ndiyavula.	Ndivul**ile**.	I opened.
Siyathunga.	Sithung**ile**.	We sewed.
Niyapheka.	Niphek**ile**.	You (plural) cooked.

If a word other than an object follows the verb, the long form is still used.

Umama uphek**ile** izolo.	Mother cooked yesterday.
USandile ucul**ile** kusasa.	Sandile sang this morning.

The short form of the past tense

IF A sentence has an object, the **-ile** is shortened to **-e**. This is called the short form of the past tense and is similar to the short form of the present tense.

subject concord	verb root	-e	object in sentence

UPiwe ubon**ile.**	Piwe saw.
UPiwe ubon**e** inja.	Piwe saw the dog.
Ndithengile.	I have bought.
Nditheng**e** ihempe izolo.	I bought a shirt yesterday.

Most verbs ending in **-ela**, **-ala**, **-ana** and **-atha**, form their past tenses as **-ele**, **-ene** and **-ethe**.

Ndihambela eKapa.	I journey to Cape Town.
Ndihamb**ele** eKapa.	I journeyed to Cape Town.
Ndiyaphatha.	I touch.
Ndiphethe.	I touched.
Sihambela eMonti.	We journey to East London.
Sihamb**ele** eMonti.	We have journeyed to East London.
Umntwana uphatha inja.	The child touches the dog.
Umntwana up**he**th**e** inja.	The child touched the dog.

An exception

THE VERB **ukuthi**, 'to say' is always used in its shortened form. You would say **ndithe**, 'I have said' and not **ndithile**.

The negative of the recent past tense

THE VERB root is prefixed with the negative subject concord and suffixed with **-anga**. This construction is used in both the long form and the short form.

negative subject concord	verb root	-anga

Umama akaphek**anga.**	Mother did not cook.
Andity**anga**.	I did not eat.

In the short form of the the negative recent past, the object following the verb loses its initial vowel except in the following instances.

- ☐ When a locative construction follows.

Izolo andiyanga **e**caweni.	Yesterday I did not go to church.

- ☐ If there is an object concord in the sentence.

Andi**ba**thandanga **a**bazali.	I did not love them, the parents.

Some examples

Sibonile.	We saw.
Sibone imithi.	We saw the trees.
Asibonanga.	We did not see.
Asibonanga mithi.	We did not see any trees at all.
Umntu uphekile.	The person cooked.
Umntu upheke isidudu.	The person cooked the porridge.
Umntu akaphekanga.	The person did not cook.
Umntu akaphekanga sidudu.	The person did not cook the porridge.
Abantwana bavukile.	The children woke up.
Abantwana bavuke kusasa.	The children woke up early.
Abantwana abavukanga.	The children did not wake up.
Ihashe libalekile.	The horse ran.
Ihashe libaleke entsimini.	The horse ran in the field.
Ihashe alibalekanga.	The horse did not run.
Ihashe alibalekanga entsimini.	The horse did not run in the field.

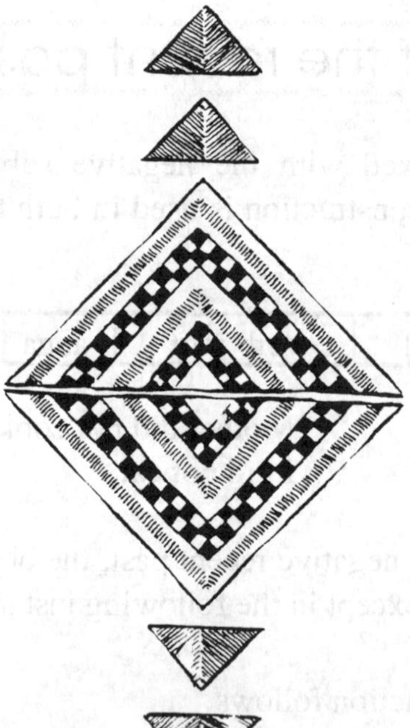

49 Stative verbs

There is a group of verbs in Xhosa called stative verbs.[1] In their infinitive they translate as 'to be' or 'to become' something. Stative verbs show the result of a process. They show a condition such as hunger, tiredness, thirst, etc., which has begun and is still continuing. Because of this they are expressed in the past tense while still having a present tense meaning. When you say 'I am hungry' in Xhosa you are actually saying 'I have become hungry'. In English these verbs are expressed in the present tense with a present tense meaning, such as 'I am hungry', 'I am tired', 'I am finished', etc.

ukubaluleka	to become good
ukubhitya	to get thin
ukucaca	to be clear
ukudinwa	to become tired
ukufa	to die
ukugoba	to bend
ukuguga	to get old or weary
ukukhululeka	to set free
ukulamba	to be hungry
ukulumka	to be careful
ukuma	to stand/ wait
ukungcola	to get dirty
ukunqaba	to be scarce
ukunxila	to get drunk
ukunxanwa	to become thirsty
ukonwaba	to relax
ukothuka	to get a fright
ukuphila	to be healthy
ukuphola	to cool
ukuqina	to harden
ukuqumba	to sulk
ukuthamba	to soften
ukuthoba	to bend
ukutyeba	to get fat
ukuzola	to become calm

1 List from Sydney Zotwana, 1991, page 124.

Using stative verbs

Ndilambile.	I am hungry.
Ndonwabile.	I am happy.
Ndinxaniwe.	I am thirsty.
Ndidiniwe.	I am tired.
Amahashe adiniwe.	The horses are tired.
Iinkomo zinxaniwe.	The cows are thirsty.

Ukuhlala, 'to sit down' is also a verb which describes a process. As a stative verb in the past tense it expresses the present tense state of having sat down. However, when used in the present tense, **ukuhlala** means 'to stay' or 'to reside'.

Ndihleli, in everyday speech, can also mean 'I'm fine' in response to 'How are you?' It could be interpreted as 'I'm sitting, all is well'.

Using stative verbs in the present tense

If a stative verb is used in the present tense its meaning alters. **Ndiyalamba** means 'I am getting hungry' or 'I am always hungry'.

Uyalamba.	You are getting hungry.
Siyaguga.	We are wearing out.
Abantwana bayangcola.	The children are getting dirty.
Iinkomo ziyatyeba.	The cows are getting fat.
UFreddy uyanxanwa.	Freddy is getting thirsty.

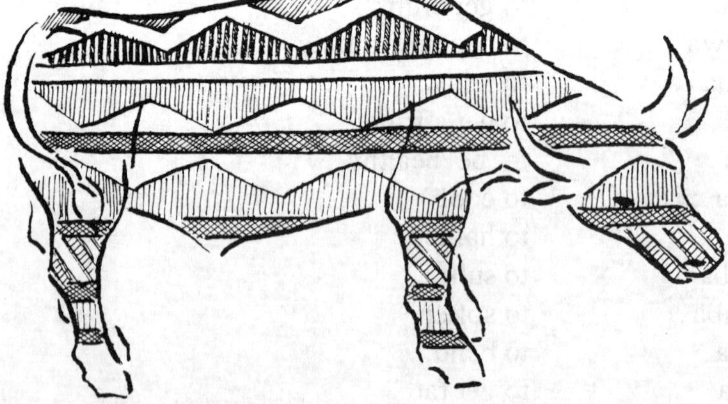

50 Absolute pronouns

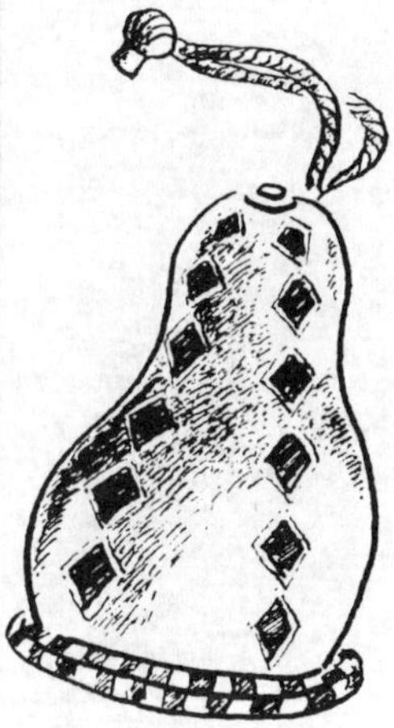

Personal pronouns have corresponding absolute pronouns which translate as 'as for me', 'as for them', 'as for us', etc. The absolute pronoun is used to emphasise the noun or to show contrast. It does not replace the subject concord but is used in addition to it.

Absolute pronouns end in **-na** and are mostly formed by suffixing **-ona** to the subject concord. The **-na** stabilises the noun by providing a second syllable. In nouns with 'weak' prefixes the absolute pronoun begins with **y-** or **w-**. Nouns with 'strong' prefixes give their strong agreement sound, the consonant sound, to the absolute pronoun. The absolute pronoun can be used with or without a noun.

Yena uThemba uyabaleka.	He himself, Themba runs.
Yena uyabaleka.	He himself runs.
Yena umama uyapheka.	She herself, mama cooks.
Yena uyapheka.	She herself, she cooks.

☐ The absolute pronoun can precede or follow a noun.

Inja **yona** iyakhonkotha.	The dog, it barks.
Yona inja iyakhonkotha.	It, the dog barks.

☐ The absolute pronoun may come before the verb, or after the verb.

Mna ndiyasebenza ngoku.	I myself, I work now.
Ndiyahamba ngoku, **mna.**	I go now, myself.

☐ The absolute pronoun can be placed between the verb and adverb.

Ndiyahamba **mna** ngoku.	I **myself** am going now.

☐ The absolute pronoun can be prefixed with **na-** to mean 'and me', 'with me', 'also me', 'even me', 'even you', etc. In such cases the final **-na** of the absolute pronoun is dropped.

Table of absolute pronouns

Class	Subject concord	Absolute pronoun	Absolute pronoun with na-
1st person	ndi-	mna	nam
plural	si-	thina	nathi
2nd person	u-	wena	nawe
plural	ni-	nina	nani
3rd person	u-	yena	naye
plural	ba-	bona	nabo
Class 1	u-	yena	naye
plural	ba-	bona	nabo
Class 2	u-	wona	nawo
plural	i-	yona	nayo
Class 3	li-	lona	nalo
plural	a-	wona	nawo
Class 4	si-	sona	naso
plural	zi-	zona	nazo
Class 5	i-	yona	nayo
plural	zi-	zona	nazo
Class 6	lu-	lona	nalo
plural	zi-	zona	nazo
Class 7	bu-	bona	nabo
Class 8	ku-	kona	nako

Using the absolute pronoun

Ndifuna **yena.**	I want him.
Ndifuna **wena.**	I want you.
Ndifumene ibhokisi **mna.**	As for me, I found the box.
UPhumeza **yena** uyeza.	Phumeza herself is coming.
Umthi **wona** uswela amanzi.	The tree itself needs water.
Imithi **yona** iswela amanzi.	The trees themselves need water.
Amahashe **wona** ayabaleka.	The horses themselves run.
Izinja **zona** ziyakhonkotha.	The dogs themselves bark.
Kona, ukutya kumnandi.	As for it, the food is nice.
Sona, isonka simnandi.	As for it, bread is nice.
Bona, ubulumko bulungile.	As for it, caution is good.

Predicates formed from absolute pronouns

IF YOU want to say 'it is *I*' or 'it is *them*', with emphasis on the pronoun, you simply attach a copulative prefix to the relevant absolute pronoun. In such cases the final **-na** of the absolute pronoun falls away. The negative is formed by prefixing **asi-** to the copulative.

Ngabo.	It is they.
Asingabo.	It is not them.
Nguwe.	It is you.
Asinguwe.	It is not you.

To have a definite subject in such a sentence, simply prefix a subject concord to the copulative prefix.

Ndindim.	I am I.
Andindim.	I am not I.
Unguwe.	You are you.
Akunguwe.	You are not you.
Unguye.	He is he.
Akunguye.	He is not he.

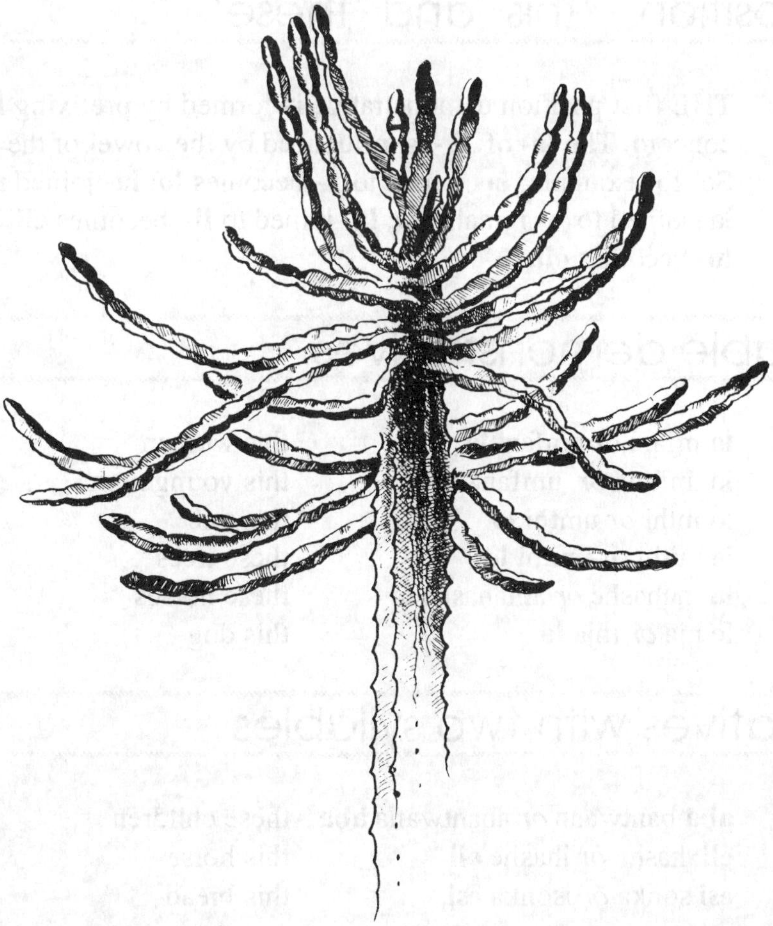

51 Demonstrative pronouns

The demonstrative pronoun is used to point out something. It shows the position of the noun being spoken about. In Xhosa there are three demonstrative positions:

- ☐ 'This' and 'these', which point to something close to the speaker.
- ☐ 'That' and 'those', which point to something not close to the speaker, but close to the one spoken to.
- ☐ 'That' and 'those yonder, over there', which point to something far away from both the speaker and the one spoken to.

When a demonstrative pronoun precedes a noun, the initial vowel of the prefix is omitted. When a demonstrative pronoun follows a noun, the initial vowel is retained and there is usually less emphasis on a demonstrative which follows a noun.

The first position - 'this' and 'these'

THE first position demonstrative is formed by prefixing **la-** to the subject concord. The **-a-** of **la-** is influenced by the vowel of the subject concord. So, for example, **la-** joined to **u-** becomes **lo**; **la-** joined to **i-** becomes **le**; **la-** joined to **a-** remains **la**, **la-** joined to **li-** becomes **eli** and **la-** joined to **lu-** becomes **olu**.

Single syllable demonstratives

lo mfazi *or* umfazi **lo**	this woman
lo mfana *or* umfana **lo**	this young man
lo mthi *or* umthi **lo**	this tree
le mithi *or* imithi **le**	these trees
la mahashe *or* amahashe **la**	these horses
le nja *or* inja **le**	this dog

Demonstratives with two syllables

aba bantwana *or* abantwana **aba**	these children
eli hashe *or* ihashe **eli**	this horse
esi sonka *or* isonka **esi**	this bread

ezi zonka *or* izonka **ezi**	these breads
ezi ntlanzi *or* iintlanzi **ezi**	these fishes
olu bisi *or* ubisi **olu**	this milk
obu buso *or* ubuso **obu**	this face
oku kuthetha *or* ukuthetha **oku**	this talking

Some examples

Lo mntwana uyadlala.	This child is playing.
Aba bantwana bayadlala.	These children are playing.
Lo mthi mkhulu.	This tree is big.
Le mithi mikhulu.	These trees are big.
La mahashe ayabaleka.	These horses are running.
Eli hashe liyabaleka.	This horse is running.
Le nja iyatya.	This dog is eating.
Lo mfazi uyapheka.	This woman is cooking.
Le mifuno midala.	These vegetables are stale.
La mazinyo makhulu.	These are big teeth.
Ezi ntlanzi ziyadada.	These fishes are swimming.
Le ntlanzi iyadada.	This fish is swimming.
Eli litye likhulu.	This stone is big.
Olu bisi lumuncu.	This milk is sour.
Obu tywala buyabanda.	This beer is cold.
Oku kuthetha kumnandi.	This talking is nice.

The second position - 'that' and 'those'

THE second position demonstrative is formed by adding **-o** to the final vowel of the first position demonstrative. When the second position demonstrative is placed directly before the noun, the first vowel of the noun spoken about falls away.

Should a second position demonstrative follow a noun, the noun remains intact. However, in the case of nouns with 'weak' prefixes (those which do not have a consonant), when the demonstrative follows a noun, the pronoun is lengthened by using either **-y-** or **-w-**. The following examples use nouns with 'weak' prefixes.

Loo mfana uyadlala *or* umfana **lowo** uyadlala.	That boy is playing.
Loo mthi mkhulu *or* umthi **lowo** mkhulu.	That tree is big.
Loo mithi mikhulu *or* imithi **leyo** mikhulu.	Those trees are big.
Loo mahashe ayabaleka *or* amahashe **lawo** ayabaleka.	Those horses are running.
Loo nja iyatya *or* inja **leyo** iyatya.	That dog is eating.
Loo mfana uyasela *or* umfana **lowo** uyasela.	That young man is drinking.

Loo mifuno midala *or* imifuno **leyo** midala.	Those vegetables are stale.
Loo mazinyo makhulu *or* amazinyo **lawo** makhulu.	Those teeth are big.
Loo ntlanzi iyadada *or* intlanzi **leyo** iyadada.	That fish is swimming.

The third position - 'that over there'

THIS IS formed by adding **-a** to the first position demonstrative. If the first position demonstrative ends in **-o**, then **-w-** is introduced after the **-o**. If the first position demonstrative ends in **-i** or **-u** then **-y-** is introduced after either of these letters.

Laa nkwenkwe iyadlala.	That boy over there is playing.
Laa mthi mkhulu.	That tree over there is big.
Laa mithi mikhulu.	Those trees over there are big.
Laa mahashe ayabaleka.	Those horses over there are running.
Laa nja iyaluma.	That dog over there is biting.
Inkwenkwe **leya** iyahamba.	That boy over there is walking.
Umfazi **lowa** uyapheka.	That woman over there is cooking.
Imifuno **leya** midala.	Those vegetables over there are stale.
Amazinyo **lawa** makhulu.	Those teeth over there are big.
Intlanzi **leya** iyadada.	That fish over there is swimming.

Using the demonstrative

☐ The demonstrative pronoun can be prefixed with **na-** to mean 'and this', 'with this', 'even this', etc.

Hamba **nalo** mfundi.	Go with this student.
Thetha **nabaa** bantwana.	Speak to those children over there.
Yitya **nalo** mntwana.	Eat with this child.
Sela utywala **nabaa** bantu.	Drink beer with those people.

☐ The demonstrative pronoun can be prefixed with **nga-** to mean 'by means of this', 'with this', etc.

Bhala **ngalo** siba.	Write with this pen.
Qhuba **ngale** moto.	Drive with this car.
Utata ufunda **ngezo** ncwadi.	Father studies with those books.

☐ The demonstrative pronoun can be prefixed with the possessive concord to mean 'of this', 'of those', etc.

Uphi utata **wale** ndlu?	Where is the father of this house?

☐ The demonstrative pronoun can be prefixed with **ku-** to mean 'at this', 'in that', etc.

Ndifunda **kwesi** sikolo. — I study at this school.
Kukho amanzi **kolo** dikeni. — There is water in that dam.
Kukho abantwana **kulaa** gadi phaya. — There are children in that garden over there.

The copulative of demonstratives

IF YOU want to say, 'it is this' or 'it is those over there', simply prefix a copulative prefix to the relevant demonstrative pronoun.

Ngulo. — It is this.
Nguloo. — It is that.
Abantwana ngabaa phaya. — The children are those over there.
Ihashe kaPiwe lelo. — Piwe's horse is that one.

Table of the three demonstrative positions

Class	this/these	that/those	yonder
Class 1	lo	lowo/loo	lowa/laa
plural	aba	abo	abaya/abaa
Class 1a	lo	lowo/loo	lowa/laa
plural	aba	abo	abaya/abaa
Class 2	lo	lowo/loo	lowa/laa
plural	le	leyo	leya/laa
Class 3	eli	elo	eliya/elaa
plural	la	lawo/loo	lawa/laa
Class 4	eso	eso	esiya/esaa
plural	ezo	ezo	eziya/ezaa
Class 5	le	leyo/loo	leya/laa
plural	ezi	ezo	eziya/ezaa
Class 6	olu	olo	oluya/olaa
plural	ezi	ezo	eziya/ezaa
Class 7	obu	obo	obuya/obaa
Class 8	oku	oko	okuya/okwaa

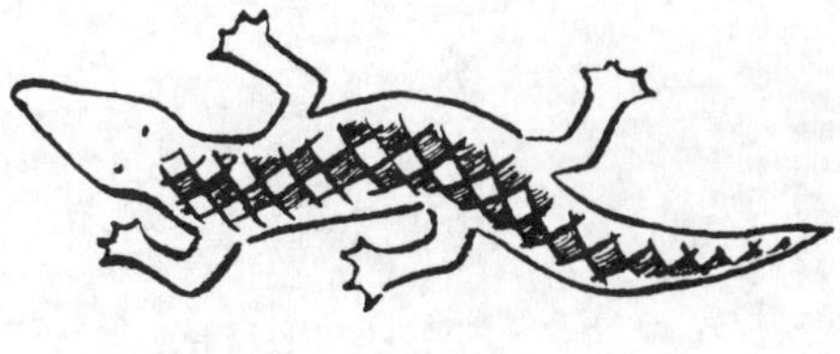

How to say 'here it is', 'there they are', etc.

DISTINCTIVE words carry the meanings 'here he is', 'there they are', etc. Like demonstrative pronouns these words have three positional types. Some examples are **nanku**, 'here he is', **nanko**, 'there he is' and **nankuya**, 'there he is over there'. The following table gives the forms corresponding to the nouns of the various classes.

A table of **nanku, nanko,** etc.

Class	First position	Second position	Third position
Class 1	nanku	nanko	nankuya
plural	naba	nabo	nabaya
Class 1a	nanku	nanko	nankuya
plural	naba	nabo	nabaya
Class 2	nangu	nango	nanguya
plural	nantsi	nantso	nantsiya
Class 3	nali	nalo	naliya
plural	nanga	nango	nangaya
Class 4	nasi	naso	nasiya
plural	nazi	nazo	naziya
Class 5	nantsi	nantso	nantsiya
plural	nanzi	nanzo	nanziya
Class 6	nalu	nalo	naluya
plural	nanzi	nanzo	nanziya
Class 7	nabu	nabo	nabuya
Class 8	naku	nako	nakuya

52 The future tense

If something is about to happen, or will happen quite soon within a definite time span, it is expressed by the near future. If something is going to happen within an indefinite future time it is expressed by the remote future.

The near future

THE NEAR future is expressed by using the infix **-za-** followed by the infinitive of the verb. The first vowel of the infinitive prefix falls away.

subject concord	-za-	ku-	verb root	-a

UNosipho **uza** kuya edolophini ngomso. — Nosipho will go to town tomorrow.
Umama **uza** kubhaka ikeki ngoku. — Mother will bake a cake now.

The remote future

THE REMOTE future uses the same construction but with the infix **-ya-** followed by the infinitive of the verb. The first vowel of the infinitive prefix falls away.

subject concord	-ya-	ku-	verb root	-a

Inkwenkwe **iya** kufika ebudodeni. — The boy will arrive at manhood.
UThandile **uya** kuya eyunivesiti ngenye imini. — Thandile will go to university one day.
Umama **uya** kuya edolophini ngenye imini. — My mother will go to town one day.

The short form

IN EVERYDAY speech, a short form is often used to express both the near future and the remote future. The subject concord and the future infix contract.

Ndofunda. — I'll study.
Sobonana. — We'll see each other.

The negative of the near future

THIS IS formed by prefixing the negative subject concord onto the infix **-za**, which becomes **-zi.**

negative subject concord	-zi-

ku-	verb root	-a

Umntu akazi kuthetha ngomso. The person will not talk tomorrow.
Umama akazi kuya edolophini ngomso. Mother will not go to town tomorrow.
Abantwana abazi kukhwela ibhasi ngomso. The children will not catch the bus tomorrow.

The negative of the remote future

THE NEGATIVE subject concord is attached to **-ya**, which becomes **-yi**.

negative subject concord	-yi-

ku-	verb root	-a

Inkwenkwe ayiyi kufika edolophini. The boy will not arrive in town.
Utata nomama abayi kubona utat'omkhulu. Father and mother will not see grandfather.

How to express purpose

Ukuza, 'to come' and **ukuya**, 'to go', are called verbs of motion and can be used to express a purpose. This is done by joining the verb of motion to the infinitive of the verb of purpose. The first **u-** of the infinitive falls away. This construction is called the infinitive of purpose and it takes the same form as the future tense, so care must be taken not to confuse them.

Ndiya kulala. I am going for the purpose of sleeping.
Ndiya kuthenga ukutya. I am going for the purpose of buying food.

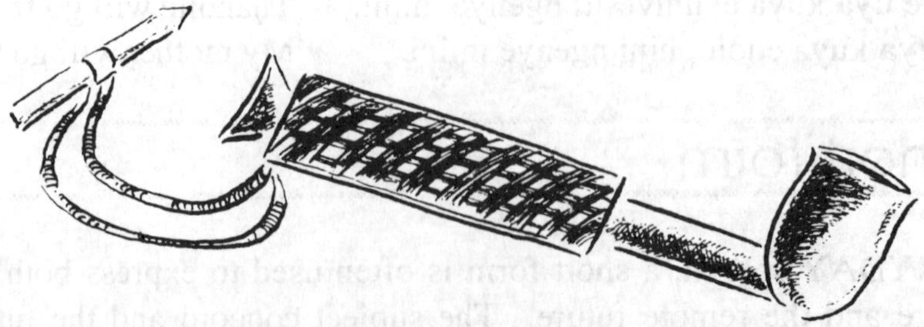

53 The subjunctive mood

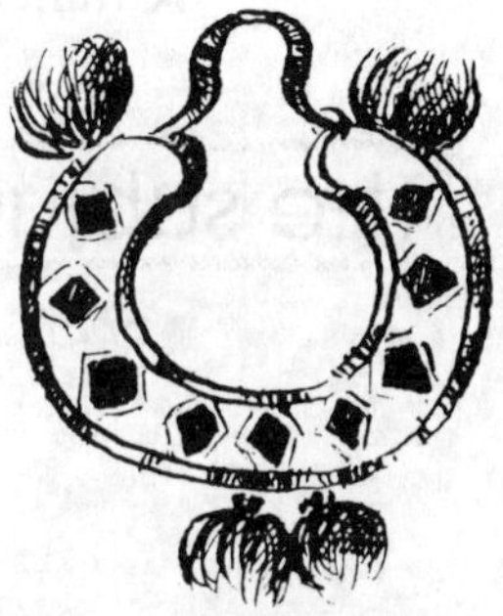

The subjunctive is a verb mood and not a verb tense. It is known as a dependent mood because it usually 'depends' on a sentence or word coming before it to give it full meaning. The subjunctive is used:

- ☐ To express a sequence of events.
- ☐ To show purpose.
- ☐ To express certain commands.

How to form the subjunctive

THE SUBJECT concord is prefixed to the verb root and **-e** is suffixed to it. The only exceptions occur in the 3rd person singular and classes 1 and 1a singular. With these, the verb is prefixed with **a-** instead of its usual concord, **u-**.

subject concord	verb root	-e

Expressing a sequence of two actions or events

THE FORMATIVE **na-** is used to translate the English word 'and' when nouns are joined together. But **na-** cannot join two sentences together as can the English 'and'. To join two sentences the subjunctive is used. The verb of the first sentence does not take the subjunctive. The subjunctive verb is in the second sentence. This second sentence becomes a clause of the first when the two are joined.

Galela ipetroli **umpompe** amavili.	Pour petrol and pump the tyres.
Inja iyatya **isele**.	The dog eats and drinks.
UMary uyapheka **athethe**.	Mary cooks and speaks.
Abantu bayathetha **bahambe**.	The people speak and go.
Ihashe liyabaleka **lisele** amanzi.	The horse runs and drinks water.

Using the subjunctive to express purpose

CERTAIN verbs which express desire, want, purpose, etc., are followed by the subjunctive.

Ufuna ukuba **ndi**buy**e** kusasa.	He wants me to return early in the morning.
Kufuneka ukuba inja **i**hamb**e**.	It is necessary that the dog goes.
Kufuneka ukuba ihashe **li**balek**e**.	It is necessary that the horse runs.
Kufanele umntu **a**fund**e**.	It is right for a person to study.

The subjunctive and verbs which end in -i

VERBS which end in **-i**, such as **ukuthi**, 'to say' and **ukwazi**, 'to be able to', do not change when used in the subjunctive.

Ngena uthi 'hayi'.	Enter and say 'no'.
Funda ukwazi ukwenza umsebenzi.	Study and be able to do the work.
Phakamisa uthi igama lakho.	Stand up and say your name.

The negative present of the subjunctive

THE SUBJECT concord of the verb does not change in the negative present of the subjunctive. **Nga-** is placed between the subject concord and the verb root, and the verb root is suffixed with **-i.**

subject concord	-nga-	verb root	- i

Yiza u**nga**theth**i.**	Come and do not talk.
Thetha u**nga**cul**i**.	Talk and do not sing.
UPiwe ufunda a**nga**theth**i**.	Piwe reads and does not speak.
UMeri upheka a**nga**thethi.	Mary cooks and does not speak.

Using the subjunctive to express certain commands

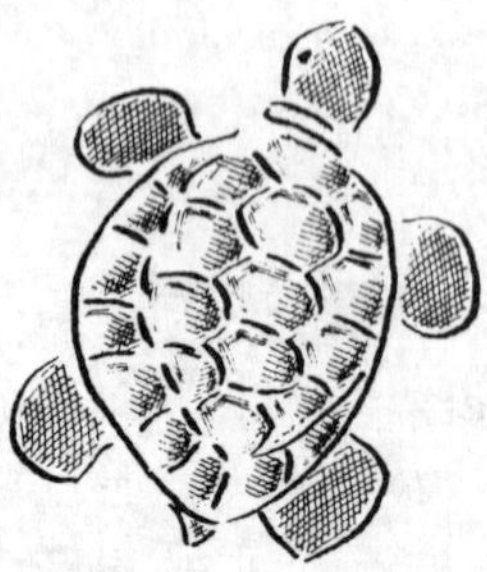

A COMMAND or direct instruction can be softened by saying 'you must' or 'you ought to'. This is done with the subjunctive. In the singular, the verb root is prefixed with **uzu-** and suffixed with **-e**. The negative is formed by placing **-nga-** between **uzu-** and the verb root, which is suffixed with **-i**. In the plural form, the verb root is prefixed with **zeni-** and suffixed with **-e**. The negative is formed by placing **-nga-** between **zeni-** and the verb root, which is suffixed with **-i**. The first vowel of the object falls away.

positive singular	uzu-	verb root	-e	
positive plural	zeni-	verb root	-e	
negative singular	uzu-	-nga-	verb root	-i
negative plural	zeni-	-nga-	verb root	-i

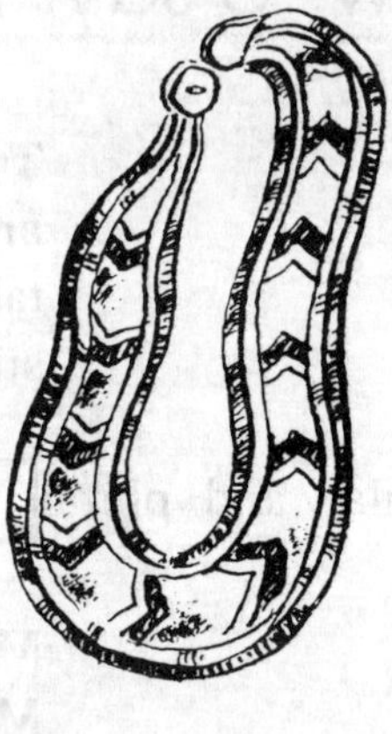

Uzubhale ileta. You ought to write a letter.
Uzungabhal**i** leta. You ought not to write a letter.
Uzuphathe ibhokisi. You ought to carry the box.
Uzungaphath**i** bhokisi. You ought not to carry the box.

The hortative

ANOTHER way to 'soften' an instruction is to say 'oh won't you do such-and-such' or 'just do such-and-such'. These persuasive instructions are called hortatives and they are expressed in the subjunctive. In the singular, **khawu-** is prefixed to the subject concord and its verb root, which is suffixed with **-e**. In the plural, **khani-** is prefixed to the subject concord and its verb root, which is suffixed with **-e**.

singular	khawu-	verb root	-e
plural	khani-	verb root	-e

Khawufonele ugqirha. Won't you phone the doctor.
Khawubethe intsimbi. Won't you ring the bell. (literally, 'beat the iron')
Khawukhaphe abantwana. Won't you accompany the children.
Khanisebenze apha. Won't you (plural) work here.
Khanifunde. Won't you (plural) learn.
Khanithethe. Won't you (plural) speak.
Khawuncokole nam. Won't you chat with me.

The hortative with vowel verbs

IN FORMING the hortative, when **uzu-**, **zeni-**, **khawu-** or **khani-** are added to vowel verbs, no part of the verb is lost. Instead the final **u-** or **i-** of the hortative prefix is discarded when joined to a vowel verb.

Uzenze iti ngoku. You ought to make the tea now.
Zenenze iti ngoku. You (plural) ought to make the tea.
Khawenze iti ngoku. Won't you make the tea now.
Khanenze iti ngoku. Won't you (plural) make the tea now.

How to say 'let me' and 'let us'

TO SAY 'let me' and 'let us', **ma-** is placed before the subject concord and the verb root is suffixed with **-e**. Although singular and plural both take the prefix **ma-**, the plural form is obvious because of the plural subject concord.

Singular and plural	ma-	subject concord	verb root	-e

Mandihambe ngoku. Let me go now.
Mandifunde ngoku. Let me study now.
Mandisele. Let me drink.
Mandilale. Let me sleep.
Masihambe ngoku. Let us go now.
Masifunde. Let us study.
Masithandaze ngoku. Let us pray now.

How to say 'please'

'PLEASE', **nceda**, also takes the subjunctive.

Nceda **uhambe**. Please go.
Nceda **upheke** inyama. Please cook the meat.
Nceda **ni**bilise amanzi. Please (plural) boil the water.

The past tense of the subjunctive

THIS IS used when a sequence of actions happened in the past. The infix **-a-** is placed between the subject concord and the verb root, which is suffixed with **-a**.

subject concord	-a-	verb root	-a

Abantwana bafike **bacela** iincwadi. The children arrived and asked for books.
Ihashe libaleke **latsiba**. The horse ran and jumped.

The negative past of the subjunctive

THIS IS formed by making the subject concord negative by beginning it with **a-**. The rest of the verb takes the past subjunctive form.

a-	subject concord	-a-	verb root	-a

UPiwe ufikile **akathetha** naye. Piwe arrived and did not speak to her.

54 Adjectives and relatives

Adjectives and relatives are said to be words which describe nouns and pronouns. Relatives and adjectives use different concords when they describe something. They do the same work however - they describe or 'qualify' nouns and pronouns.

In Xhosa, 17 descriptive words are known as adjectival stems and they are not whole words as such. They include the numerical stems 1 to 6.

Although there are only 17 adjectival stems in Xhosa, there are many more 'descriptive words'. All Xhosa descriptive words other than the 17 adjectival stems are called relatives.

The adjectival stems

-bi	bad/ugly
-hle	beautiful
-khulu	big/great/large
-ninzi	many/much
-tsha	new/young/fresh
-dala	old/stale
-futshane	short/very short
-fuphi	short
-ncinci	small
-ncinane	small/young/very small
-de	tall/long/high
-nye	one
-bini	two
-thathu	three
-ne	four
-hlanu	five
-thandathu	six

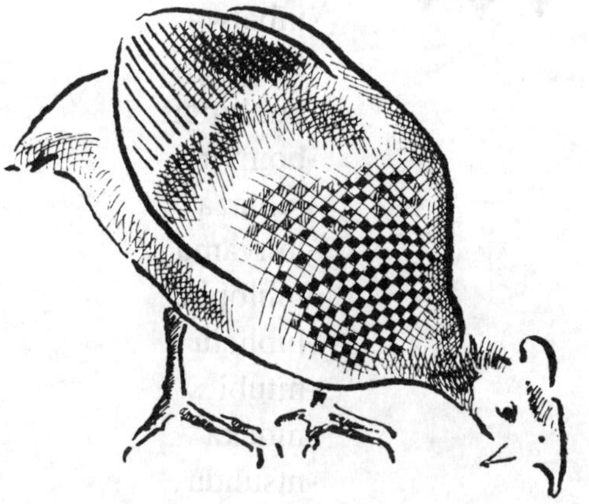

How to form simple adjectives

TO FORM the adjectival concord, the letter **a-** is prefixed to the full prefix of the noun which is being described. This is then prefixed to the adjectival stem. The adjective follows the noun it is describing.

a-	noun prefix	adjectival stem

abantu **aba**dala	old people
abantu **aba**bi	bad people
abantwana **aba**khulu	big children

Relatives

THE MOST common relatives describe degrees of warmth, sadness and heaviness and include all the colours.

-manzi	wet
-mdaka	dirty
-shushu	hot/warm
-dikidiki	lukewarm
-bukhali	sharp
-buthuntu	blunt
-lukhuni	hard
-lula	light/easy
-nzima	heavy/difficult
-mnandi	pleasant/sweet
-krakra	bitter
-muncu	sour
-nje	like this
-njalo	like that
-ngaka	as big as this
-ngakanani?	how big?
-ze	empty/naked
-mbalwa	few
-thile	certain
-buhlungu	painful
-bomvu	red/red-brown
-luhlaza	green/blue
-mnyama	black
-mhlophe	white
-lubhelu	yellow
-mtubi	egg yellow
-mdaka	dark earth brown
-ntsundu	brown
-luthuthu	ash-grey
-luhlaza	green or blue

The name of green and blue is the same, **-luhlaza**, although **-blowu** has been taken over from the English, 'blue' or perhaps the Afrikaans, 'blou'. The colours **-orenji**, 'orange' and **-pinki** 'pink' have been taken from English and function as relatives.

Relatives in action

THE relative concord is formed with **a-** and the subject concord of the noun being described. Because of vowel elision a secondary vowel forms. In 'strong' nouns the secondary vowel is prefixed to the subject concord and the relative stem. In 'weak' nouns the secondary vowel is prefixed to the relative stem without a subject concord.

'Strong' nouns	secondary vowel	subject concord	relative stem
'Weak' nouns	secondary vowel		relative stem

inkomo **emhlope**	the white cow
ingca **eluhlaza**	the green grass
ilanga **elim**tubi	the light sun
intyatyambo **ebomvu**	a red flower

Making simple sentences

SIMPLE sentences can be made with adjectives and relatives without using a verb. To make a sentence using an adjective, the basic prefix of the noun being described is prefixed to the adjective. The initial vowel of the class prefix falls away, except for class 5 nouns, when the full class prefix is used. In this usage, the adjective can be placed before or after the noun.

To make a simple sentence using a relative, the subject concord of the noun being described is prefixed to the relative stem. In this usage the relative can be placed before or after the noun.

Bumnyama ubusuku.	The night is dark.
Intyatyambo ibomvu.	The flower is red.
Kushushu ukutya.	The food is hot.
Inyoka inde.	The snake is long.

Table of adjectival and relative concords

Class	Noun prefix	Subject concord	Adjectival concord	Relative concord
Class 1	um-	u-	om-	o-
plural	aba	ba-	aba-	aba-
Class 1a	u-	u-	om-	o-
plural	oo-	ba-	aba-	aba-
Class 2	um-	u-	om-	o-
plural	imi-	i-	emi-	e-
Class 3	ili-	li-	eli-	eli-
plural	ama-	a-	ama-	a-
Class 4	isi-	si-	esi-	esi-
plural	izi-	zi-	ezi-	ezi-
Class 5	in-	i-	en-	e-
plural	izin-	zi-	ezin-	ezi-
Class 6	ulu-	lu-	olu-	olu-
plural	izin-	zi-	ezin-	ezi-
Class 7	ubu-	bu-	obu-	obu-
Class 8	uku-	ku-	oku-	oku-

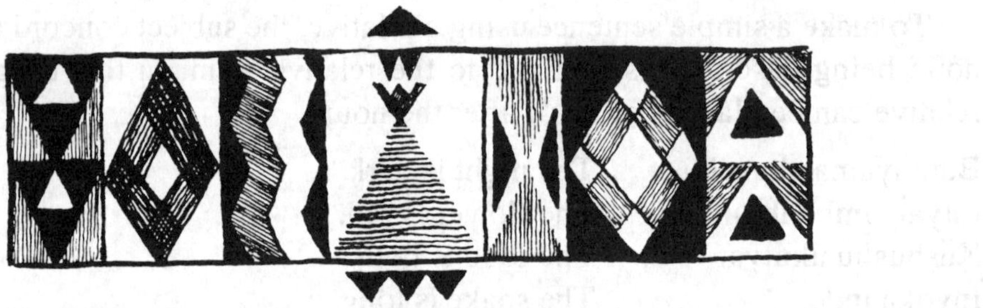

55 Big and small

To describe a thing as small, the suffix **-ana** is added to the end of a noun, with appropriate coalescence.

indod**ana**	a small man
amazw**ana**	small voices
intw**ana**	a small thing
isikhukwaz**ana**	a pullet

To describe something as very small, the suffix **-anyana** is added to the end of a noun.

inja	inj**anyana**	a very small dog
ubuso	ubusw**anyana**	a very small face
isonka	isonk**anyana**	a very small bread
inyama	inyam**anyana**	a very small piece of meat

To describe something as big, the suffix **-kazi** is added to the end of the noun.

indlovu	indlovu**kazi**	a very big elephant
indlu	indlu**kazi**	a very big house
induli	induli**kazi**	a very big hill

Degrees of comparison

IN XHOSA there is no direct equivalent of the English 'loud-louder-loudest' or 'fresh-fresher-freshest' to show degrees of comparison. Instead, degrees of comparison are expressed by using the formative **kuna-**. The thing which is of the higher degree is placed first in the sentence and **kuna-** is prefixed to the lesser thing. Vowel elision occurs.

IRhini ikufuphi **kune**Komani ukusuka eKapa.	Grahamstown is nearer than Queenstown from (leaving) Cape Town.
Iindlovu zinkulu **kune**empuku.	Elephants are bigger than mice.

56 Quantitative pronouns

The quantitative pronoun is used to express number or quantity. In Xhosa there are three types of quantitative pronouns. These express:

- ☐ 'All', 'every' or 'the whole of'.
- ☐ 'Alone' or 'only'.
- ☐ When using the numerical roots from 2 - 6 to denote 'both', 'all three', 'all four', etc.

All, every and the whole of

THE STEM **-nke** is used to express 'all', 'every' and 'the whole of'. This pronoun is formed by prefixing the subject concord to **-o-** plus the stem **-nke**. As usual, vowels will modify when they come together.

subject concord	-o-	-nke

umntu wonke	every person
bonke abantu	all the people
iapile lonke	the whole apple
iinkomo zonke	all the cows
zonke iimini	all the days

Only and alone

THE STEM **-dwa** is used to express 'only' and 'alone'. This pronoun is formed by prefixing the subject concord with **-o-** plus the stem **-dwa**. There are three exceptions: The first person, second person and class 1. These prefix the subject concord **-e-** instead of **-o-**. Vowels will modify.

subject concord	-o-	-dwa

ihashe lodwa	the horse only
ukutya kodwa	the food only

Quantitative pronouns with numeral stems

THE NUMBERS 1 to 6 are known as adjectival stems and they function as adjectives. They are used with quantitative pronouns to mean 'both', 'all three', all four', etc.

Bafika bobane.	All four arrived.
Ndibona iinkomo zontathu.	I see all three cattle.

Quantitative pronouns used before nouns

IF A QUANTITATIVE pronoun is used in front of the noun to which it refers, the final vowel of the pronoun is dropped.

Zonk' iinkomo.	All the cattle.
Zontath' izimvu.	All three sheep.

57 Adverbs

Adverbs 'add' to verbs. They tell more about an action by telling 'when', 'how' or 'where' something happened. Adverbs do not change form when used and usually follow the verb.

Adverbs of place

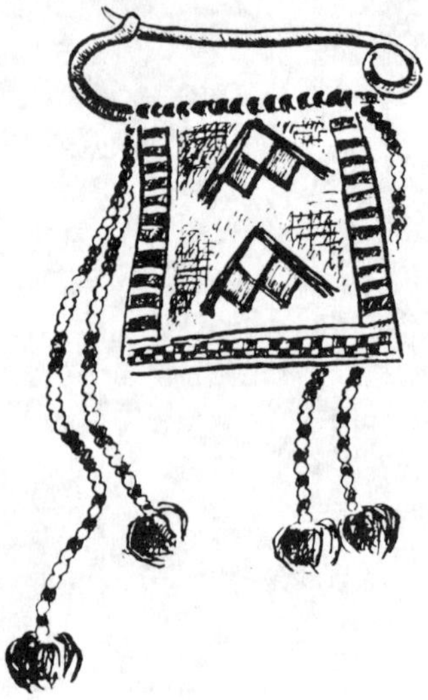

phaya	yonder
kufuphi/ kufutshane	near
kude	far off
emva	behind
phambile	in front
phandle	outside
phakathi	inside
apha	here
apho	there
nganeno	on this side

Kwa- often follows certain adverbs of place as in **phezu kwa**, 'on top of' and **phantsi kwa,** 'underneath'. It is used in the sense of 'of' in such cases.

ngasentla kwa-	higher up/above
ezantsi kwa-	lower down/below
phesheya kwa-	on the opposite side

Adverbs of time

futhi	often
kade	long/late
kakade	long ago
kamsinyane	soon
kamva	after/afterwards
kanjalo	again
naphakade	never
tanci	first/earlier
emva	after/behind

Adverbs of manner

THESE adverbs add to a verb by saying in what way a certain action is done.

kanene	really/truly
kuhle	well/beautifully
kamnandi	sweetly/pleasantly
njalo	in this way
ngokunjalo	accordingly
kwakhona	in the same way/again
nje	in this way/ thus

Some simple sentences

Inja iphuma **phandle.**	The dog goes outside.
Umama uya **futhi** edolophini.	Mummy often goes to town.
Utata ufika **kade** emsebenzini yakhe.	Father comes late from his work.

Sentences can be formed using adverbs as predicates. A verb is not needed in such sentences. The subject concord is prefixed to the adverb. In this way the subject concord and the adverb function together as a predicate. The adverbs **apha** and **apho** take **-l-** between themselves and their subject concords.

Indlu **ikude.**	The house is far off.
Inja i**lapha.**	The dog is here.
Inenekazi li**phaya.**	The lady is over there.
Abantu ba**lapho.**	The people are there.
Indlu i**phaya.**	The house is over there.
Isonka si**phezulu kwe**tafile.	The bread is on the table.

Turning adjectives into adverbs

ADVERBS can be formed by adding the formative **ka-** to adjectival stems.

Adjectival stem		**Adverb**	
-de	long	kade	long ago
-hle	beautiful	kakuhle	beautifully
-khulu	big	kakhulu	greatly
-ngaka	great	kangaka	so greatly
-lusizi	sad	kalusizi	sadly
-ncinane	slight	kancinane	slightly
-ninzi	many	kaninzi	many times
-nzima	difficult	kanzima	with difficulty

58 Owning things

The possessive is used to show ownership. In English the possessive is expressed in two ways:

- ☐ By using an apostrophe with the letter *s*, as in 'the mother's child'.
- ☐ By means of the preposition *of*, as in 'the child of the mother'.

In Xhosa the possessive is expressed by using the particle **ka-** with class 1a nouns and by using the particle **a-** with all other nouns. **Ka-** and **a-** both translate as either ***'s*** or ***of***.

The possessive particle **ka-**

KA- IS PLACED in front of the possessor, the person who owns. **Ka-** is only used in front of proper names of persons and for the words in class 1a for father, mother, uncle, etc. **Ka-** is governed by the class of the thing which is owned. If the prefix of the noun is 'weak' (does not have a consonant, but is made up of a vowel and **n** or **m**), **ka-** stands alone with the possessive noun. If the prefix of the noun is 'strong' (has a consonant), it needs the 'softening' sounds of the subject concord of the thing owned placed in front of **ka-**.

'Weak' noun

ka-	class 1a noun

'Strong' noun

subject concord	-ka-	class 1a noun

Umama **ka**Saul.	Saul's mother.
Inkomo **ka**bawo	Father's ox.
Ihashe **lika**Piwe.	Piwe's horse.
Iinkomo **zika**bawo.	My father's cattle.
Isikolo **sika**Toto.	Toto's school.

The possessive particle **a-**

THE PARTICLE **a-** is used in front of all nouns other than those of class 1a, which use **ka-**. The particle **a-** is always used in front of the possessive noun (the noun which is the owner), but it is 'governed' by the noun which is owned. The particle **a-** is always attached to a letter or letters representing the prefix of the governing noun. This combination of letters is called the possessive particle.

The first vowel of the governing prefix is not dropped as it would be when using **ka-**. Instead it elides with the vowel of the possessive particle, so **i-** before a vowel becomes **y-** and **u-** before a vowel becomes **w-**.

subject concord	-a-	noun

inkosi **y**abantu	the people's chief
abantu **b**elizwe	the people of the land

Possessive pronouns

☐ My

'My friend' translates literally as 'friend of me'. The Xhosa word for 'of me' is a possessive pronoun which matches the word for the thing which is owned. For words which begin with the prefix um- the possessive pronoun is **wam**.

umhlobo **wam**	my friend
umlomo **wam**	my mouth
umlenze **wam**	my leg

For words which begin with the prefix **ama-** the possessive is **am**.

amantombazana **am**	my girls
amakhwenkwe **am**	my boys
amaso **am**	my beads

For words which begin with the prefix **imi-** or **in-** the possessive is **yam**.

iminwe **yam**	my fingers
inja **yam**	my dog
ikati **yam**	my cat

For words which begin with the prefixes **aba-**, **ili-**, **isi-**, **izi-**, **izin-**, **ulu-** and **ubu-**, the possessive is formed by taking the consonant of the noun prefix and adding it to **-am**.

ilizwe **lam**	my country
isizwe **sam**	my nation
abantu **bam**	my people
usana **lwam** (lu- + a- = lwa-)	my baby

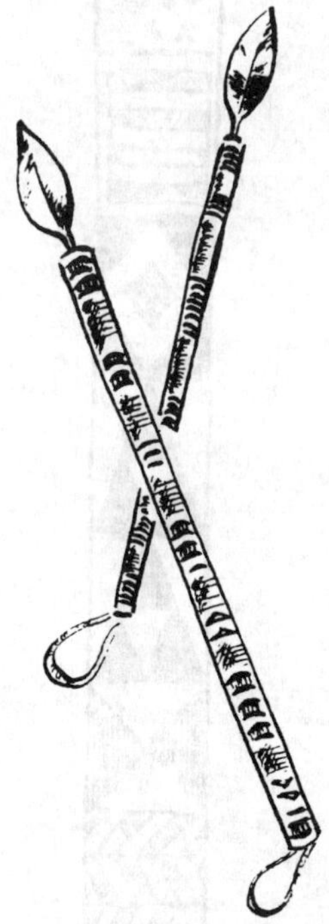

☐ Your (singular)

'Your friend' translates literally as 'friend of you'. 'Of you' is translated by **-kho.**

abapheki **bakho**	your cooks
ilizwe **lakho**	your country
isikolo **sakho**	your school
izihlangu **zakho**	your shoes
umlenze **wakho**	your leg

☐ Your (plural)

'Your (plural) friend' translates literally as 'friend of you'. If the thing belongs to more than one person, 'of you' is translated by **-inu**. Vowel elision occurs.

abaqhubi **benu**	your drivers
isicaka **senu**	your servant
isitulo **senu**	your chair
iihagu **zenu**	your pigs
indlu **yenu**	your house

☐ Our

'Our house' translates literally as 'house of our'. 'Of our' is translated by **-ithu.**

abaqhubi **bethu**	our drivers
ilizwe **lethu**	our country
isicaka **sethu**	our servant
izihlangu **zethu**	our shoes
iinkomo **zethu**	our cattle

☐ His, hers, its

'His/her/its house' translates literally as 'house of him/of her/of it'. 'Of him/of her/of it' translate as **-khe.**

abapheki **bakhe**	his cooks
ilizwe **lakhe**	his country
isikolo **sakhe**	her school
isitulo **sakhe**	her chair
iinkomo **zakhe**	his cattle

☐ Theirs

'Their house' translates literally as 'house of them'. 'Of them' is translated by **-bo**.

abapheki **babo**	their cooks
ilizwe **labo**	their country
isikolo **sabo**	their school
uluthi **lwabo**	their stick
izihlangu **zabo**	their shoes

☐ Possessive pronouns of the classes

These are formed by attaching the subject concord of the noun to the possessive particle **-a-** . This is then attached to the absolute pronoun without the stabiliser **-na**. As usual, vowels will modify.

Ihashe alibaleki. Umlenze **walo** ubuhlungu. The horse does not run. Its leg is sore.

Owning more than one thing

IF THE possessor owns more than one thing, the possessive is used for the first item only, followed by **na**, 'and', which is prefixed to the other items owned.

Indlu yamadoda, nendoda, nonyana.	The house of the men, the man, the son.
Imizi yabantu, nelizwe, nabantwana.	The homesteads of the people, the country, the children.

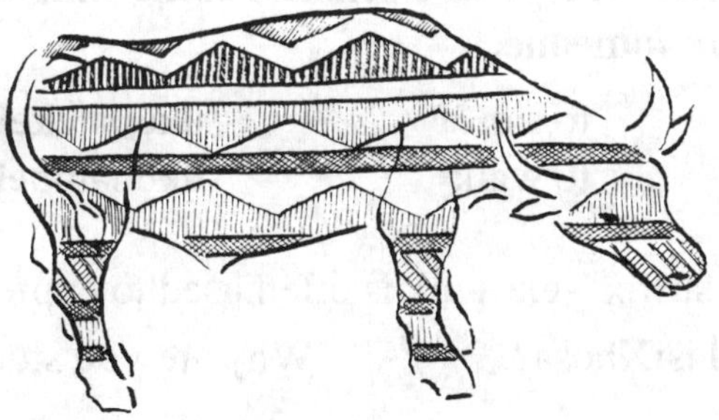

59 Playing with verbs

Xhosa verbs have the ability to subtly alter their meaning with the addition of various suffixes. In other words, the root of a verb may be changed in various ways to make new forms of that verb. New verbs made from the roots of existing verbs are called derived verbs, or derivatives. They are the 'children' of the original verb. There is a similarity between parent and child verb, but a new meaning appears in the derived verb. Derived verbs can function quite independently of the verbs they were 'born' from. They function as fully as all other verbs, in all tenses and moods.

☐ **The suffixes -eka and -akala describe a condition.**

ukuthanda	to love	ukuthand**eka**	to be loveable
ukubona	to look	ukubon**akala**	to be visible
ukuhleka	to laugh	ukuhlek**eka**	to be laughable

Some verbs use both **-eka** and **-akala**.

ukunceda	to help	ukunced**eka** *or* ukunced**akala**	to be useful
ukufihla	to hide	ukufihl**eka** *or* ukufihl**akala**	to be mysterious

☐ **The suffix -ela gives a sense of something being done on behalf of or for someone.**

ukubaleka	to run	ukubalek**ela**	to run for
ukuhamba	to walk	ukuhamb**ela**	to walk for

The verbal suffix **-ela + ni** is often used to express 'why?'.

Ufund**elani** isiXhosa?	Why are you studying Xhosa?

☐ **The suffix -ana denotes a mutual action, as in the English 'one another' or 'each other'.**

ukulandela	to follow	ukulandel**ana**	to follow one another
ukuthanda	to love	ukuthand**ana**	to love each other
ukubona	to see	ukubon**ana**	to see one another

☐ **The suffix -isisa expresses speed or swiftness of action and can also express persistence.**

ukuhamba	to go	ukuhamb**isisa**	to travel fast
ukubaleka	to run	ukubalek**isisa**	to run fast

☐ **The suffix -isa means 'to cause to' or 'to make to do'.**

ukulala	to sleep	ukulal**isa**	to put to sleep
ukusebenza	to work	ukusebenz**isa**	to use
ukuphakama	to rise	ukuphakam**isa**	to raise
ukuza	to come	ukuz**isa**	to bring
ukufunda	to learn	ukufund**isa**	to teach
ukubona	to see	ukubon**isa**	to show
ukuthenga	to buy	ukutheng**isa**	to sell

For some verbs which end in **-ka**, the **-ka** falls away and the derived verb takes the ending **-sa** instead of **-isa**.

ukusuka	to go/ come off	ukus**usa**	to remove
ukuvuka	to get up	ukuv**usa**	to arouse

Other verbs which end in **-ka** take the ending **-za** instead of **-isa** in the derived form .

ukudilika	to fall down	ukudiliza	to break down
ukukhathala	to be concerned	ukukhathaza	to trouble
ukusondela	to approach	ukusondeza	to bring near

This form of derived verb can also express communal action when suffixed with **-ana.**

Abahlwempu bayanced**isana**. — Poor people help one another.

☐ **Some verbs in Xhosa express the undoing, or reversing, of an action. They are similar in sound to their opposites and so are easy to remember.**

ukuvula	to open	ukuvala	to shut
ukambatha	to put on clothes	ukambula	to take off clothes
ukandlala	to lay a mat	ukandlula	to roll up a mat

☐ **Verbs can be doubled to give them an additional emphasis. Any verb can be doubled to get this effect.**

ukubhekabheka	to look in all directions
ukubuyabuya	to go backwards and forwards
ukucholachola	to pick up here and there
ukucumbacumba	to tickle
ukufunafuna	to seek about for
ukuhambahamba	to go to and fro

Forming nouns from verb roots

SOME NOUNS are formed from verb roots and are called derived nouns. Derived nouns which name people generally end in **-i**. Derived nouns which name things generally end in **-o**.

Verb		**Noun**	
ukuhamba	to walk	umhambi	a traveller
		uhambo	a journey
ukulwa	to fight	umlwi	a fighter
ukuphatha	to rule	umphathi	a ruler
ukubonga	to praise	imbongi	a poet
ukudlala	to play	umdlalo	a game
		umdlali	a player
ukuthanda	to love	uthando	love
ukuthemba	to hope	ithemba	hope
ukusebenza	to work	umsebenzi	a worker
ukufunda	to teach	isifundo	a lesson
		umfundisi	a teacher
		imfundiso	an instruction
		umfundi	a student
ukuhlala	to sit	isihlalo	a seat
ukutshixa	to lock	isitshixo	a key
ukulumka	to be careful	ubulumko	wisdom/caution

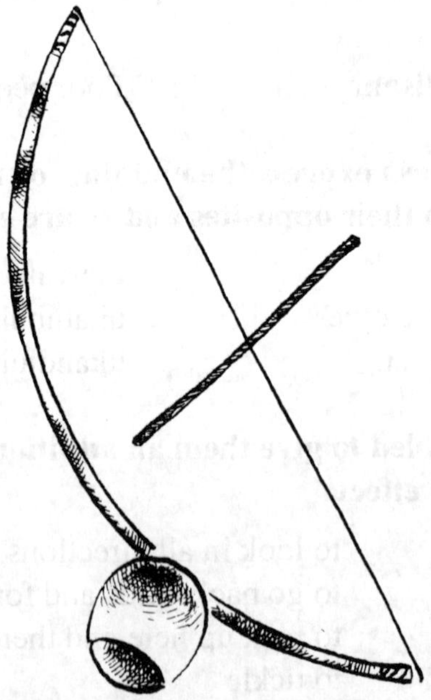

60 The passive

The passive is a verb voice. When a verb is in the passive, action is being done *to* the subject of the sentence and not *by* the subject. The passive can be used in the present and past tenses and in the positive and the negative. There is a short form and a long form in the passive.

Present tense long form

THE PASSIVE is formed by suffixing the verb root with **-wa**. The long form takes the infix **-ya-** between the subject concord and the verb root and is used when a word does not follow the verb.

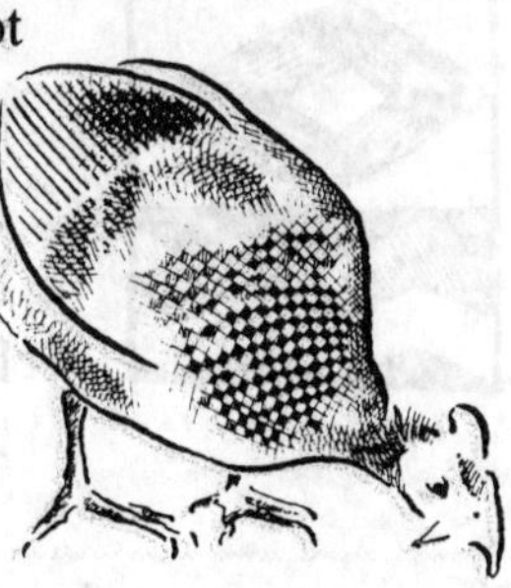

subject concord	-ya-	verb root	-wa

Isidlo si**ya**phek**wa**. The meal is being cooked.
Amanzi **ayabiliswa.** The water is being boiled.
Abantwana **bayathandwa.** The children are being loved.

Present tense short form

THE SHORT form does not have the infix **-ya-** and is followed by an indirect object or other word. The copulative is used to show the doer of the action.

subject concord	verb root	-wa

Isidlo siphek**wa** nguNomsa. The meal is being cooked by Nomsa.
Amanzi abilis**wa** eketileni. The water is being boiled in the kettle.
Abantwana bathand**wa** ngoomama. The children are being loved by their mothers.

Long form of the past tense

THIS IS formed by suffixing the verb root with **-iwe**. It is used when a word does not follow the verb.

subject concord	verb root	-iwe

Isidlo siphek**iwe**. The meal was cooked.
Amanzi abilis**iwe**. The water was boiled.
Abantwana bathand**iwe**. The children were loved.

Short form of the past tense

THIS IS formed by suffixing the verb root with **-we** and must be followed by a word.

subject concord	verb root	-we

Isidlo siphek**we** nguNomsa. — The meal was cooked by Nomsa.
Amanzi abilis**we** eketileni. — The water was boiled in the kettle.
Abantwana bathand**we** ngoomama. — The children were loved by their mothers.

Vowel verbs and monosyllabic verbs

VERBS which have only one syllable and verbs which begin with a vowel have only one form in the present passive and one form in the past passive. There is no long or short form of these verbs. The verb root is suffixed with **-iwa** in the present and **-iwe** in the past.

Isidlo siyaty**iwa**. — The meal is being eaten.
Ikofu iyenz**iwa.** — Coffee is being made.
Ikofu iyenz**iwa** ngumama. — Coffee is being made by mother.
Isidlo sity**iwe.** — The meal has been eaten.
Isidlo sity**iwe** nguPiwe. — The meal has been eaten by Piwe.

The negative of the passive

THIS IS formed by prefixing the negative concord to the passive verb.

Akufunw**a.** — You are not wanted.
Akudlal**wa** ngezinto zokudlala. — The toys were not played with.
Amahashe **aka**khwel**wa.** — The horses were not ridden.

Nouns and signs

NOUNS can be formed by the passive as follows.

isithandwa	a beloved one
umthunywa	a messenger/an angel
ukuhlwa	evening

The negative infinitive of the passive is often used on signs which forbid something.

Akungenwa.	No entry.
Akumiswa.	No stopping.
Akungxolwa.	Silence. No shouting.
Akutshaywa.	No smoking.
Akungcoliswa.	No littering.

61 The remote past tense

The remote past is used to relate events in the distant past. It is used when you're not quite sure of the exact time something happened, only that it was long ago. By comparison, the time is always definite and fairly recent when the perfect tense (near past tense) is used. The remote past tense is mostly used in story telling and other narratives, particularly the **iintsomi**, folk tales traditionally told by grandmothers. It is also used to relate historical facts. In spoken Xhosa the remote past tense and the recent past tense are often used interchangeably.

This tense is characterised by having an **-a-** after the subject concord. Because of this the vowel of the subject concord must adapt. The ending of the verb is **-a**.

subject concord	-a-	verb root	-a

ndi + a ndathetha
si + a sathetha
u + a wathetha (**u + a** gives a semi-vowel **w**)
ni + a nathetha
u + a wathetha
ba + a bathetha

UThixo **wadala** ilizwe. God created the world.

The negative

THE NEGATIVE of the remote past is formed in the same way as the negative of the recent past, that is, by prefixing **a-** to the subject concord and suffixing **-anga** to the verb root.

a-	subject concord	verb root	-anga

Umbona **awufikanga** nabelungu. Maize did not arrive with the white people.

A traditional folktale

Ufudwazana nocikilishe[1]	**The tortoise and the lizard**
Kwathi ke kaloku ngantsomi kwakukho ufudwazana.	Once upon a time there was a tortoise.
Ngenye imini lo fudwazana wagqiba ukuba aye edolophini.	One day this tortoise decided to go to town.
Wahamba ke esiya kuthenga ingxowa yetyuwa.	He went to buy a bag of salt.
Wayifumana wayibopha ingxowa leyo ngentambo ende wayityatha egxeni wagoduka.	He found it and tied up the bag with a long strap on his shoulder to go home.
Ufudwazana ke kodwa wevu ukuba yayingasekho ingxowa emhlana!	But tortoise felt that the bag was not on his back!
Wagqiba ukuba ajike aye kuyifuna.	He decided to turn back to look for it.
Waya kuyifuna ke.	He went to look for it then.
Kamsinyane wabona ucikilishe.	Soon he saw lizard.
Yho! Elo sela! Lalityethe ingxowa kafudwazana!	Indeed! That thief! He was carrying tortoise's bag.
Wakhwaza wathi ke ufudwazana: "Kutheni ukuba uthathe ingxowa yam?"	Tortoise shouted and said: "Why did you take my bag?"
Ucikilishe waphendula esithi waye ezibonele ngxowa le ilele nje endleleni ngoko ke wazicholela yona!	Lizard answered and said he saw the bag lying on the road and decided to take it for himself!
Kweveki elandelayo ufudwazana naye wabona ucikilishe.	The next week tortoise saw lizard.
Yena ucikilishe waye engamboni ufudwazana lo konke.	Lizard did not see tortoise at all.
Wayesitya iimpukwane umsila wakhe ulele phezu kwelitye.	He was eating flies, his tail was lying on top of a stone.
"Heke," wacinga watsho ufudwazana. "Ndiza kumbonisa lo rheme!"	"Good," tortoise thought and said. "So! I am going to teach this guy a lesson!"
Heke! Nanko ufudwazana enqumla loo msila!	Indeed there is tortoise cutting that tail!
Yho! Wothuka kakhulu ucikilishe wakhwaza wathi:	Yho! Lizard got a big fright and shouted:
"Shu! Uwunqumleleni umsila wam?"	"Ouch! Why have you cut off my tail?"
Waphendula ke ufudwazana wathi waye ezibonele loo msila uhleli nje phezu kwelitye elo.	Tortoise replied that he saw that tail just lying on the stone.
Ngoko ke wazicholela wona!	Therefore he picked it up for himself!
Phela phela ngantsomi!	And there ends the tale!

1 Kirsch and Skorge, 1990, page 251.

62 The participial mood and the continuous past tense

The participial is a verb mood which allows a sentence to describe two actions which are happening at the same time. The participial always deals with two verbs - while something is being done, something else is happening. The main action is placed first in the sentence and the second action then follows. The subject of the sentence does not have to be doing both actions. The participial can also translate as the English '-ing', as in 'I saw my friend buying shoes'. The second verb takes the normal subject concord except in the 3rd person singular and plural, classes 1 and 1a, singular and plural and class 3 plural. These exceptions are shown in the table.

Table of the participial

Class/person	Subject concord	Participial concord
1st person	ndi-	ndi-
plural	si-	si-
2nd person	u-	u-
plural	ni-	ni-
3rd person	u-	**e-**
plural	ba-	**be-**
Class 1	u-	**e-**
plural	ba-	**be-**
Class 1a	u-	**e-**
plural	ba-	**be-**
Class 2	u-	u-
plural	i-	i-
Class 3	li-	li-
plural	a-	**e-**
Class 4	si-	si-
plural	zi-	zi-
Class 5	i-	i-
plural	zi-	zi-
Class 6	lu-	lu-
plural	zi-	zi-
Class 7	bu-	bu-
Class 8	ku-	ku-

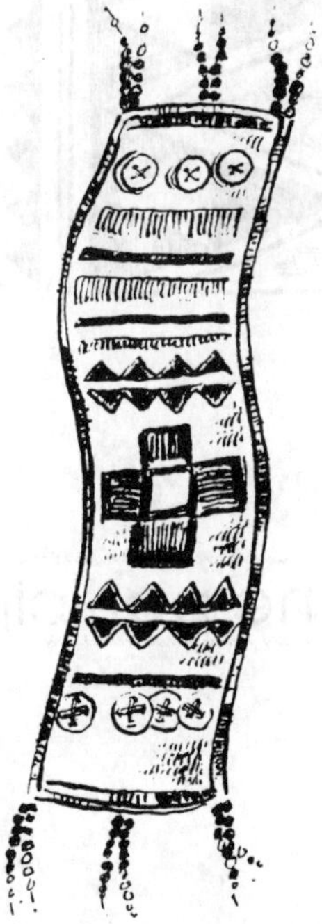

Ndifunda ndicula.	I study while singing.
Ufunda ecula.	He studies while singing.
Umama ucula epheka.	Mother sings while cooking.
Abantwana badlala **be**hleka.	The children play while laughing.
Amahashe abaleka ekhala.	The horses run while neighing.
Ndiyababona bapheka **be**ncokola.	I see them cooking while chatting.

The negative of the participial

Nga- is placed between the subject concord and the verb root, and the verb root is suffixed with **-i**. One or other of the two verbs is negativised, not both.

subject concord	-nga-	verb root	-i

Umama upheka e**nga**culi. Mother cooks while not singing.
Abantwana badlala be**nga**hlek**i**. The children play while not singing.

The participial with monosyllabic verbs

MONOSYLLABIC verbs take the infix **-si-** to form a bridge between the subject concord and the verb root.

subject concord	-si-	verb root	-a

Ndifike ihashe **lisi**fa. I arrived while the horse was dying.
Ndilile umthi **lisi**wa. I cried while the tree fell.

In the negative, monosyllabic verbs drop the infix **-si-**.

Ndibone abantwana bengatyi. I saw the children not eating.

The participial with vowel verbs

THE INFIX **-s-** is used to separate the subject concord and the vowel verb.

subject concord	-s-	verb root	-a

Ndifike umama **es**enza isopholo. I arrived while mother was making supper.

In the negative the infix **-s-** is not used. The negative is formed by placing **-nga-** between the subject concord and the verb root. The verb root is suffixed with **-i**.

Ndifike umama engenzi isopholo. I arrived while mother was not making supper.

Other uses of the participial

THE PARTICIPIAL is also used in the following instances:

☐ **After the conjunctions xa, which means 'when', 'whenever' and 'if'; noxa, meaning 'even if' and nangona, meaning 'although'.**

Xa umntwana **e**fika mse kuMama kwangoku. — When the child arrives, take him to mother at once.

Noxa bafunda imini yonke abazi kuphumelela. — Even if they study all day, they won't pass.

Nangona amanzi enqabile, balimile. — Although water is scarce, they have planted.

☐ **After the interrogative kutheni? which means 'why?'.**

Kutheni abahlobo bakho **be**funda isiXhosa? — Why are your friends studying Xhosa?

☐ **After the adverb of time, kudala, which means 'it is a long time' and 'for a long time'.**

Kudala oomama **be**zama ukupheka isonka. — For a long time the mothers have been trying to make bread.

☐ **After se-, sel'- and sele-, which mean 'already'.**

Umntwana **sel'e**fike? — Has the child already arrived?

☐ **After -soloko, which means 'always'.**

Usoloko ethetha eklaseni. — He is always speaking in the classroom.

The continuous past tense

THE CONTINUOUS past tense makes use of the participial form of the verb and because of this is known as a compound tense. It gives a sense of an action still in the process of happening. It translates as 'used to do something' or 'was doing something'.

The continuous past tense takes different forms for 'strong' and 'weak' subject concords. 'Strong' subject concords contain a consonant and their continuous past is formed by prefixing **be-** to the participial form of the verb.

Besisiya edolophini. — We were going to town.

Izolo **be**zisoyika imipu. — The animals were scared of the guns.

'Weak' subject concords have no consonant. To form the continuous past, they are prefixed to **-b-** which is followed by the participial form of the verb.

Inkwenkwe i**bi**lungisa ibhayisekile yakhe. — The boy was fixing his bicycle.

Ubawo e**be**funa ukuthenga imoto entsha. — Father wanted to buy a new car.

63 The gestures of language

"In polite language any gift is described by the recipient in hyperbole, so that a fowl killed for a visitor's dinner is spoken of by him as though it were a sheep of eight teeth, and a goat as though it were an ox. On the other hand, the giver belittles his gift, and might describe a goat he is giving as **le nkukwana ilusizana,** 'this sad little chick'."[1]

Xhosa speech abounds with figurative language and metaphorical expressions. Words and phrases can have subtle, alternative meanings, and conversation can be peppered with sarcasm, wit, exaggeration and the sting of a sharp tongue. In describing a greedy man you could say, **uyingcuka**, 'he is a wolf', that is, his disposition is that of a wolf. Of a strong or hard working man one could say **uyinkabi**, 'he is an ox', that is, he is as strong as an ox. If a person always smokes a pipe, he could be called **Nqawe** or **Nonqawe**, 'Pipe'; someone who always wears a hat could be called **Mmnqwazi** or **Nomnqwazi**, 'Hat'. Similarly a personal characteristic could be used as a name, so a sympathetic person might be called **Thandabantu,** 'Lover of people' or **Nobuntu**, which is a name formed from **ubuntu**, the human quality. A person with a fiery temperament might be called **Nopepile**, 'Pepper'. A builder might be called **Skonkwane**, 'Nail', and a speedy, energetic and fast working person could be called **Jujuju,** after the sound made by a steam train.

Here are some examples of how words and expressions can be used literally and figuratively.

	Literal	**Figurative**
ukucudisa	To squeeze a wound or ulcer to get the liquid out.	To destroy a man by taking his cattle.
ukucwisha	To tear off meat from bones.	To tease one.
umnzwi	The level rays of the rising or setting sun.	The breathing of someone dying.
isiqwashumbe	A wild turnip.	A corpulent person.
isibidi	Sediment or dregs.	Disagreeable things.
gqumgqum	Full of wind in the stomach.	To be boastful.

1 W.G. Bennie, 1939, page 163.

isigxala	An unhealed wound.	To feel wounded in spirit.
isitata/ isitati	A distant flame seen at night.	A nobleman by birth.
ingcala	A flying ant.	Uncommon dexterity.
umkhonto	An assegai.	A thing of value. [2]
ukuqhawuka	To be snapped assunder.	To be dead.
umsila	A tail.	A court messenger.
ukuzidla	To consume oneself.	To be proud.

Ideophones

IN THE same way that we use our hands when we speak in order to be more emphatic and descriptive, so too we use linguistic gestures such as ideophones and interjections to add emphasis, texture, humour or exclamation to everyday language. Ideophones and interjections are best described as gestures of speech.

The ideophone is an outstanding characteristic of all Bantu languages. It is descriptive and usually imitates the sound of the action described or associated with it. Ideophones have no equivalent in English and are difficult and sometimes impossible to translate. Onomatopoeic words such as 'clatter', 'ting', 'gong', 'bang', 'boom', 'clang', 'dong' and 'ding' are close parallels. Ideophones are dramatic and are frequently used by traditional poets, performers and literary artists because of their aesthetic value. They enhance the imagery of the language, allowing all kinds of occurrences to be described with emotional effect. The descriptive ideophone usually follows the word **ukuthi**. When used this way, **ukuthi** does not translate as 'to say' but merely introduces the ideophone.

Loo bhotile yewayini **wayithi hlasi**, mho, mho, qongqololo, jwi-i phaya, wathath' ibhatyi yakhe wahamba.	That bottle of wine he grabbed, (drink from the bottle, the sound of liquid as it goes out the bottle) - **mho**, **mho**, (drink it up quickly) - **qongqololo** (and throw it away) - **jwi-i,** he took his jacket and went.[3]
Ukuthi gaga na.	To bump up against unexpectedly.
Ukuthi sa.	To be scattered.
Ukuthi nqa.	To be surprised.
Ukuthi xha.	To stick in the throat.
Ukuthi cwaka.	To be quiet.
Wathi cwaka.	He was quiet.

2 Spears were once used as money. "Before they came to know the Europeans javelins, (assegais) appear to have replaced the absence of money and also to have served this purpose for trading. The javelins hold their own in value because their production is laborious and troublesome on account of the scarcity of more suitable tools being available; and they are lost in hunting and on other occasions and therefore have to be produced again." L.Alberti, 1807, page 71.

3 S.Z. Zotwana, 1991, pages 181-182.

Interjections

INTERJECTIONS are exclamatory and emotional and have no effect on the grammatical construction of a sentence, like saying 'wow!' or 'man!' or 'damn!' in English. The best known is probably **Yho!** which has found its way into South African English as a gesture of surprise, outrage or shock. Xhosa makes free use of a wide variety of interjections.

Aa!	Hail!
Au! Awu! Athike!	Alas! Oh! To express sympathy, pain, regret.
Bayethe!	To greet a chief.
Be!	Goodness!
Cha!	Certainly not!
Chosi!	Hush! Peace!
Ehla!	Well, really! Or to express protest.
E!	To express dislike.
Ewu!or Iwu!	Hallo!
Gxebe!	By-the-by!/Really!
Ha!	Hurrah!
Hayi!	No!
He! Heke!	So! Denoting agreement/Well done!
Hee!	To express approval.
Heyi!	There!
Hi!	But! Suppose! As an exclamation of surprise.
Hina wena!	Hello you!
Ho!	To express indignation.
Huntshu!	Victory!
Kwowu!	To express astonishment, dislike, or protest.
Qa!	Woe!
Nantso ke!	Well done!
Nci!	Dear me!
Ngxatshi ke!	Well done!
Tshotsho!	Serves you right!
Tshu!	He's in a hurry!
Tyho!	Oh!
Tyhu!	To express surprise.
Tyhini!	You don't say!
Yazika!	There you have it!
Wa!	Used to call attention - Hello you!
Wena ke! Wenani!	Still!
X!	To express contempt/Stop it!/Don't!

Mawo! and **Bawo**! the vocative forms of **umawo**, 'my mother', and **ubawo**, 'my father', are often used interjectionally, especially **Mawo!**, in order to say 'wonderful!' or 'strange!'.

Man with pipe by Julius Mfete

64 Idioms

Idioms are expressions which characterise a language. All languages have unique idioms. They are often not logically or grammatically explicable, but they add texture and depth to a language. They often have more than one meaning, a literal one and a hidden, more subtle one.

Idiom	Literal meaning	Idiomatic meaning
Kuhle ngomqolo.	It has gone down by the spine.	I am still hungry.
Intloko uyiphethe ngesandla.	He is carrying the head in his hand.	He is acting foolishly.
Uyibetha ngoyaba.	He is beating it with silence.	He is ignoring it.
Undibetha ngemfe iphindiwe.	He is beating me with a sweet cane doubled.	He is cheating me.
Unyawo alunampumlo.	The foot has no nose.	Beware of unkind actions, they have a way of turning against the doer.
Ilahl'el'nothuthu.	A live coal (covered) with ash.	A placid person with a hidden violent temper.
Amanz' eendonga.	The water of the banks.	Beautiful, light brown.
Ihlathi leentonga.	A forest of sticks.	An inexhaustible source of supply.
Ubuhle bakhiwane.	The beauty of a wild fig.	Beauty of complexion only.
Abahlobo bezinyo.	Friends of the tooth.	Casual friends.
NguNongqawuse.	It is Nongqawuse.	It is an impossibility, it is wonderful.
Akukho kufa kunjani.	There is no death (like) it is now.	There is no way of escaping death.
Yajal'ipudini.	The pudding has turned sour.	Pleasant times have changed for bad.
Ukhasel' eziko.	He is crawling towards the fireplace.	He is heading for dangerous trouble.
Unesandla.	He has a hand.	He is expert in a particular craft.
Uneminwe.	He has fingers.	He is skilful.
Unoluthi.	She has a stick.	She has a tall, straight figure.
Akabaleki, ushiy' izinja zengqina.	He does not run, he leaves the greyhounds.	He runs incredibly fast.
Akamhle, lilanga liphuma.	She is not beautiful, it is the rising sun.	She is wonderfully beautiful.
Akanasithunzi.	He has no shadow.	He cannot command respect.
Ukufa uhleli.	To be dead while living.	To be useless.

Ukubila usoma.	To sweat and dry up at the same time.	To be very busy.
Ukulala ngenxeba.	To sleep by a wound.	To accept one's fate.
Umtya nethunga.	The string and the pail.	Very close friends.
Unomvundla.	He has a rabbit.	He is very light headed.
Imaz'enethole.	A cow with a calf.	A big thank you.
Umbele wenkuku.	Teat of a fowl.	A rarity.
Ngumpha ochutywe walahlwa.	He is a mealie cob shelled and thrown away.	He is quite destitute.
Ndingumpha.	I am a shelled cob.	I have been robbed of my last cent.
Yinkuku emanzi.	It is a wet fowl.	He is dejected.
Akahlalwa mpukwane.	He is not sat on by a fly.	He is scrupulously neat, a dandy of a fellow.
Ngumde ngeentonga.	He is tall by means of fighting sticks.	He is short of stature, but of outstanding intellectual ability.
Galela ukuthetha.	Pour out speaking.	Speak with eloquence.
Ukwahlulwa ziinduduma.	To be separated by thunder.	To be inseparable. (Mostly of people in love.)
Amehlo amnyama.	Black eyes.	Eyes blinded with emotion or glare.
Ngumhle nezandla.	He is beautiful, even the hands.	He is spotless, without blemish.
Inyoka nesele.	The snake and the frog.	Bitter sworn enemies.
Amabal'engwe.	Spots of a leopard.	Salient points.
Umsila wengwe.	The tail of the leopard.	A court summons.
Isandla semfene.	Hand of a baboon.	The left hand.
Unyawo lwemfene.	The foot of the baboon.	A dark and suspicious move.
Imbabala yolwantunge.	The buck of the wide forest.	A wayward person.
Amaphuth'ahlathi.	Bucks of the same forest.	Good friends.
Inqweme lenkawu.	The entrails of a monkey.	A limited supply of something precious.
Umtsi wenkawu.	A leap of a monkey.	A short trip.
Umdudo woononkala.	The dance of the crabs.	A disorderly commotion.
Yinyoka.	It is a snake.	He is dangerously treacherous.
Yimfene yam leyo.	It is my baboon that.	I can use him for my own ends.
Lilulwane.	It is a bat.	He is a fly-by-night, a shady character.
Lunwabu.	It is a chameleon.	He is very slow of movement.
Ngumkhombe.	It is a rhino.	He is dangerously angry.
Yindlovu.	It is an elephant.	He has great strength.
Akukho ndlovu isindwayo ngumboko wayo.	No elephant finds its trunk too heavy to carry.	We should be able to bear our own troubles.

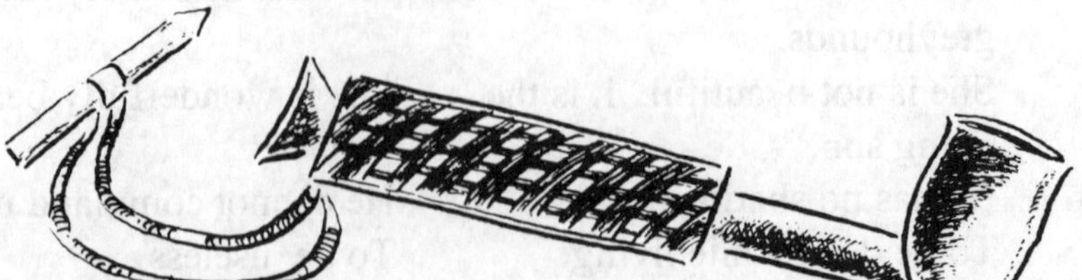

65 English words of Xhosa origin

Many South African English words are derived from Xhosa. Here are a few.

basella/bonsella: A present, a gratuity. From **ukubasela**, 'to give a present'.

bombella: A third-class train. Trains transported newly-recruited migrant workers from the rural areas to the cities. Probably from **ukubamba**, 'to take'.

comtsotsi: Gangster who sees himself as a political comrade.

dagha: Cement, mortar or any of several mixtures for building. From **udaka**, 'mud'.

donga: A dry, eroded watercourse running only in times of heavy rain. From **udonga**, 'washed out ravine'.

fanakalo: Pidgin language used as lingua franca on the mines. Made up of English, Xhosa, Zulu and Afrikaans elements. From **ngu-fana-ka-lo**, 'it's like this' or 'be like this'.

fundi: An expert, a wise guy, from **umfundisi**, 'a teacher'.

galla: To want very much, to crave. From **ukurhala**, 'to be greedy for'.

gogga/goggo/rhorho: Small insect, creepy-crawly. From **irhorho**, 'insect'.

hamba: Harsh command to go away, 'push-off'. From **ukuhamba**, 'to go'.

indaba: A meeting or conference. From **indaba**, 'a tribal meeting'.

intombi: A young girl. From **intombi**, 'a marriageable girl'.

khaya: A house or shack. Often used to name servants'quarters. From **ikhaya**, 'a home'.

kwedini: A young boy. From **inkwenkwe**, 'an uncircumcised boy'.

kwela-kwela: A police pick-up truck. Also the name for a taxi. From **ukukhwela**, 'to climb in' or 'to ride'.

mabela: Millet porridge. From **amabele**, 'grain sorghum'.

quagga: The now extinct wild ass related to the zebra but different in its markings. From **iqwara**, 'zebra' or 'something striped'.

shushu: Hot. From **shushu**, 'hot'.

skebenga: A gangster, rogue, robber. From **isigebenga**, 'a giant'.

Man on a horse by Julius Mfete

songalolo/ chongalolo: Shiny black millipede. From **ukusonga**, 'to roll up'.

suka: Rude command to tell someone to leave, get out. Although it can also translate as 'get on with you!', from **ukusuka**, 'go away'.

tokoloshe: Bad spirit. From **uthikoloshe**, 'a mischievous dwarf', 'an elf who lives in rivers'.

tollie: A castrated bull calf. From **ithole**, 'a calf'.

tsotsi: A street thug or urchin, a thief. Originally a flashily dressed street thug. From **ukutsotsa**, 'to dress in an exaggerated style'.

twalie: Head lice. From **ukuthwala**, 'to carry on the head' and **intwala**, 'a louse'.

66 How did the prefix develop?

Noun prefixes are not a mere collection of arbitrary syllables whose only purpose is to distinguish nouns into certain classes. It is thought that singular prefixes were originally a group of independent nouns.[1] These nouns probably had meanings closely related to the noun classes which the modern prefixes now belong to. In the same way that the modern prefix serves to identify which class a noun belongs to, so their ancestral nouns would have also identified words. These ancestral nouns came to be attached to other nouns as determinatives. In some cases it is still possible to trace the original form and exact meaning of these nouns.

The prefix **um**(u)- of class 1 was probably an independent noun, **mu**, meaning 'man' or 'human being'. It is probably connected with the noun **ubomi**, meaning 'life'.

The prefix **um-** of class 2 is probably connected with the adjective **umi**, 'living', and its primary use was to denote things which the Xhosa looked upon as living things but which were not human or animal. Thus we have **umthi** (a tree) and the great majority of names for trees, plants and rivers. However, rivers with names of Khoikhoi origin were mostly included in class 5. The following words were all seen to have some sort of existence: **umoya** (wind), **umbane** (lightning), **umlilo** (fire), **umhlaba** (earth), **umzimba** (body), **umphefumlo** (breath). Fleshy and muscular parts of the body were also thought to have an existence, as in **umlenze** (leg) and **umhlana** (back).

In class 2 are also found a large number of words denoting locality and time, such as **umgaqo** (passage or track of animals), **umhadi** (a pit), **umgangatho** (floor), **umhla** (day or date) and **umnyaka** (a year).

The prefix **ili-** of class 3 was probably originally a noun meaning something hard, such as a stone or fruit. The following words show how, even in words where the prefix has contracted, **ili-** stands for something hard: **ilitye** (a stone), **igaba** (a hoe), **igobolokondo** (a cliff), **igongoma** (bone of the forehead), **igubu** (calabash), **igugu** (jewel), **iligxa** (shoulderblade), **igongo** (a lump), **igidiva** (heavy object), **igalagala** (Cape boxwood) and **igada** (a clod).

The prefix **isi-** of class 4 is perhaps connected with the root which we find in such words as **siza** (come to the aid of) and **isisa** (kindness). The following words show how often the prefix is used in the sense of

1 This chapter is drawn from J. McLaren, 1944, page 191.

something used for a certain purpose: **isibambelelo** (a thing to hold on by), **isibambiso** (a trap), **isibambo** (pincers), **isibane** (a thing for producing light), **isibatha** (a snare), **isibazelo** (an anvil), **isibethelelo** (a switch) and **isibulelo** (thanksgiving).[2]

The prefix **in-** of class 5 uses its original form, **ni** and **ny**, in front of vowels, in words such as **inyathi** (buffalo), **inyama** (meat) and **inyoka** (snake). This prefix is probably connected in origin with the word **into**, (a thing). It is used as a prefix to name things in general which do not belong to some other class, but especially to the names of animals. It is significant of the generalised use of this prefix that words derived from other languages are usually included in this class. This is possibly why names of rivers of Khoikhoi origin are found in this class instead of in class 2 with the names of other rivers.

The prefix **ulu-** of class 6 includes nouns naming long objects. It is probably connected in origin with the words **lee** (far) and **ele** (beyond) as well as with the word **de** (long) which is **le** in many of the other Bantu languages. The following words illustrate the use of **ulu**, even in words where the prefix has contracted, as denoting long objects: **ubambo** (rib), **udonga** (wall), **ukhuni** (log of wood), **uluthi** (rod), **ukhuko** (sleeping mat), **uhadi** (Xhosa single-string harp), **ulwimi** (tongue), **uphondo** (horn), **unyawo** (foot), **ulusu** (entrails) and **uxande** (an oblong house). The metaphorical meaning of 'long' is also found in words like **uluhlu** (a row), **uhlanga** (a race) and **usapho** (family).

The prefix **ubu-** of class 7 is probably connected to the verb **ukuba** (to be). It denotes the quality or essence of a thing, as in **ubulumko** (wisdom), **ubuhle** (beauty), **ubuntu** (humanness), **ubuntwana** (childhood) and **ubuthi** (the essence of a tree, hence the poison derived from it).

The prefix **uku-** of class 8 is probably the same in origin as the preposition **ku,** which was originally a noun meaning distance. Used to denote action, it probably originally meant 'occasion' as **ukubona** (the occasion of seeing) and **ukuthetha** (the occasion of speaking).

2 The root of the meanings of **isibambelelo, isibambiso** and **isibambo** is probably **-bamba** which means 'to grasp', 'to seize', 'to catch hold', 'to keep', 'to restrain', 'to arrest', etc. There could also be a connection with **ubambo**, 'a rib', 'pectoral muscle' or 'the band on a wheel'. All these 'keep' or contain something inside.

67 The first Xhosa dictionaries

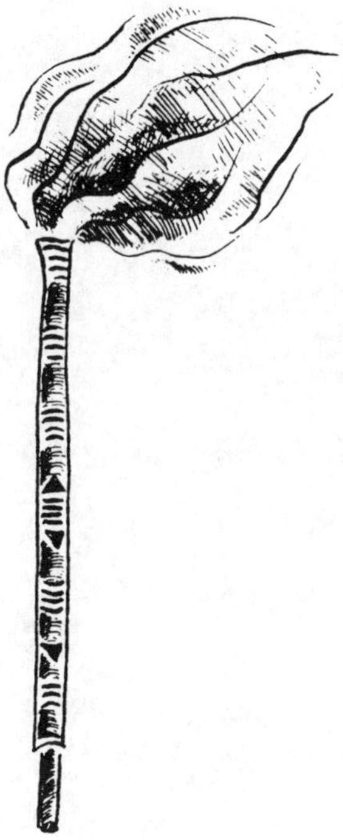

Housed in Cory Library at Rhodes University is a small, stained and very worn Xhosa-English dictionary. Although it has no cover, it is stitch-bound in old thread and the original binding knots, more than a century old, still hold the pages together. There is no title page or preface, but in the top left hand corner, written in faded pencil, is the date 1826. Its identification has been confirmed by the South African Library as *'A Systematic Vocabulary of the Kaffrarian Language'*, by John Bennie, printed at Lovedale Mission in 1826. Only words beginning with **b**, **p**, **d** and **t** are listed.

This little book is probably the dictionary to which Rev. Albert Kropf refers in the preface of his own dictionary as a "small but trustworthy vocabulary, partly printed and partly in manuscript", which was used by the missionaries of the early part of last century. It is probably also the vocabulary mentioned in the minutes of the Glasgow Missionary Society's 36th Year's report, which are quoted from in chapter 22.

The first Xhosa dictionary was probably the *'Woordenlijst'* compiled by Dr Johannes van der Kemp in 1801. This was later described by Rev. Albert Kropf as "more of a curiosity than a help to the student"[1] when he began compiling a vocabulary for his own use soon after his arrival in the Eastern Cape in 1845. He was urged by the Board of Revisers of the Xhosa Bible to prepare his vocabulary for publication. At the time he was unwilling and unable to undertake such a great task. In 1889, at the United Missionary Conference held in King William's Town, it was proposed by a Mr Andrew Smith that "the lexicon should be printed, if only as a memorial of the Xhosa language which would soon be supplanted by English". Still Dr Kropf hesitated and it was not until 1893, when the Brethren of the Free Church of Scotland Mission urged him strongly to prepare the manuscript for publication, and Lovedale offered to print at its own risk, that he agreed to go ahead with the work. Printing began in 1895 and extended over four years, during which time he collected more words which he added as an appendix. It was published in 1899 as *'A Kafir-English Dictionary'*.

In 1911 Rev. Robert Godfrey was asked by Principal Henderson of Lovedale to edit a new edition of Dr Kropf's dictionary. He was given the use of Dr Kropf's annotated copy of the dictionary which had been

1 Kropf, Preface, 1899.

bequeathed to Lovedale. Many notable scholars helped him in his work, including Horatio Isaiah Bud-M'belle, Rev. J. Lennox, Rev. J.H. Soga, J. McLaren and W.G. Bennie. The Misses Ross of Pirie, daughters of Dr Bryce Ross, also helped him. He was able to accurately list the Xhosa names of mammals, birds, trees and plants through help given by mission pupils, staff of the Albany and Transvaal museums and various books on the flora, fauna and mammals of South Africa. Printing of the revised edition took over two years. On July 14th, 1915, when the dictionary had been printed as far as page 368, "our joint labours were nearly consumed in smoke by a fire breaking out in the engine-room immediately beneath the place where the printed sheets were stored. The presence of mind of one of the workers enabled him to deal effectively with the cause of the outbreak and Mr Atkinson, the printer, at great personal risk fought the fire, being badly burned but saving the dictionary!".[2]

In his later life Godfrey worked on a third edition of the Kropf-Godfrey classic dictionary. He eventually finished it in the late 1940s, just before he died, and although it was the crowning achievement of his life's work it was unfortunately never published. Fort Hare University holds Godfrey's manuscript.[3]

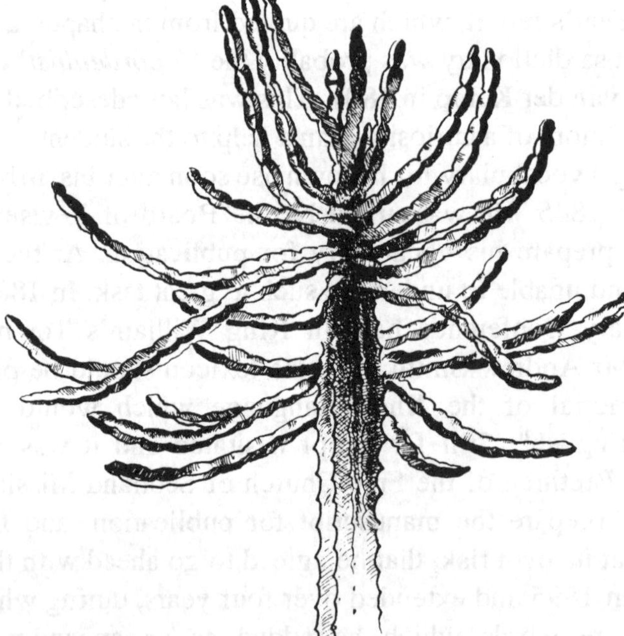

2 Godfrey, Preface, 1915.
3 Interview with J.B. Peires on his discussions with Professor Pahl, Umtata, 1990.

Bibliography

African National Congress. **Unity in action: A photographic history of the African National Congress of South Africa 1912-1982.** ANC, London, 1982.

Alberti, Ludwig. **Account of the Tribal Life and Customs of the Xhosa in 1807.** Translated by Dr W. Fehr from the original manuscript in German of **The Kaffirs of the South Coast of Africa.** Balkema, Cape Town, 1968.

Alexander, Lucy. **Frederick I'ons Retrospective Exhibition.** King George VI Art Gallery, Port Elizabeth, 1990.

Appleyard, Rev. John W. **The Kafir Language.** Wesleyan Missionary Society, King William's Town, 1850.

Axelson, E. (Editor) **Dias and his Successors**. Saayman and Weber, Cape Town, 1988.

Basson, H.N., Gaqavu, J., and Xayimpi, E. **Xhosa for English-speaking pupils.** Modules one, two and three, Masithenge isiXhosa simnandi series. Shuter and Shooter, Pietermaritzburg, 1994.

Bennie, John. **A systematic vocabulary of the Kaffrarian language**. The Lovedale Press, 1826.

Bennie, W.G. 'Xosa Orthography. Memorandum on the Proposed Changes', in **The South African Outlook**, April 1st, 1931.

Bennie, W.G. (B.A.) **Notes on the New Xhosa Orthography**. The Lovedale Press, 1937.

Bennie, W.G. (B.A.) **A Grammar of Xhosa for the Xhosa-speaking**. The Lovedale Press, 1953.

Branford, Jean and William. **A dictionary of South African English**. Oxford University Press, Cape Town, 1991.

Broster, Joan A. **Amagqirha: Religion, Magic and Medicine of the Transkei.** Via Afrika, Cape Town, 1982.

Broster, Joan A. **Red Blanket Valley**. Hugh Keartland Publishers, Johannesburg, 1967.

Broster, Joan A. **The Tembu: Their Beadwork, Songs and Dances**. Purnell and Sons, Cape Town, 1976.

Broster, Joan A. 'Joan Broster talks to Mary K.', in **Cape Librarian**, April, 1986.

Bull, Bartle. **Safari, a Chronicle of Adventure**. Viking (Penguin Group), London, 1988.

Costello, Dawn. **Not Only For Its Beauty: Beadwork and its cultural significance among the Xhosa-speaking peoples.** University of South Africa, Pretoria, 1990.

Crawshaw, C.J. **Crawshaw's First Kaffir Course.** Juta, Cape Town, 1894.

Dapper, Dr O. **Kaffraria or Land of the Hottentots (1668)**, reproduced in **The Early Cape Hottentots**, Van Riebeck Society, Cape Town, 1933.

Dargie, David. **Xhosa Music - its techniques and instruments with a collection of songs.** David Philip Publisher, Cape Town, 1988.

Davis, Rev. William J. **A Dictionary of the Kaffir Language: including the Xosa and Zulu dialects.** The Wesleyan Mission House, London, 1872.

Dohne, Rev. Jacob Ludwig. **Zulu-Kafir Dictionary etymologically explained with**

copius illustrations and examples. G.J. Pike's Machine Printing Office, Cape Town, 1857.

Glasgow Missionary Society. Thirty-Sixth Year's Report. 14th April 1831. Cory Library, Rhodes University, Grahamstown, Manuscript No.10,632.

Godfrey, Rev. Robert. **Bird-Lore of the Eastern Cape Province.** 'Bantu Studies' Monograph Series No.2. Witwatersrand University Press, Johannesburg, 1941.

Gordon-Brown, Alfred. **Pictorial Africana.** Balkema, Cape Town, 1975.

Hendrikse, A.P. **Xhosa Through the Ear: Grammar Notes and Excercises.** Dept. of African Languages, Rhodes University, Grahamstown, 1977.

Huskisson, Yvonne. **The Bantu Composers of Southern Africa.** South African Broadcasting Corporation, 1969.

Jennings, Lionel E. **The Concise Trilingual Dictionary in English, Xhosa and Afrikaans,** The Lovedale Press, 1966.

Jordan, A.C. **A Practical Course in Xhosa.** Longmans Southern Africa, 1966.

Jordan, A.C. **Towards an African Literature: The Emergence of Literary Form in Xhosa.** University of California Press, 1973.

Kaschula, Russell H. 'Xhosa Oral Poetry: A Changing Tradition', in **Rhodes Review,** Grahamstown, 1989.

Kaschula, Russell H. 'Imbongi in Profile', in **English in Africa** 20 No. 1 May, 1993.

Kaschula, Russell H. 'Power and the Poet in Contemporary Transkei', in **Journal of Contemporary African Studies,** Vol. 10 no. 2 , 1991.

Kaschula, Russell H. 'The role of the Xhosa oral poet in contemporary South African society', in **South African Journal of African Languages,** 1991. 11 (1).

Karis, Thomas and Carter, Gwendolen (Editors). **From protest to challenge: A documentary history of African politics in South Africa 1882-1964,** Hoover Institution Press, Standford USA, 1973.

Kirsch, Beverley and Skorge, Silvia. **Masithethe isiXhosa.** Citadel Press, Cape Town, 1979.

Kirsch, Beverley and Skorge, Silvia. **Masithethe IsiXhosa.** 1990.

Kropf, Rev. Albert. **A Kafir English Dictionary.** First Edition, The Lovedale Press, 1899. Second Edition edited by Rev. Robert Godfrey. The Lovedale Press, 1915.

Riorden et al. **Lumko self-instruction course in Xhosa.** The Lumko Institute, Lady Frere C.P. 1969.

Lloyd, G. Owen. 'A Study of Some Xhosa Words of Afrikaans Origin', in **The South African Outlook,** The Lovedale Press, June 1955.

Lodge, Tom. **Black politics in South Africa since 1945.** Ravan Press, Johannesburg, 1983.

Maclennan, Ben. A **Proper Degree of Terror - John Graham and the Cape's Eastern Frontier.** Ravan Press, Johannesburg, 1986.

Mahlasela B.E.N. **A General Survey of Xhosa Literature from its Early Beginnings in the 1800's to the Present.** Working Paper No. 2. Department of African Languages, Rhodes University, Grahamstown, 1973.

Mahlasela, B.E.N. **Some Xhosa Idioms and Expressions.** Occasional Paper No 22 I.S.E.R. Rhodes University, Grahamstown, 1977.

Malherbe, Candy. **Men of Men.** Shuter's History Reference Library. Shuter and Shooter, Pietermaritzburg, 1983.

Mertens, Alice and Broster, Joan. **African Elegance.** Purnell, Cape Town, 1973.

Mini, Prof. B.M. **The Life and Work of Professor H.W. Pahl.** Fort Hare Papers, Volume 10, November. University of Fort Hare Press, Ciskei, 1990.

McLaren, J. **A Grammar of the Kaffir Language.** Longmans Green and Co. London, 1919.

McLaren, J. **A Xhosa Grammar in the New Orthography,** edited by G.H. Welsh, Longmans Green and Co. London, 1952.

McLaren, J.A. **A Concise Kaffir-English Dictionary** 1915. Revised edition, **A Concise Xhosa-English Dictionary** 1936. New edition, **A New Concise Xhosa-English Dictionary,** Longman Southern Africa, Johannesburg, 1971.

Mncube F.S.M.(M.A.Rand) **Xhosa Manual.** Juta., Cape Town. No date.

Molema, S.M. **The Bantu - Past and Present.** Green and Son, U.K. 1920.

Moll, Glen. **Table Mountain - a natural wonder.** Western Cape branch of the Wildlife Society of South Africa, Kirstenhof, Cape Town, 1987.

Mostert, Noel. **Frontiers. The epic of South Africa's creation and the tragedy of the Xhosa people.** Jonathan Cape, London, 1992.

Mtuze, Prof. P.T. **Tasks and Challenges Facing the Indigenous Literatures in Southern Africa.** No date.

Oosthuysen, P.J. **Xhosa Conversation Manual.** Oudiovista Productions, Cape Town. No date.

Opland, Jeff. **Xhosa Oral Poetry: Aspects of a black South African tradition.** Cambridge University Press, 1943.

Oxford Encyclopedic English Dictionary, The. Edited by Joyce M. Hawkins and Robert Allen. Clarendon Press, London, 1991.

Pahl, H.W. with Jafta, D.N. and Jolobe J.J.R.**Xhosa Literature. Its Past and Future.** The Lovedale Press, 1971.

Peires, J.B. 'The Lovedale Press: Literature for the Bantu Revisited', in **History in Africa,** 6 (1979).

Peires, J.B. **The House of Phalo: A History of the Xhosa People in the Days of their Independence.** Ravan Press, Johannesburg, 1981.

Peires, J.B. **The Dead Will Arise: Nongqawuse and the Great Xhosa Cattle-Killing Movement of 1856-7.** Raven Press, Johannesburg, 1989.

Pinnock, Don. **Orality and Writing.** Cultural Studies Working Paper No 2. Department of Journalism and Media Studies, Rhodes University, Grahamstown.

Pinnock, Don. **A History of the Black Press in South Africa.** Lectures, 1983-1994, unpublished.

Pinnock, Patricia Schonstein. **The Trojan Elephant,** unpublished.

Plaatje, Sol. T. 'Suggested New Bantu Orthography', in **The South African Outlook.** May 1st 1931.

Potenza, Emilia. **The Broken String: An integrated approach to Southern African history.** Maskew Miller Longman, Cape Town, 1992.

Raper, P.E. **Dictionary of Southern African Place Names.** Jonathan Bull Publishers, Johannesburg.

Raven-Hart, Major R. Editor. **Before Van Riebeeck.** Struik, Cape Town, 1967.

Reader's Digest. **Illustrated Guides to Southern Africa: Southern and Eastern Cape.** The Reader's Digest Association, Cape Town, 1983.

Reader's Digest. **Illustrated History of South Africa: The real story.** The Reader's Digest Association, Cape Town, 1988.

Roberts, Martin. **A History of Southern Africa.** (Longman History Studies in Depth.) Longman, London, 1990.

Shepherd, Robert H.W. **Lovedale South Africa, The Story of a Century 1841-1941.** The Lovedale Press, 1940.

Shepherd, R.H.W. **Lovedale and Literature for the Bantu, A Brief History and a Forecast.** The Lovedale Press, 1945.

Soga, John Henderson. **The Ama-Xhosa: Life and Customs.** The Lovedale Press, 1931.

Spamer, Conrad. 'The Richtersveld: Hope Without Glory', in **Via Winter** 1991. T & R Special Editions, Cape Town.

Stewart, James. **Lovedale Past and Present - a Register of two thousand names.** The Lovedale Press, 1887.

Stewart, James. **Outlines of Kaffir Grammar.** Lovedale Mission Press, 1901.

Switzer, Les and Switzer, Donna. **The Black Press in South Africa and Lesotho : a descriptive bibliographic guide to African, Coloured and Indian newspapers, letters and magazines 1836-1976.** G.K. Hall and Co., Boston, Mass. 1979.

Weldon, Gail. **George Grey and The Xhosa: Fact and Opinion.** Heinemann-Centaur, Pietermaritzburg, 1993.

Zotwana, Sydney Z. **Xhosa in Context, from Novice to Intermediate.** Perskor Publishers, Cape Town, 1991.

Unknown compiler. **English-Kaffir Vocabulary.** Bound, hand-written manuscript. Cory Library, MS16.555. No date.

Note on titles. Until the early years of this century, the words 'Kaffir', 'Kafir' and 'Caffre' were generally used to refer to the Xhosa. I have discarded these terms when quoting early writers in the main text, but could obviously not do so in the bibliography. The different spellings 'Xosa' and 'Xhosa' reflect the different orthographies in use at the various times of publication.

Sources of illustrations

William Fehr Collection, Castle, Cape Town - *Sandile's Kraal in the Amatole* by Thomas Baines

1820 Settler Museum, Grahamstown - *Xhosa women, Xhosa chief and his wives, Xhosa woman in skirt, Eastern Cape flora* and *Scene at the Kariega River* by F.T. I'Ons; *Wagons in Market Square, Grahamstown* by Thomas Baines; *Fish River* by unknown British soldier; *Hoopoes* by Mrs F. Barber - all photographed by **Cathryn Pinnock**

Museum Africa, Johannesburg - *Xhosas watching for the return of their dead warriors* by F.T. I'Ons

African Image, Cape Town - *Woman smoking a pipe*; *Young, beaded couple*; *Beaded man*; *Scarified woman*

Dakawa Arts and Culture Project, Grahamstown - *Imbongi* by Noluthando Beyi; *Voting at farm* by Joel Sibisi

Julian Cobbing - Photograph of students protesting during the 1980s, Grahamstown; photograph of UDF activist Gugile Nkwinti and comrade at political funeral during the 1980s, Grahamstown

Julius Mfete - Wooden carvings - *Man on a horse* and *Man with pipe*

Cathryn Pinnock - Photograph of Ntombi Mzuzo, Grahamstown

Gaelen Pinnock - Photograph of a Xhosa youth, Grahamstown

Don Pinnock - Photograph of a child, Dimbaza

Larry Strelitz - Photograph of a woman playing a jew's harp, Tsakana; Photograph of an old woman, Tsakana

Daguerreotype of woman wearing a kaross, unknown photographer - courtesy **Robyn Riddle**

Despite extensive efforts, we have not been able to trace the owners of the originals of some of the illustrations in this book. Should they contact us, we will acknowledge them in future editions.

p2: Mandela - Thembu (Madiba) clan name
Winnie - Pondo
Hani - Xhosa
p4: Pondo last to come under colonial admin
Ciskei/Transkei

7 Hottentot - gibberish
The clicks!
8 sheep: Xhosa use Khoi
Zulu use old Xhosa

p9 Xhosa derivation
angry men

All of page 11.
amaXhosa
amaThembu
amaMpondo
p12 iZolabudd.

p12 large grey mongoose etc

Names p14

Covers p14

p24 skin not cloth
still ceremonial dress

dassies used
tobacco bags 27

scarification of
children to
identify kids 29
carried on

White + red.

beads value p30

p43-44 travel
+ fortification for

p45 trad. months
Canopus - Saturn ↓ p48

p50. healing
Magaliesberg elephants
+ lions p51
Isitsikamma p52
extinction p52
birds p54
Medicinal plants p60
to
hlonipa = revere

p64.
cattle names p65
p70 music → dock
w - Zulu.

names of rattles p71
English as unifying language p82
*** Britain iNtshonga p85
hymn p89

p107. plural for beer

iqudu - kudu
p111 really Khoi/Khoi
p112 isiBhulu - Afrikaans